Raising Children
Who Refuse To Be Raised

Parenting Skills
and
Therapy Interventions
for the Most Difficult Children

Dave Ziegler, Ph.D.

Executive Director,
SCAR/Jasper Mountain,
Jasper, Oregon

SCAR/Jasper Mountain,
37875 Jasper Lowell Rd.,
Jasper, OR 97438-9704.
E-Mail: davez@scar-jaspermtn.org
Website: www.scar-jaspermtn.org

ISBN 0967118727
LCCN 2002401104

Printed in the United States of America

Cover design by The Cricket Contrast
Published by Acacia Publishing, Inc.
Phoenix, Arizona
1-866-265-4553

This volume is dedicated to my parents,
Guy and Rosemary Ziegler,
who provided me with every tool necessary
to take on the world and pursue my dreams.

Guy, the real author in our family, instilled in me
the ethic of hard work, discipline, and a code of ethical behavior
that did not include compromise.

Rosemary, the inspiration for my advanced educational work,
provided me with support, intuitive understanding,
and a desire to live a life of service to others.

The fruit does not fall far from the tree.
If I have been able to some degree
to lighten the load of the children and adults
with whom I have had the privilege to work
over the last three decades,
much credit must go to such quality root stock!

Acknowledgments

Writing a book takes little time compared to learning everything needed to start writing in the first place. I have been at the business of learning from difficult children going on thirty years (where has the time gone?). For a little over one year I have been compiling some of what I have learned in these pages. Time is an important commodity to me. When I am alone at my computer, I am not spending that time with my family. So I appreciate the support and the time to put into this project from those around me.

I want to thank my wife Joyce, who never questioned the importance of this effort. She has always graciously shared my time with projects such as this. Thanks also to Judy Littlebury, the Director of Jasper Mountain, where much of my learning has taken place. Judy has the highest of standards when it comes to children, and I feel fortunate to have periodically met those standards. I am grateful to my parents, Rosemary and Guy Ziegler, to whom this volume is dedicated. They taught me how to listen and be a student of those around me. I also want to acknowledge my brothers and their families: Mick Ziegler, John, Devin, and Abby Ziegler, Steve and Jamie Ziegler, other family members Hugh, Erin, Zoe, Azraia, Tiffany, Brett, Nika, and many lifetime friends.

Thanks to Karen Gray for her direction of this effort, and to Janet Gielow for her review of the text. I am frequently inspired by Kiva Michels, one of our program directors who is a constant student learning each day about herself and her work. I appreciate Don Landauer for his steady hand on the fiscal wheel. My thanks to our program's Board of Directors, Steve Cole, John Lively, Sharon Sandgathe, Linda Beach, Brent

Andersen, Chuck Davis, Mike Kelly, Frank Papagni, Gary Buss, and Board member and my psychology mentor and supervisor Dr. Debi Eisert.

Thanks to all the staff who have joined in our work with children and families over the years. Many have shared how enriching it has been for them in every way other than financially.

And most importantly, I wish to thank the frightened, traumatized, and angry children I have worked with for all they have taught me. The honesty of their struggles overrides the sharpness of their tongues. The resilience these children display even in their rage is life affirming to me, and a lesson to anyone with an open heart. To all parents who are willing to follow this road less taken, and to take up this cross, I acknowledge and applaud your optimism and love.

Contents

Raising Children Who Refuse To Be Raised

A Guide for Parents and Therapists

Foreword

It is my belief that being a healthy and successful human being is a *very difficult* job. But an even *more difficult* job is to be a parent and produce a healthy, successful person. And the world's *most difficult* job is to take into your family, through adoption or foster care, a child who has few or none of the characteristics of a healthy individual, and assist him or her through the labyrinth of human development and socialization.

There is another difficult job, and that is guiding parents on this difficult journey. Usually this job is done by professionals, but it can also be done by wise and experienced friends or members of the family. I call this job "coaching" the family to be a therapeutic agent for the child. The coach helps the parents to help the child.

This book is about the struggle of raising children who work against your every effort as a parent or clinician to help them succeed in the world. There are many books and parenting programs that are very good. However, I know of no approach to parenting that claims to work with all children, and I would be suspicious of one that did.

This book is about the children who often do not respond to approaches offered in books and parent training programs for "normal" children.

There are other books that address individual categories of special needs children, such as hyperactive children, sexually abused children or any number of other problems that make

i

parenting extremely challenging. Much more rare is help with parenting a child with multiple problem areas.

From my experience, it is seldom that special needs children come to a family with only one primary problem. Hyperactive children often have learning problems, histories of trauma, and conduct problems. If children cannot be categorized into neat boxes, then parents need help with a multitude of problem areas rather than going to the library researching each problem area one at a time. This book is intended to give parents and therapists some of the most essential elements of working with children with multiple problems and to provide a practical guide for the most common challenges presented by special needs children.

In a very real way, this book is playing the role of a mouthpiece for all the children who have let me into their world over the years. The issues that will be raised in these pages do not come from my knowledge; they come from my observations and the listening I have done not only to words but to the energy and the spirit of the children I have been privileged to work with. You will quickly see that some of the ideas expressed make perfect sense, but more often they may initially make no sense at all, from a logical perspective. This is one of the reasons why well-meaning and very competent people can find working with children with multiple disturbances so difficult and even maddening.

This is also a reason why parenting programs that work so well with "normals" can have the opposite effect on children with many of the problem areas that will be covered in these pages. As one parent once told me, "I am having to throw out everything I know about raising children and learn it all over again." This may be one reason why I have observed successful parents of their own children and parents who have been successful with adoptive children have a much more difficult time with behaviorally and emotionally disturbed children than parents with little or even no experience. This is due to the challenge of unlearning and relearning. If we come to trust our ideas and approaches, we just may be creating a problem for ourselves when the parameters change. If there is one position to avoid in learning how to be successful with the children discussed in this book, it is the belief that "I know exactly what will work." Many parents of very troubled children will find out that this belief can lead to some quick lessons in humility.

From the outset I want to say that I believe that parenting a child is the most challenging job an adult will ever have. The only challenge that is greater is to parent a child who has been confused, traumatized, or had a bond of trust seriously broken by another adult. In these cases, you are not starting from scratch, but the starting point is to first tear down the substructure of mistrust and then build from a deficit. The complexity of this task is more troublesome than most parents will want to consider.

If foster or adoptive parents really knew what it would take to reach and help turn around children with serious disturbances, would they choose to start the journey in the first place? Many adoptive parents have asked me the question, "How long will it take to turn my child around?" My response is almost always to ask, "How long does it take to raise a normal child to become a successful social and moral individual?" After they consider this question, my estimates of five to seven years of constant effort hopefully will seem less daunting.

There are no short cuts that I have found in raising these children. The magic medication, the latest therapeutic technique, or the two week intensive cures have been and will always be promoted by the "get there quick" crowd. I am often asked about these new approaches that claim remarkable results. The question reminds me of the story of a westerner asking an eastern spiritual teacher how to know when someone is offering the truth or another false and empty promise of wisdom, to which the teacher replied, "If they charge money for it, look elsewhere."

I have often wondered about this eastern wisdom when considering western psychotherapy. Surely a healer can fairly charge for the healing. I have partially resolved this by believing that if the price for the healing is signing on to one way of thinking, believing and acting that is in accord with a prescribed system, then it may well be wise to look elsewhere. Most parenting systems will have built-in reasons why failures are really successes in disguise. This is a partial answer to how anyone could get hooked into a cult and find themselves leaving family, waiting for the apocalypse, or drinking poisoned Kool Aid. The best advice may be to never suspend healthy skepticism or stop asking questions, or you may end up like too many parents who have had to ask themselves, "How did we spend all our money to help our child and have so little to show for it?"

This advice includes anything you read in this book--be skeptical, question, ask what the cost is to do what is suggested. Surrendering our common sense is not required; however, learning to think in some different ways may be essential. Of course, I am suggesting that you try some of the approaches that will be offered; however, I do not suggest that you do something over and over if it does not produce the results you are looking for. I remember a psychologist who once said that parenting seems to be one of the only times that otherwise intelligent parents do the same things continually and then complain it never works, for example, "I have told you a hundred times to pick up after yourself." After 99 times (or more like 9 times) it may be time to try a different approach.

I have found no one approach that works every time with any child. Parents of difficult children need a "bag of tricks," not the "one approach fits all" strategy offered by some well-meaning professionals, authors or systems.

The structure of the following pages is to review the various issues that most frequently confront parents who want to do a good job in situations that feel impossible, as well as therapists who are called upon to help when nothing has worked. The truth is that both parents and therapists need help, and the help they need is to be able to do the Vulcan Mind Meld (the mind reading approach used by Mr. Spock of Star Trek fame) with the children they are trying to raise. Since it takes a long time to learn the language and the inner world of challenging children and their various forms of problems, this book is offered as a type of Rosetta Stone to understand the hieroglyphics of troubled children.

Within many of the issues covered, there will be general comments and information presented specifically to parents and also to therapists. The two will often be addressed separately because they both have distinct roles and jobs. So why not separate the two in two different publications? For one important reason: in order to take on the challenge of raising the children discussed in the pages to come, parents need to know what therapists know, therapists need to know all the parents know, and both need to understand the issues faced and the possible ways to improve the chances for success.

I have attempted to address professionals in terms that will be understandable to parents, so parents are not only free to read the section written for professionals, it is important that they do so. It may be that periodically the parents may lose their way and the therapist can help by pulling out a road map. In the same way, the therapist may lose his/her bearings and need the parent to get him/her back on track toward the important role of "coaching" the family to better understand and help the child. Parenting is truly a team sport; it may take everyone at his or her best to produce the results everyone wants. There is little room here for the know-it-all expert.

There are just too many one-of-a-kind kids who need adults who are ready to learn and use one-of-a-kind solutions.

One question that may immediately come up is, "How do the ideas in this book relate to the many popular parenting programs?" First of all, the ideas discussed here are not a rehash of any of the many parenting systems. I was first exposed to parenting programs in 1972 when I had the opportunity to be trained and be a trainer in Thomas Gordon's Parent Effectiveness Training. I was intrigued by providing parents with a number of tools that fit together into a system of parenting. After working with PET for two years, I believed parents deserved to receive some of the same counseling training I had received in graduate school, particularly the parents of children who did not always respond well to PET techniques.

I wrote my first training program for parents in 1974. The program was essentially training in positive discipline combined with a crash course in basic active listening skills taught in grad schools. The program was a hit with the parents I had as clients. It was gratifying to hear from a colleague fifteen years later who ran across my original parenting training program, used the approach in a training program for parents, and wrote to tell me how effective it was. I find it comforting that good parenting ideas have more staying power than many things in our world such as fashion trends and computer software.

Ever since that first effort in working with parents, I have believed that we need to provide parents with all the tools that are available for understanding and working with challenging children. It remains my belief that throughout human history, except for the last 100 years (when we invented the therapist) the problems of children have been primarily addressed by parents or grandparents. With all due respect to Sigmund Freud and a hundred years of subsequent head shrinkers, most families over thousands of years raised children quite successfully without a therapist. It still seems clear to me that when everything is said and done, the most impact on a child's life will be made by the parent(s) regardless of how wonderful teachers, therapists, and other family members may be for the child. For nearly three decades, my focus as a family therapist has been to train parents to become therapeutic agents for their children. If my work has been at all successful, I believe it is due to helping parents make an even more positive impact on children than without my help.

Over the years I have continued to study and be trained in other systems of parenting such as Systematic Training In Effective Parenting or STEP. Over the last eighteen years my focus has moved to the most challenging children, who are generally the exception to every parenting rule. No credible parenting program would say that it helps all children. In fact, there is often fine print in parenting programs that usually says something to the effect of, "if serious problems persist or if the child becomes violent or tries to hurt self or others, get professional help or consider a residential treatment center designed to work with extreme issues in children." Having run such a program for nearly two decades, I see that if we worked with two, three or even four times the number of children referred to us, we would still have a waiting list.

After ABC's 20/20 ran a story on our program in 1998, we began to get requests for help from across the United States and other countries as well. I began to feel the burden of the many letters, emails, and out-of-state calls I was receiving from desperate parents looking for any help they could get. Some time later, I mentioned to a colleague that one day I needed to take the time to write a book and offer help to the thousands of parents of exceptional children (kids that are the exception to every rule) and to therapists who at times can feel helpless and ineffective with these children. To my surprise, the colleague took me to task for not already having written such a book regardless of how busy I was. After a few days of thinking he had a lot of nerve, I decided he was right. Not long after this encounter, I realized that it was time to make this effort a priority.

I know better than to claim that the ideas and approaches mentioned here will work with every child. However, I will go so far as to say that parents should be better able to understand their difficult child if these principles are used. But the fact remains that many parenting programs are available, and most will vary considerably from thoughts contained in this book. A good parenting system will give the parent the tools to implement and evaluate the approach to determine if it fits the challenges provided by their child. A good parenting program will not say, "The approach is right; it must be what you are doing that is wrong." This is the old circular argument of psychology--it can't be a flaw in the therapy or the therapist; if it doesn't work, it is a flaw in the client. Despite the fact that you and many parents of difficult children like yours want and need to believe in help that is available, beware of the above message from any professional.

While I am at it, I will make more professional trouble by calling into question parenting approaches that rest on the solid rock of research. Research has many important uses, but one I question is its use as a marketing tool to sell a particular point of view. It is more and more popular in psychology to have theoretical approaches be science- or research-based. It is important to be grounded in what we know to be truth rather than what we want to believe is true. At the same time, research has become something of a "sacred cow" in psychology. Too often, if research supports a particular perspective, some want the discussion to end there. But this is a misuse of research and not the foundation of scientific inquiry. Questioning theories, questioning the research design, replication, and working to disprove is still the basis of science.

There are approaches to working with children that claim to be science- and research-based, as if to say they are better than other methods. Examples are parenting approa- ches that focus almost solely on behavioral methods, which happen to be the easiest way to use observable measurement. But it does not take research, only common sense, to see that human beings are so much more than behavior. While outcome research can be an important aspect of a successful approach, there are also limitations to psychology as a science that are reflected in the state of considerable psychological research.

The more I learn about research, the more true it appears that all research has its flaws, some much more than others. I will not go into this in detail here other than to men- tion a few *caveat emptors* (consumer beware). The first truth about research is that there are no flawless studies. You can design a study to avoid a Type I error only by increasing your chances for a Type II error and vice versa. Or to put this in plain language, you can avoid believing that there is a signifi- cant impact to your subject when there is not, only by increasing the chances of believing there is no impact when there actually is. Basically, you can't have it both ways.

The second consumer alert is the whole issue of objec- tivity. Few of us went through school to have our teachers let us give ourselves our own final grades. One of the reasons for this is that we lack objectivity over our own work. I believe the same issue needs to be raised with psychological research. Is the researcher objective, or is the researcher studying his/her own work and beliefs? I believe it is common sense that the more a person is investing in anything, the less objective she becomes. The issue here can roughly be pointed out by the "research" of Pepsi when the company reports the finding of its taste tests indicating that Pepsi is preferred 3 to 1 over Coke. Three to one is pretty compelling, until Coke releases its research, which shows Coke is widely preferred over Pepsi. The reason such research is not helpful is that it is not conducted by an objective party with no stake in the results. This is marketing disguised as research. Under these circumstances, when researchers test their own theory or system and find that it does not perform well, these results are essentially never published. Do you think you will ever have Coke come out and admit most people like Pepsi better, regardless of the results of research?

The final Caveat is to avoid theories or systems that say, "Our system works and everyone else's does not work." The first question to raise, given such an arrogant claim, is whether the research was conducted by an independent objective party with no stake in the results (such as Consumer Reports doing a cola taste test, instead of one of the cola companies). The second question is to ask, "What research has shown the system not to be effective in certain situations and why not?" And the final question is, even if the system has proven useful in some situations, "What evidence is there that other systems are not effective in some situations as well?" On this last point, I would have to say that good researchers are very careful people who are slow to speak definitively because they know the weaknesses of all research. My measuring stick is that the researcher who lacks humility also lacks credibility.

The other limitation of research-based approaches is that no amount of research guarantees that something will help your child. As interesting as research is, there is only one study that is of primary importance to the parent and therapist of a challenging child, and that is what proves to be useful in this "single subject study"--your child. The effectiveness of any approach to raising children still must make its case one child at a time. The best advice is to see if the approach works with your child. This advice includes anything in this book. The fact that these approaches have worked with hundreds of very difficult children over the last eighteen years does not say that success with your child is guaranteed. But you might look at it this way: what do you have to lose to test some of the enclosed ideas? One helpful idea may be more than worth the price of the book, and if you find two or more helpful ideas you just may come out ahead.

As you have already figured out, it is my intention to say exactly what I think and believe. As a young person I was taught to speak directly and say what I thought. Very quickly I was labeled "tactless," and I had ample teachers over the years to help me say things in ways that were more easily accepted by others. As I spend more time in the business of helping families, I find myself going back to saying things directly.

Although there are still many people who react negatively to hearing it straight, I have found that parents of difficult children prefer and need this approach. These parents are tired of carefully couched terms and suggestions from professionals so unsure of themselves that they need to leave themselves an out by being vague or conditional. Tired, frustrated parents just want to hear what you have to say, and they can judge for themselves whether it will be helpful for them.

I plan to say it straight in these pages. In fact, I may seem to go overboard a bit at times. I was very surprised as I completed my doctoral work that so few professors wanted or even allowed me my own thoughts or personal synthesis of situations. I found that I was supposed to continue the many years of American education to parrot back what the professor had said or wanted to hear. Challenging was not a hallmark of the hallowed halls of my university, to my surprise and sadness. Even in my own definitive academic project, the dissertation, I was not allowed to say what I believed or give even a limited opinion. I may be making up for that in these pages. After so many years working with difficult children, I have a lot to say, and I plan to respect the reader by saying it plainly and not being careful in a professional or political sense. I am not surprised when others disagree with me; I expect it. It tells me that they are taking me seriously and thinking for themselves.

In the pages ahead, you will find some heavy issues at times treated in a light or humorous way. It is not my intention to offend people who might see very little humor involved in the predicament of either the child or the parent. However, it is my intention to challenge the need for continuous struggle by coming up for a little air now and then. My defense for my sense of humor may come from nearly two decades of living with hundreds of very troubled children. I could say, "Try it and see if you don't end up like me."

With all due respect given to the serious nature of the task of parenting and coaching parents, the goal in this effort is not to make it to the finish line, it is to cross the finish line with a smile on your face. My goal is not just to survive but to thrive. A sense of humor and an ability to take myself and my struggles less seriously at times are ways I have found to thrive when the situation would suggest otherwise. It is important that we first direct our humor at ourselves. The humor of Bill Cosby resonates in a much more universal way than the humor of Don Rickels. If we can laugh at ourselves, we might be able to bring a smile to other faces as well, and many people could lighten up a little more -- OK, even me.

You will see in the table of contents that the topics I will cover are divided into three Parts. Part I - Emotional Disturbances, Where It All Begins includes the first three chapters:

Chapter 1 Emotional Disturbances -- The Two Main Forms

Chapter 2 Childhood Trauma and the Aftermath

Chapter 3 Attachment

I see these initial chapters as a condensed version of the entire book. If you only have time to read a few chapters, the first three are recommended. They provide a background, a method of formulating the battle lines of working with challenging children, and they address the primary causes of emotional disturbances.

Part II - Behavioral Disturbances -- There is More than Meets the Eye has less of a focus on causes and discusses the challenges of working with serious behavior problems. Even if you understand some of the reasons why a child has developed problems, you still need to know how to respond when he or she acts out. Three chapters make up Part II:

Chapter 4 Anti-Social Behavior in Children

Chapter 5 Conduct Disorders

Chapter 6 Attention Deficit Hyperactive Disorder and Bipolar Disorder

Part III - Advanced Parenting Skills and Challenges is an attempt to cover the many other possible problem areas and potential combinations of difficulties. It would be impossible to cover all the permutations parents and therapists are faced with; however, Part III includes both specifics in many areas and general methods of dealing with challenges not covered in detail. Part III has six chapters:

Chapter 7 Sexual Problems with Children

Chapter 8 Other Challenges with Difficult Children

Chapter 9 Parenting Children with Multiple Impairments

Chapter 10 Strategies for Successful Parenting or How to Maintain Your Sanity

So I invite you to put on your thinking cap, roll up your sleeves (and perhaps your pant legs, it can get pretty deep some times) and let's get started.

Part I

Emotional Disturbances

Where It All Begins

Chapter

1

Emotional Disturbances --
The Two Main Forms

Before discussing general categories of problems in children, I believe it is important to say a few things about the climate of today's mental health service delivery system. To begin, I will share some observations of the professional community in the area of diagnosing children. After these contextual comments, I will move into the two general types of emotional disturbances in children.

The Helping Professions

Psychiatry and psychology are not exact sciences, although because of something of an inferiority complex with respect to physical medicine, they would like to be. Change may come somewhat slower in psychology than in the "hard sciences," but change is very visible to both practitioners and outside observers. Twenty years ago, many branches of psychology took exception to psychiatry and its labeling of people. Many psychologists preferred not to use diagnostic categories and disorders and attempted to avoid "putting people into boxes." The preference was to individualize every case and every client (avoiding even using the medical label "patient"). This preference can still be found among some in the practice of psychology, but for the most part psychology has given in to the societal acceptance and

1

legitimacy of the medical model. This evolution has received substantial prodding by medically-dominated managed care. Some even see the medical model as useful.

At a time when medical doctors are having a more difficult time with the pragmatics of their practices than they have had since the days of bleeding patients of their evil humors, psychology is coming on strong, and in some ways psychologists are the new high priests of normal and abnormal.

In a practical sense, medicine has killed the goose with the golden eggs by pricing itself out of the market. Not long ago, a young medical student would have been a fool not to specialize because that was where the status and the big money were. But that picture has been changing. The specialty of psychiatry, which has had a particularly difficult time of it, will be mentioned later. In the view of the AMA, managed care is to blame for the economic woes of psychiatrists, physicians and clinics. But reform in some manner was inevitable to break the monopoly of physicians in the healing arts.

Learning a lesson from medicine, psychology has worked to corner the market in some areas. Managed care has actually helped psychology through the uniquely managed care question, "what is the cheapest way to treat the problem?" The answer is seldom psychiatry. The largest federally subsidized mental health program, Medicaid, actually in practice turned the tables on psychiatrists by giving them an important role in approving treatment plans, diagnoses, and managing medication, but it all but prevents them from actually doing therapy with the patient because of the pragmatics of cost. But not so for psychologists, who are now in many cases the highest degreed professionals who can actually treat clients under managed care and Medicaid.

Amid this backdrop, psychologists have directly worked to keep licensed therapists from being the therapists of choice for managed care, which physicians did to psychologists in the past. They have done this by initially opposing the licensing process for anyone other than PhDs, and then attempting to take the precious ability to diagnose the problem away from "lesser" mental health professionals. Being in both these professional fraternities, I can only say that psychologists need to beware of having the same fate as psychiatrists -- pricing themselves out of the market.

Understanding the Use of Diagnoses

The changing dynamics of diagnosing clients is mentioned here because, for the most part, diagnosis is back in a big way. In many cases, the treatment is not authorized (meaning paid for) unless the diagnosis sticks. Because of this, children are once again subjected to the categories and boxes of the DSM-IV (Diagnostic and Statistical Manual 4th edition), or the ICD-9-CM (International Classification of Diseases -- 9th Clinical Modification). Instead of trying to understand children outside of the medical model, children are now understood through the new "flexibility" of the DSM-IV, the newest face of the old problem of medical model pigeonholes for patients.

I actually find the DSM-IV a big improvement over its predecessor, but in some ways it is a new coat of paint on the same old jalopy of medical diagnosing. It does not appear that anytime soon we will return to understanding the individual outside the medical model boxes. With this in mind, a practical approach would be to understand as fully as possible how children are diagnosed. I will not go into the details here of DSM-IV five axis diagnoses, but readers are encouraged to review this topic on their own.

With the strong return of diagnosing, bearing in mind that some camps of healing professionals never strayed in the first place, comes the inevitable complexity of labels. An old dynamic of the diagnosis de jour has reappeared with the new legitimacy of diagnostic categories. Over the years, this dynamic has been seen in children when all of a sudden throughout America, young people have caught mental health calamities with names like minimal brain dysfunction (although passé, it appears that we still have both children and adults whose brains are not fully engaged, but I am not sure we can always blame it on their brain), hyperactivity, learning disability, attachment disorder and serious emotional disturbance, to mention a few. There does appear to be some progress in these labels; we seem to be more willing to consider problems that are less rigid and more treatable.

The general term most often used for children with significant mental health problems at this point is a child with a mental and/or emotional disturbance. We all know that some people with mental disturbances get better with no help just as physical disturbances often get better on their own. Emotional disturbances can be even more transient than medical problems. In addition to the children who improve without help, most children with mental and emotional disturbances show improvement with the right kind of attention and treatment.

General Types of Emotional Disturbances

Before discussing specific types of problems in children, let's start with some generic terms. In general, I like to discuss emotional disturbances in two practical types: the explosive type and the implosive type. In other words, emotions and behavior that are aimed outward toward objects, other people or the world in general; and emotions and resulting behavior that are aimed inward at the self.

Explosive Type

Explosive disturbances are by far the easier to identify. In fact, they are quite difficult to overlook. To a greater or lesser extent, explosive disturbances in children erupt and disrupt everyone and everything going on in the child's environment. These are the children well known to the school principal, and the children who consume the majority of the time for social

4

workers. Typical manifestations of explosive disturbances are anger, rage, violence, and destructiveness.

Although many adults think these children intend to hurt others and destroy property, they are often much like other explosions in nature: the pressure builds to the point that it must come out. Typically pressure comes out unplanned and often with little premeditation by the child. Even children who look like they target their explosive energy are often not as they appear. The general cause of explosive disturbances is an internal pressure that may be caused by a multitude of factors. To the child, relief comes only from reducing the pressure. Much like seismic pressure in the earth, stress relief only comes after a considerable release of energy. For explosive children, pressure release is usually the goal, not destructiveness or making anyone in particular's life more difficult.

It is important to imagine the inner world of explosive children. When adults say that a child does not care about the consequences of her behavior, often it is more accurate that the consequences are the last thing on her mind. Many of these children are apologetic and remorseful after an explosive outburst. But for them the devastating results of the pressure release are only apparent to them after they have externalized a great deal of energy. Like the San Andreas Fault line, this gives them some momentary internal relief of the pressure, allowing for a momentary ability to be more aware of people and events outside them. This is why right after a cathartic emotional outburst many people are more present than any other time. This is very often true with violent children.

For adults who have trouble understanding what an explosive internal state must feel like for children, they need only recall times in their own life when events were beyond their control, and the only thing they could do was react internally or perhaps externally. Some examples may be receiving an emergency phone call, anticipating negative results from a medical test, having a partner indicate a desire to leave the relationship, or other events that make everything else in life go into suspended animation. For many explosive children, their world is a series of emotional pressures that comes from their experience of life being completely out of their own control. In a way, it is even worse than this, because these children often do not experience being in control of themselves, much less their environment or their life. The only outlet for temporary relief of this pressure is release of large amounts of energy.

It seems logical that the target of the explosive energy is the nearest object or person. It is a common dynamic that explosive children strike out toward objects and people they care about. To some adults it does not make sense that these children damage their favorite toy or possession, or hurt the person who is their greatest advocate and protector. But the explanation for such behavior is generally no more complicated than striking out at the most available target. When this involves targeting a person, these children often pick the safest person to strike out at while leaving themselves least vulnerable, which often means either a younger or smaller child or an adult who cares for them.

Although recipients of rage-filled outbursts often feel this explosive energy quite personally, the incident is often not personal at all to the explosive child. Carefully consider the child's internal experience before assuming that she "intentionally" exploded, which is close to being a contradiction in terms. It is true that children can learn to relieve stress in a functional way, as adults do by activities such as sleeping, sports, hobbies, exercise, and sex. But this is an important learned skill that takes a good deal of self-awareness and belief that personal control of stress is possible. Believing internal pressure can be managed is a belief that comes only from successful experience.

To many explosive children, successful relief of pressure has only been experienced from exploding outward to provide at least momentary inward calm. Once again, this is why an explosive child may often be quite available immediately after an explosion that is high on the Richter scale. It is as if the internal fog lifts momentarily and the child may see things more clearly -- that is, with some help from a caring adult.

The explosive style of handling internal pressure can have multiple causes. It can be the result of trauma, when children learn to strike out at others before someone strikes out at them. It can come from behavior modeled by adults in domestic abuse situations. Explosive reactions can also be the result of insufficient guidelines as the child matures and produces the continuing responses of "the terrible two's" long after this phase has passed developmentally. But there is a whole other category of disturbance quite different than the explosive type.

Implosive Type

The second type of emotional disturbances are implosive behaviors that direct energy inward. Unlike children who explode, implosive children do not primarily show anger and rage as their main emotional states. Children who implode take out frustration, depression, anger, disappointment and even boredom on themselves. Some would never consider doing to someone else what they do to themselves, making the golden rule meaningless in teaching these children moral development.

Many of these children are convinced that what they have been told by abusive or at least unsupportive adults is true -- they are the problem. Each day, when the struggles of life present themselves, these children once again prove to themselves that they are in fact the problem. They convince themselves continually of this truth with the fact that they do not succeed in getting the things they want. They ensure that they are not successful in accomplishing the things they hope for. It does not take long before it is clear and factually true that they are the major stumbling block to their own success, and the downward cycle continues.

Manifestations of implosive emotions include self-injury, depression, eating disorders, academic failure, substance abuse, suicide issues, self-sabotage, and much more. As children grow older, this can turn into serious eating disorders, self-mutilation, drug and alcohol abuse, high risk activities and behaviors, and chronic self-depreciation and abuse. In a general sense, explosive disturbances fill our criminal justice system, and implosive disturbances fill our mental health treatment centers.

Implosive children have internally accepted the dictum that they are to blame for the things that go wrong around them, and they are to be punished for present as well as past problems. Implosive children do not need a good reason to abuse themselves, making their behavior often very difficult to understand. It is as if they have had an implosive microchip implanted in their brain which becomes the default mode in their internal hard drive of thinking and feeling.

The technician planting this psychological microchip is nearly always an abusive parent or caregiver. The implosive style is almost always the result of trauma due to targeting oneself. If the implosive pattern is very entrenched, it is generally a good idea to look for significant emotional or physical abuse at some point in the child's past. In addition, there is growing evidence that childhood neglect may be the most damaging type of abuse. Neglect seems to send to a child a deeply held message that "I wasn't important enough to have my needs met by others." This internal set point may follow the individual throughout a lifetime.

Of the two general types of emotive styles, explosive types get the majority of the attention, funding and programs. But the implosive child is typically far more difficult to reach and help. However, both types of responses are critical to understand when working with children with emotional

8

disturbances. There are also those unlucky parents who have children who alternate between these emotive states, making it very difficult to stay one step ahead of the next episode. My suggestion with both emotive styles is to make sure you can translate the message and the meaning of the child's symptoms. Without having some sense of what the child is communicating by his behavior and affect, you cannot know how to best intervene.

Chapter

2

Childhood Trauma and the Aftermath

Childhood trauma is one of the most insidious, disabling experiences a human being can experience. At a time when children experience complete dependence and vulnerability, they reach out for protection and nurturing and find the opposite. For the rest of their life, vulnerability will be associated with terror. Trauma inflicted by a primary care provider, usually a parent, appears to produce the most lasting scars.

My work with abused children has taught me that neglect and other types of abuse by a parent are far more lasting and serious for a child than more substantial abuse by most anyone else. I have found it odd that neglect seems to play a disproportionate role in behavioral and emotional disturbances when compared to substantial physical and at times even sexual abuse.

But from one perspective, this makes some degree of sense. Physical abuse is scary and painful, but neglect can be more emotionally damaging, in that it creates the ongoing question of whether one's basic survival needs will be met. Faced with the choice between a bruise or burn and survival itself, what would you prefer? Neglect appears to be a betrayal of confidence in a care provider that can have intense long term impact on an individual's ability to truly count on or have confidence and belief in another human being.

It is likely that as far back as one can go in the history of humans, trauma has been an important factor. It is hard to imagine that an unexpected encounter with a saber tooth tiger did not leave a lasting impression on Homo Erectus -- that is, if the human was lucky enough to get the better of the encounter. It appears clear from physiology that the internal stress response was important for survival, enabling the "fight or flight" response.

It also appears that as long as humans have been on the planet, they have been busy warring with other humans. Undoubtedly war also made lasting impressions on at least some warriors, although the understanding of trauma produced by war is a relatively recent discovery. At the same time, it appears to have always been the case that some external experiences may produce little lasting trauma for one person, but may incapacitate another person. The study of trauma and its effects on people first began due to pervasive effects of world wars. But after decades of study, it is still somewhat of a mystery how some soldiers are able to come through the horrors of war with little or no significant trauma, while others have been forever scarred by the experience.

One potential explanation of the differential effects of trauma is how the individual cognitively processes the experience. One of the essential clinical criteria for traumatic stress is the experience of a profound or life threatening event. Therefore, it appears that if the individual does not define and thus experience the event as traumatic, it may not produce the same stress response, or be stored in the mid brain in the way we now know traumatic experiences are remembered.

The ability of humans to use their cognitive abilities to define their external and internal experience can literally define their reality. For example, thrill seekers or proponents of "extreme" sports pursue the rush of experiences that would traumatize others. The experience of white-water rafting can be very frightening to one person and thrilling and enjoyable to another. Although the physiological experience is the same, the cognitive process defines the meaning and long-term significance of the situation.

A number of years ago, I collaborated with Michael Reaves, a psychiatrist with significant experience with post traumatic stress disorder in war veterans, in a review of the similarities and the differences in Post Traumatic Stress Disorder (PTSD) in war veterans and in young sexually abused children. The results were shared at the annual conference of the Society for Traumatic Studies in Los Angeles. I was somewhat surprised that there were far more similarities than differences between veterans and children.

However, there was one defining difference: most of the children did not have a cognitive paradigm to define their experience, whereas most of the veterans did. This tended to result in children viewing their experience as random and unpredictable and from an egocentrist position (they were the personal target of the abuse). Therefore, since the event could reoccur at anytime, the experience was never really over. Times of non-abuse were merely interludes before the next episode.

The traumatized child has an experiential open wound. As bad as war can be, veterans at least to some degree have a context into which to place the experience, and they cognitively know that they leave the danger behind when they return home. But where do children go to escape trauma that occurs in their home, often at the hands of a parent? Unlike veterans, who had life experiences before the experience in war to compare it with, some young children know only a world in which trauma is ever present.

The point being made here is that the ability of individuals to be aware of their physiological and emotional state, and more importantly to cognitively define the meaning of external and internal experience, are keys to solving the puzzle of trauma and its effects on children.

Ψ The Challenge for Therapists

With a few exceptions, the potent aspect of psychotherapy is the therapeutic relationship with the client. When working with children who have experienced trauma, a relationship is very important. However, knowing how to form a bond with a traumatized child and knowing when a bond has been formed can be more complex than may be anticipated.

A relationship can be defined as a mutual connection between two people where social and emotional needs are met and no one is used or abused. With this definition in mind, forming a relationship with a traumatized person, particularly a traumatized child, can be a minefield.

The most common mistake of inexperienced therapists is to believe a relationship has rapidly developed, when they are actually far from it. Forming a bond with a traumatized child is actually not the first rung of the therapeutic ladder as in most other therapeutic alliances. It is actually one of the top or last rungs. Keeping in mind the fact that traumatized children remain in the "war zone" of potential abuse in their minds, a number of steps must occur to form the foundation of a true relationship. In my work I have found the Building Blocks of Treating Emotional Disturbance (Figure 1) a useful road map.

Ψ Safety

The internal question of the child is, "Will I be safe in a nonviolent environment where my basic needs are uncon-ditionally met?" Of course, the child is seldom consciously aware of this question. He more likely assumes that he is not safe and thus is hypervigilant and suspicious of the people around him as the next potential source of abuse. Even if the child believes that you will not be the next abuser, he must

Figure 1. Building Blocks of Treating Emotional Disturbance

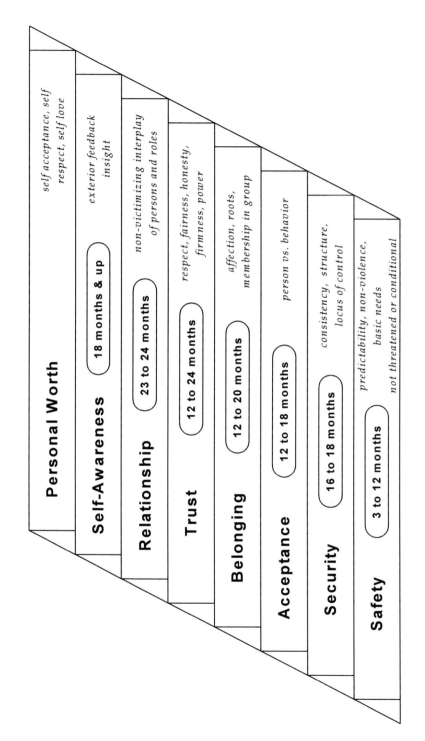

Personal Worth — *self acceptance, self respect, self love*

Self-Awareness (18 months & up) — *exterior feedback insight*

Relationship (23 to 24 months) — *non-victimizing interplay of persons and roles*

Trust (12 to 24 months) — *respect, fairness, honesty, firmness, power*

Belonging (12 to 20 months) — *affection, roots, membership in group*

Acceptance (12 to 18 months) — *person vs. behavior*

Security (16 to 18 months) — *consistency, structure, locus of control*

Safety (3 to 12 months) — *predictability, non-violence, basic needs not threatened or conditional*

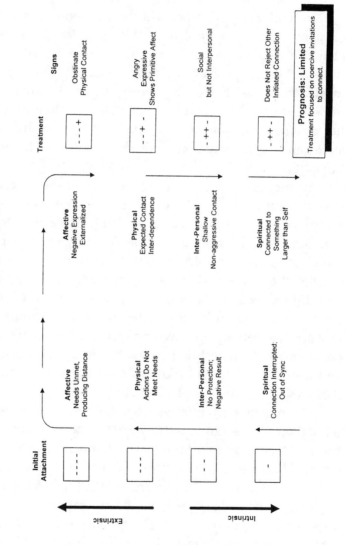

Figure 5. Foundations of Attachment
No Attachment Bond

determine that you will be able to protect him from his former or future sources of abuse.

An environment that communicates safety to an abused child has several essential characteristics:

Nonviolence -- all aspects of the environment must be free of signs or hints of violence. This includes the presence of someone who wants to take you where you do not want to go (how a child might view a prying therapist). The energy from individuals must be for the most part calm, supportive and understanding. The child must experience: room to be him or herself, the space and time to share what he or she wants to share, and in the way that he or she chooses to share (seldom initially with words).

My suggestion is to consider the physical environment of your therapy space. Most therapists are aware of child-friendly signs such as furniture that is comfortable and sized for children, as well as pictures, objects, and games that interest the child. Less often do therapists consider that closing the door to the office during the initial stages of therapy can be very threatening to the child. It can also make a difference if the therapist sits or stands between the child and the door, perhaps viewed by the hypervigilant child as blocking an escape route. I suggest that doors remain open at least a crack, and insure that the child knows she can exit the room even though she may never feel a need to.

A nonviolent environment lets children know that being who they are is not upsetting to the adults around them, because these children know what happens when adults get upset. Although this may not be done obviously, an abused child will carefully read the energy of the therapist and his/her hypervigilance will signal if the therapist is pleased or displeased with what is going on. This will then be personalized to the therapist being displeased with him or her.

Touching the child client is a complex issue and one that must always be considered individually. I would not say to avoid touch, but how and when you touch the child is important. Often, abused children have an approach avoidance reaction to touch. On a deep level, they like touch, and it fulfills a basic need. On a protective level, they are wary of touch and often attribute incorrect meaning to it. The best course of action is to signal the meaning of supportive friendly touch with your energy. Your words will mean very little, so always communicate the fact that you are a safe person with your energy, not your words. Abusers often tell the child one thing and the abuser's actions tell a very different story.

Do not be reluctant to set some physical boundaries using physical touch. For example, if the child becomes destructive of property in the office, calmly and firmly step in and stop the behavior. Or if the child begins to hurt himself or herself, again calmly hold the child to prevent any harm. It is through this physical touch that children learn that you are powerful enough to protect them from others and from themselves.

These children will be looking for any inconsistency in you, and they may react strongly when they find it. This can come as a surprise when, for example, the child is very upset when you arrive at 9:05 after having said, "I will see you at 9." Therapists often wonder how such a minor issue becomes major, and one of the answers is that the child is looking for the next characteristic of a safe environment -- predictability.

Predictability -- With abused children, when things happen that they did not anticipate and do not understand, their reaction is generally negative. Knowing their world and anticipating events are among the few factors that reduce hypervigilance, which takes a great deal of stressful energy. A person cannot be safe if they anticipate something bad happening at any time.

In therapy, predictability means having a routine: not changing appointments frequently, having a familiar and consistent place, and greeting the child with consistent supportive energy. If the process is going to change, leave sufficient time to help the child understand the change. Remember, to many of these children, if it is different, it is bad. Having a session opening and closing "ritual" of some kind may help with predictability. In this way, the child is reminded at the beginning of the session that this is the place where good things have happened, and at the end is warned that we are about to finish today's session.

Boundaries -- Physically and sexually abused children have experienced that their most basic boundaries have been violated. Adults have not respected limits on physical punishment and have inflicted pain and injury. Sexual abusers have violated their most intimate and private spaces. Establishing boundaries does not just mean that you respect the child's space by asking for a hug or asking permission to touch. It also means that you require the child to respect your space and follow basic rules in the office.

Being open and supportive as a therapist does not mean letting the children do what they want. The children learn that there are rules that will be enforced, and this provides an important element of safety. The child may intrude on the therapist's space and it may seem counterintuitive, but unless the therapist establishes and maintains his/her space, the child will not feel safe. Some sexually abused children have been taught to offer themselves sexually, and to act seductively. If you do not establish this boundary, you are not protecting the child's space which adults have taught the child not to protect for herself.

There should always be rules in the therapy office. An essential rule is no violence, which includes targeting people or things. There is a difference between a child expressing anger by pounding a doll identified as an offending parent, and the child trying to destroy the doll as an aggressive act. There will probably be places in the office that are off limits, such as client files on your desk. There will often be items in the office that are not available to play with or even touch, such as artwork or the therapist's personal property like a purse or briefcase. Unlike some who suggest not having items in the therapy room that are off limits, I would suggest having such items to show that there are limits that will be enforced. Limits and rules that are respected and taken seriously provide a sense of boundaries, and therefore safety, to an abused child.

Ψ Security

The next step in the journey toward relationship is the child being secure in the people and the environment. In therapy, building security means having consistent aspects of the counseling process the child can count on. Change will often be met with resistance and usually with suspicion. If there is a change in the day you are to meet the child or even the time of day, it is generally best to let the child know well in advance. Circle the new date on a calendar and let the child take it home. Just the fact that you take the time to let him/her know helps with the need for security.

The other essential aspect of security is structure. As a general rule, the more anxious the child, the more structure he or she needs. Structure is important not only for children but also for adults in the therapy process. Part of the structure of therapy are the rules. Overall, the best way to enhance security is through consistent structure in the therapy process.

Ψ Acceptance

Hypervigilant children are extremely aware of the reaction adults have to them. They know that as a therapist, you are an important person in their life. How you respond to them in large and small ways will be greatly amplified by them. It is not unusual for the child to believe that anytime you are displeased with something they have done and you mentioned it, you are "yelling at them." The important point of acceptance is that there is a differentiation between the behavior and the child. Do not assume the child understands this distinction if, for example, you correct the child's behavior for perhaps violating one of the therapy rules. It is important each time to correct the behavior but let the child know that you believe in her and her ability to abide by the rule in question.

Consider your therapy style. Do you reward children when they easily share with you, and subtly punish those who withhold from you? Many years ago, I was asked to meet individually with an eleven year old female who was having problems with family members, peers and her teacher. She managed to go the entire first session without saying a word to me, and in fact would not look in my direction. This became a challenge for me, and the next session I was prepared for the silent treatment. However, after several weeks of trying all my tricks to even have the child look at me, I received the same response from her -- no response.

I met with her parents and told them nothing was working. Shocked at my assessment, they had just the opposite point of view. They explained that from the first session, the vast majority of the problem behaviors had disappeared, and they pleaded with me to keep doing exactly what it was that was making such a huge difference. I nodded knowingly and agreed to continue despite being confounded by such a strange therapeutic relationship. Over the next ten sessions, I continued a variety of strategies and on one occasion I even brought in a newspaper and began to read it to the child.

After fifteen sessions that in my experience were all one way communication, we terminated, the therapy having been a huge success in the parent's view because all problem behaviors were gone at both home and school. However, no matter what I did, this child never once acknowledged my presence in the room, said not a word to me, or even said good-bye when we terminated.

To this day, if I can believe that our time together had anything to do with her behavioral turnaround, my only theory is that she felt accepted by me even though she ignored me the whole time. It could also be important that the parent took the time to give her the attention of bringing her to a therapist. Despite my confusion as to her response to me, I continued to be there for her. To her, our time was hers to do with what she wanted, even if that was ignoring me. I thought about calling it newspaper therapy and going on the lecture circuit, but I knew some graduate student would ask how it worked and I would not know how to answer.

Abused children always have dark secrets about the abuse. You may think you know from the file what they have been through, but at best you know only some of the external facts. There is always more that the child went through, not to mention how she experienced it on the inside. Part of the therapy process is providing the child a place to communicate her experience in her own way. If she chooses to let you in on her dark secrets, it is essential that you listen to her without strong reaction on your part. Unless you can hear about terrible abuse without reacting, the child may not sense that you can handle and accept what she has been through. Some children provide small details and gauge your response. If you have a strong response, "Oh, you poor thing, that must have been terrible," the child will assume you cannot handle the rest. Other children may exaggerate some details to see how you handle it.

The best course of action when the child tells you about abuse is to remain interested but not to react emotionally. To the children, if you cannot handle the secrets, how can you accept "what they have done"?

One of the aspects of abuse that weighs on children is that they have been involved. Their behavior caused mommy to hit them, or it was their body that made daddy come in late at night. Many children perceive that they were actively involved in the abuse, even when the opposite is true.

Throughout the process of therapy, continue to reflect to the child the strengths you see in him. Do not ask him to acknowledge these strengths; it is likely that he will not agree with you. However, this is a way that you can mirror back to the child aspects of him that you value. This process can strengthen the child's feeling your acceptance.

Ψ Belonging

To a child who feels that she does not belong anywhere, the challenge is to help her feel like she belongs in your office. You will need to find individualized ways to accomplish this. It may mean that the child keeps one of her belongings in your office while you work together; or it could be that the child likes the toys placed in certain ways. You may seek permission to put some of the child's art on your wall, or ask if she would like to make any changes in the room while she is there. Whenever possible, I attempt to externalize the goal I am trying to achieve in therapy. In this case, the interpersonal experience of belonging can be externalized by a tangible symbolic representation that has meaning to the child.

Ψ Trust

By this point in the relationship-building process, you may be thinking that surely the child knows you are there for him and a relationship has been established. But consider that some sexually abused children were the objects of grooming by the offender for six months or even longer. It only makes sense that many of the methods you use to gain a child's trust may have also been used by an offender to gain trust as well.

Once I was facilitating a group for children who had been sexually abused. After the first session, I noticed an upset mother ushering her two children, who were new to the group, into her car. I intercepted her to hear the mother's anger and tears that the children's offender had said and done many of the same things we were doing in the group, and how was she to know if this would have a different result? I simply said, "You will know because you can be here the entire time."

Unlike some children's groups, I have always made trauma groups available to non-offending parents. Knowing they can come is often enough security that they don't feel a need to be there the whole time. In the therapy process, trust is not only an issue with the child, but it is important between therapist and parents as well.

Other aspects of trust can be enhanced by giving the child straight information. It may seem odd, but trust can be built particularly by being honest in giving bad news to the child. Trust is built by being firm and enforcing (previously discussed) boundaries. Trust is also strengthened when the child experiences you as consistently the same person each time he meets with you. An abused child is accustomed to adults who are unpredictable, which raises his stress and often spells trouble because he cannot anticipate when he may be hurt next. To build trust, accept the child's reactivity and let her know you expect her to need reassurances along the way.

I am often asked how long this process takes to develop a relationship. Managed care does not give you fifteen sessions to form a relationship and thirty more to address the problem areas. It is difficult to put time frames on such a complex process, but the relationship building and therapy are not separate steps.

In the Building Blocks of Treating Emotional Disturbance, there are timelines mentioned that I have found in my work. You will quickly see that in fact the time mentioned (for relationship it may take six months) does not fit into the managed care paradigm. Some medical and psychological issues can be addressed with Band-Aids; others cannot. Trauma work does not easily fit the managed care mindset.

Ψ And Finally, Relationship

Now you have taken this journey with the child and sufficient time has expired that each of the building blocks have been climbed by both of you together. In my mind the word relationship can begin to be accurately used to describe what you have with your young client. If you are saying to yourself, "I can do it much quicker with my traumatized kids," I would ask you to reconsider your position. Does the child give you what he thinks you want to hear? Does he act the way you let him know you want him to act? Does she comply out of anxiety? Does she share scary things when she would rather not? If any of this is true then what you have does not meet the definition of relationship where there is a mutual bond, with room for both people; and where no one is used, not even for therapeutic reasons. There is much of therapeutic value that you have accomplished on the way to a relationship, but don't believe you have arrived at a relationship until you actually have.

Ψ Other Issues In Treating Traumatized Children

We come from a culture that measures everything. Even psychology gives more credence to measurement or quantitative rather than qualitative analysis. In this culture of measuring everything, we attempt to quantify trauma with less than helpful results. The nature of trauma is not in the external event but in the internal meaning and experience of the event.

A common mistake of professionals in law enforcement and psychology is to consider the seriousness of the external event. Unless you know the meaning of the event to the child, you will not know the level of the trauma. It is common to have one child go through profound abuse and at times be less haunted by it than another child whose abuse appears on the surface to be much less significant.

Do not attempt to measure the seriousness of abuse; it will only predispose you to a belief about how the abuse has translated into trauma. The problem with your belief is that you may be accurate 50% of the time, which could be achieved by guessing. The importance of a traumatic event is solely in the mind of the person who went through it. Put your energy into learning how traumatized children tell you about their pain, and remember that pain is an internal experience which at times has little to do with external events.

Some therapists confuse support with emoting for the child. Others confuse sympathy with empathy. As in medicine, the first dictum is "Do no harm." In trauma therapy, this starts with "don't make the problem worse with mistaken signs of emotional support through sympathy." Remember the child's trauma is in part based on the meaning he ascribes to the event. Don't make statements that are very appropriate in other therapy situations, such as "that must have been terrible for you," or "I bet you felt very sad and alone." Let the child let you know by words or symbolic communication what it was like.

As a therapist, your words are not the only important communication to the child; your energy and your nonverbal messages are very important as well. You must learn to hear about abuse and not let your face tell the child that it is hard for you to listen to his or her story. Many abused children will protect you from further details if they believe it is difficult for you. Particularly in the early stages of treatment, learn to listen to the child as you were listening to the weather report, and leave your evaluation of the event to yourself. This can help avoid the child considering the abuse more traumatizing than he first thought.

It should be clear by now that it is important not to rely on words as the primary communication. Children often do not have words to describe events or experiences even if they wanted to let you know in words. There are many symbolic methods of communication that children are more comfortable with and may even enjoy. These include play, art, stories, movement, sand tray work, and puppets, to name a few. Professional training is offered for these methods, which can be important aspects of the therapist's bag of tricks.

One of the roles I played for years was to work with children who would not open up to child protective service workers, and particularly to law enforcement officers. I quickly learned that if I approached the child as the investigators did, I would likely end up with the same results. So my first job when meeting the child was to establish a method of play.

When young children interact with peers and adults, they often do so with toys. One of the most effective toys in my office turned out to be a large plastic alligator, which had a mouth that opened. Seldom did the child hold back when I spoke through the alligator as I opened its mouth. The children were usually fascinated and spoke freely to "Ally." I would not have chosen this rather fierce looking toy, but it was the only toy handy one day and it was just odd enough that it worked very well, so I used it often.

There is no question that law enforcement and child protective service workers have difficult and unenviable jobs. However, I do have a problem with some aspects of typical investigations, in that the goal is not to help the child, it is to get something from the child -- in this case, information.

Many investigators believe that putting together a good forensic case does help the child. My clinical experience is that investigations and court cases do as much harm as good for the child. Don't confuse what we in our society want (justice or revenge, depending on your perspective) from what the child wants, which is generally to be left alone and to forget bad experiences.

Done poorly, an investigative interview can definitely be further traumatizing, and be experienced by the child as just another adult using him for their own purposes. The investigator is, in fact, using the child for information.

Some would defend investigators by saying their job is to get the facts. Perhaps so, but it is important that therapists not go in search of facts and miss the child. Seldom are facts important in trauma therapy. For this reason it is very important that therapists not do what investigators do, which is to ask the child to open up and be vulnerable when it is not clear that the child feels protected and supported when you are not around. We should never ask the child to let down her defenses if she will need them when she leaves your office. It may take you some time to determine how supported the child feels in her living situation before beginning to encourage her to open sensitive doors to personal trauma.

Ψ How Abused Children Think

It is helpful for parents from time to time to remember back to their own childhood. Not so much in your thoughts, but in your emotions. The time of childhood is not primarily a time of thinking, but a time of sensing and feeling. As children, we remember things based on our senses, not thoughts. We remember our hometown by the way it smells; we remember times of our lives by sounds and music. Some forms of touch remind us of positive memories, and others of less positive ones. It is not always clear to adults why there is a preference for one texture over another, or why most people have aversions to things but are not sure why. The probable causes of such internal "set points" are childhood experiences that your body remembers, but your conscious thoughts do not.

A difficulty that arises when adults remember back to their childhoods is their cognitive attempt to make sense of this time in their life -- where they lived, was it a good time or bad time, where they lived at what age, what grade in school, what defining events were going on either in the family or in the world. However, this is not going back to childhood; this is using the documentary approach to looking back in a linear way.

To be a child is to see, feel, touch and taste the world without it all making a meaningful whole. If we are able to do this as adults, we have a chance to touch the experience of terror at being lost in the department store when you believe you will not be found. You may remember a pet dying and feeling the deepest level of loss as if you will not recover. Children do not feel halfway; they only learn to do this as they grow up. When the child does not get what she wants, it is the end of the world right then. Children live in the now, and in their feelings, not their thoughts. Fortunately all adults have had experience as children, but unfortunately, adults seldom are able to truly recall what it was like.

Adults have a variety of ways to make their lives routine. Routines or rituals are ways that people make sense of the world; they provide people with some sense of understanding, and therefore control. All cultures have rituals that are designed to communicate to the members of the group that life is not random and without meaning. We can make sense out of it through defining our experience in certain ways.

One of the truly innocent aspects of a child becomes evident when he experiences something for the first time. The toddler who tastes the lemon, the excitement of going to the zoo and seeing all the creatures up close. Our treatment program is 50 miles from the ocean, and on every trip to the beach we seem to have a child who has never seen the ocean. I remember one eight-year-old child who stared at the Pacific Ocean for the first time and said, "I didn't know it was so big." Of course there is no way to let the child know how truly big the ocean is because he has no frame of reference for this understanding. This experience of just letting the world in is an ability we both teach children to move beyond as they mature and one we admire at the same time.

However, as adults, we believe that experiencing things as if for the first time is just not functional for living. Living this way would distract us from our work, or from the serious content of daily life. Spiritual systems would disagree. In Christianity the Bible admonishes that "unless you become as a little child you cannot enter the kingdom," and in Buddhism there is the concept of "beginner's mind," which is to

28

experience everything as if you are a beginner doing something for the first time.

Children must rely on adults to provide this security of understanding the context and meaning for them. If a child is unfortunate enough to be raised by an adult who is randomly abusive, the world becomes a frightening war zone for the child, and the enemy is not just the abusive adult but potentially all adults. Abused children take the childlike qualities of experiencing the world one step farther than other children. The child's survival instincts are heightened by abuse, because abuse, particularly by a care provider, tells the child that it is essentially up to her to survive. This complex situation combines the experience of going through life leading with one's feelings and experiences (seeing foreground without seeing background), and the hypervigilance of being on guard against threatening experiences and people.

Without the ability to explore the world within the context of the safety of a protective adult, abused children go through the world often avoiding experiences, people, and places rather than exploring them. What this does to children is to rob them of the innocence of childhood. There is no question that they are chronologically and maturationally children, but they cannot afford to let life happen to them without insulating themselves and essentially assuming the role of self-protection. This creates anxious, hypervigilant, moody, easily irritated, demanding, controlling, rage-filled, and reactive children. Does this sound like any children you know?

Within the context of this complex issue of how children experience the world, it is still helpful to know what abused children are thinking. Because of the factors discussed above, these children will flip from thinking to feeling frequently. Triggers in their environment can suspend their basic thought processes instantly, and primitive reactions take over.

Although some professionals believe that there are certain types of children characterized by explosive tendencies, I have not found this to be the case as much as I have seen the switch from reactive emotions to cognitively mediated behavior more apparent in some children than others. There is generally a reason for this pattern, and it is the presence of trauma in the child's life.

In describing the internal process of abused children, I am reminded of the six year old boy who was taken to the "adoption fair" by his caseworker. This was an event where prospective adoptive families and children available for adoption were brought together to meet and do a variety of activities designed to have families look for children in whom they were interested (a concept, by the way, which I have never supported). The afternoon was filled with food, fun, balloons and games. When this six year old returned to our program, I asked him how the party was for him. He said some of it was OK, but the adults kept getting too close to his private parts. This assessment of the event would never have been considered by the organizers, his caseworker, or any of the parents at the event. However, knowing the inner experience of this sexually abused child, puts the many encounters and hugs lovingly given by adults at the party into an entirely different perspective -- his.

Abused children get stuck in certain patterns, not unlike adults. The child defines her situation in primitive terms (more precisely feelings) of good and bad. It is good to go now, it is bad to wait five minutes. Enough is not a developed concept -- enough food, enough TV, enough attention. In Gestalt terms, the child does not place the foreground in the context of the background. Therefore this moment is the defining event in her short life -- if you said yes the last ten times, the fact that you are saying no this time is all that matters. The child does not experience continuity; your love for him must be proven every day with every action.

Since survival is ingrained in the base brain, getting, grabbing, taking and consuming are much more developed than any signs of waiting, delaying, or letting someone else go first. In a precognitive way, the child needs to get to the drinking fountain first because he cannot be sure that there will be water left when it is his turn. If that seems silly, watch adults leave a stadium after the game or try to get out of the church parking lot as if Godzilla were expected at any time. Because *now* is all a child experiences (foreground), the fact that there has always been more water in the drinking fountain does not enter into the internal process that drives the child's choices and behavior.

Abused children do not experience their own controlling and demanding behavior as a problem. They experience any barriers to their needs and wants being met as problems. In other words, adults who set limits are perceived as threats. In a type of reverse logic, safe adults become the biggest targets for their wrath. This occurs because unsafe adults are to be watched and avoided, if possible. And it is safe adults who make it possible to express what they really feel, which is general negativity toward adults who set boundaries and limits. This appears to be true for parents and therapists, and whoever takes the time to enter and try to understand the world of an abused child. These caring, sensitive adults will often be rewarded with hostility and at times aggression from the child.

The therapist has two primary roles with traumatized children: first, to establish a safe place for children to explore their exterior and interior world as they wish, and second, to become a therapeutic coach to the people who can make the most healing difference in the situation -- the parents.

I have already covered a number of issues concerning the role of creating a safe place. It is important to remember to individualize every case: learn the language of the child, don't ask him to let down his protections unless he is currently in a supportive environment at home, don't be in a hurry, and don't mistake manipulation and the child's following your lead for a true relationship.

The second role deserves some attention -- that of being a "coach" to the family. Therapists often overestimate the importance of what they do, and underestimate the impact they could have on the environmental scene. Too many therapists opt for seeing the child alone as the treatment of choice for young abused children. They believe they can create the conditions necessary for the child's healing during an hour every Wednesday morning at eleven. This type of thinking generally overestimates the effect they will have.

Opting to work with the child, who is the one who has been traumatized, and not work with the parents is overlooking the opportunity for maximum therapeutic impact. But isn't it the child who needs the therapy, not the parents? Correct, so save your therapy for the child, and with the parents learn how to be a good therapeutic coach.

The role of a coach is rather specific. No one would assume that Michael Jordan or Mia Hamm do not know what to do in the stadium. However, it takes the coach to bring out the best in the athlete. The coach never goes onto the field, but does send in plays and provide external eyes for the athletes to see themselves and how they can improve. A therapeutic coach's role is very similar. The coach knows that it is the parents who must play the most important role in the child's healing, because parents create the environment that will either support or further traumatize the child. Even if the parents are not particularly skilled at parenting, they deserve the chance to improve through your coaching, and the child also deserves to have more skilled parents.

The coach assesses the family environment and makes important adjustments. Like other coaches, therapeutic coaches look in from the outside and call in a play. Therefore, the family must agree in advance to the arrangement of relying on the therapist as coach. Most parents are very eager to help, if they know what to do, and know that, in fact, what they are doing is helpful to the child. It can be very complex to understand what the child needs to live with the counterintuitive aspects of the way the child thinks. Without a coach, few parents are prepared to do their best job as a therapeutic agent for the child.

Many parents resist "therapy," but few will resist an experienced coach who will help them be better at accomplishing this extremely difficult task. The tone of this book is coaching. I do not assume that you as a therapist do not know your business, or that parents do not know their own child; but I do believe that focusing attention on specific issues can improve the quality of your therapy and their parenting.

The final point for therapists is knowing when to get help with a case. Too many inexperienced therapists believe that asking others for help is a sign of a lack of competence or confidence, when the opposite is true. All the best therapists know when to seek some coaching for themselves because they, like all world-class athletes, understand that some outside input can usually improve their understanding and their performance. It is a good idea for all therapists to have a supervisor in the form of either an individual or a group of peers who provide group supervision. The supervisor does not need to be more experienced or more knowledgeable; she just needs to have an objective third party perspective. It is amazing how clearly we can see how others can improve, and how difficult it is at times to know what to do when *we* become stuck. Therefore, the answer to when should the therapist seek external input and coaching is "frequently."

Parenting the Traumatized Child

Although the role of being a therapist can be challenging, it cannot compare to the difficulty of being the parent of a traumatized child. Among other differences, if a therapist believes she is not accomplishing the treatment goals, she can refer to another therapist. A parent who believes she is not getting through to a child cannot refer the child to another parent.

It is the parent's role to provide, to teach, to understand, to admonish and discipline, to provide structure, to play and have fun, and to nurture the child. At times, some of these tasks feel mutually exclusive. Many times the child seems to be doing his or her best to obstruct the process rather than cooperate and work with the parent. This is the reason for the title of this book. The parents of the majority of children have a huge job on their hands, but the parents of traumatized children have the same job under much more difficult circumstances.

The Building Blocks for Treating Emotional Disturbances were discussed in the last section in relation to the role of therapists. It will be important to revisit these areas in regard to the role of the parent. A number of characteristics and examples of children will be mentioned. Some might sound extreme and worse than what you face in your home. If so, appreciate this fact because some children are every bit as challenging as my examples, and some children even more so.

Not all of the characteristics mentioned will be true for all children. But I trust that you will find examples that sound like your little darling at home, who has you reading this book and who is making you earn your parenting stripes. You will notice that additional building blocks have been added to the parent's task, just so you don't get bored with the task!

Safety

It is typical for traumatized children, years after their abuse has ended, to continue to, at least subconsciously, wonder when they will be abused again. It is also common for these children to overreact to limits or discipline, and at times to claim you are abusing them. It is true that in life we usually find what we are looking for -- if not in reality, then at least in our own mind. Abused children continue to experience abuse when there is none.

Traumatized children have an inner radar that sizes up adults in their world. An oddity about these children is that they do not always avoid such adults. At times their protective method is to get on the good side or make friends with an individual they find threatening. A fact that may be hard for some to accept is that in more severe abuse cases, children will frequently pursue abuse, and act in ways to recreate previous traumatic events. It is as if their world is one where abuse is ever present, and rather than be anxious about from whom and when the next abuse will come, they act as if they want to get it over with.

Another pattern of abused children is to escalate their behavior until they become dangerous to others or to themselves and need adults to prevent harm by holding them. When protecting the child requires the parent to physical hold the child, it is at this point the adult will often be rewarded with the child calling the parent an abuser. After two decades of this experience, and sufficient understanding to know better, it is still difficult for me to hold an out-of-control child as he screams that I am hurting and abusing him. Although this experience may be frequent enough for my mind to understand what is really happening, it remains upsetting to my body and my emotions, and never completely becomes routine. Perhaps it is good not to become hardened to this experience.

Another aspect of demonstrating to the child that the environment is safe is to show the ability to contain the child's explosions (or implosions). Although the adult will usually be punished by the child (biting, scratching, kicking, or calling you things like an abuser), these children must test whether you can handle violent situations. It is another example of counterintuitive logic that children are anxious about violence so they become violent to see if they are safe. When this happens, it is the adults' job to take charge of the situation and not to let the child hurt anyone or anything. Frequently, abused children will resort to damaging or destroying their possessions, often their favorite things.

Some adults let this happen to have the child learn from logical consequences. I suggest that you not do this. When the child tests you by pushing the limits of violent and destructive behavior, use this opportunity to demonstrate your ability to maintain a safe environment, as well as your ability to protect the child while staying calm yourself. This is the quickest way to stabilize the present situation and resolve the need for further testing of this nature. Understand that when abused children attack you or others, they may be less motivated by a desire to hurt you (regardless of what they look like or say) and more interested to see if you can keep them and others safe. Strong adults who stay in control of themselves and the situation receive much less testing from children.

A safe environment is one where the child's basic needs will be met. In particular, children who have experienced neglect are constantly concerned that there will be insufficient food, that their clothing will be less than what they need, and that other basic needs will go unmet, creating stressful vigilance. It is not unusual for one of these children to horde food years after there has been any sign of neglect. This comes from the child's unconscious belief that this meal may be the last, so it is a good idea to stock up and if possible take some with you.

Safety is communicated from messages throughout the environment. To ensure a message of safety, consider any forms of violence in your world such as movies and entertainment, verbal interchanges, playful expressions, and how pets and animals are treated. In our treatment program, we have always served a meatless diet, not because we are vegetarians, but because we need a ranch that is safe for the children, for chickens and other animals as well. On a family farm like ours, children tend to have a better idea where the milk and the meat come from.

Although the typical American household is desensitized to violence, such as hundreds of violent incidents on prime time TV each night, do your best to consider any messages of violence in your home. If "Lethal Weapon 8" or horror movies are your style, watch them alone, or at least talk to your children about the difference between real and pretend, although you will probably not be very successful.

Safety also requires clear guidelines and rules. Make sure that your household has clear and specific rules. This helps provide a structure that is critically important for abused children. Start with firm limits; you can always back off later. When in doubt, err on the side of firm structure. Children will let you know with their calm energy when the exterior structure can be loosened and their own inner structure is ready to take over.

A final point on safety is to avoid punishment, discipline, or consequences that get too close to basic needs. For example, it is not advisable to discipline a previously neglected child with the loss of food, such as being sent to bed during dinner. Although they will survive with fewer calories on a particular day, you need to consider what this may do to their inner anxiety. Some parents will lock a constantly intrusive child out of the house to get some space. While the frustration of the parent can be understood, it should be clear why this may have counterproductive results, with the child's anxiety likely producing more intrusiveness. To have a safe environment, all basic needs must be met unconditionally, regardless of the child's behavior, attitude, or cooperation.

Security

If you have had an abused child in your house, you know that she seldom likes surprises. Most children have a desire to know what is going on, but these children have a need to know, and often a need to control. It must be made very clear and consistently demonstrated who is in charge of your household. Although the child will attempt to take over, it is vital that the adults maintain the power base of the home.

Structure and routine are important aspects of predictability, which translates into security. When children have difficult days, weeks or months, I almost always suggest tightening the structure of the household. Try this and see if within a short period of time it helps stabilize the energy of the home. Predictability means paying attention to small details -- when supper is served, when bath time happens and the bedtime routine -- all of which provide the child some peace of mind by being able to anticipate what will happen next. Remember, in the child's past when things changed, it was often hurtful for the child.

Consistency is an important concept to discuss. Raising a child who makes it difficult for you to parent requires more than standard skills. You must become aware of and proficient at some advanced parenting skills. Consistency is a good example. This concept is the foundation of most parenting courses, as it should be. Consistency assists with safety and security. However, some children use parental consistency to their manipulative advantage in order to beat the parents at their own game -- power and control.

When possible, be as consistent as you can, which means be consistent when this produces the results you are looking for. When children are constantly working to take control of the family and the mood of the house, another concept may be important -- creative inconsistency. This means that in specific ways the parent varies the situation to actually throw off the plan of the manipulative child. The goal here is to keep the manipulative intent of the child off-balance. Although this sounds inconsistent with the points made previously, it is a paradox, not a contradiction.

The greatest need of the children for safety and security is to have the adults in charge. When they have been successful at taking control of the household, everyone loses. At times like this, being specifically unpredictable as a parent can tip the balance of control back in favor of the adult, and everyone comes out ahead.

Manipulative children love to learn the rules of the house and then use the rules for their own purposes of control. In these cases, the parent must assert the parental right to change the rules when this is deemed necessary. In this way, the manipulative child is not sure where the battle line is and what to fight against.

Another example of creative inconsistency is letting the child know his choices and the consequences of the choice, i.e., telling the child that if he continues to use poor manners when eating out, the family will just stay home. The manipulative child would much rather control the family than have a nice meal. Creative inconsistency would recommend avoiding telling the child in advance what the consequences will be in order to avoid giving the child the power in the situation to determine the outcome. Control is a much higher motivator for some children than losing a privilege. Remember creative inconsistency is to be used sparingly, and only when it is a tool to maintain the control of the environment within the hands of the parent. It is not an excuse to be an inconsistent parent.

Acceptance

The next step on the climb of healing the trauma of abuse is working to have the child feel acceptance. It means little if you accept the child but he does not experience it. These children have often been rejected by their own parents, and due to their behavior, by their extended family, school and community as well. With that past track record, most of us would not only feel unloved but also unlovable. Many of these children have learned that regardless of how hard they may try to be accepted, rejection is the likely end result. As one child told me once in a rage, "If my mom doesn't love me, why would anyone?" A good question indeed, from her point of view.

The shortcut to all the pain of rejection is to get it over with and be rejected outright. At least the child feels somewhat in control when she acts in ways to elicit rejection from others. It is important to sense when a child is doing his best to have you not like him. As long as you have this possibility in your mind, it is often rather easy to spot.

Sexually abused children have learned that they were a part of something very wrong. Few young children fully understand that it was not their fault. In their experience, to be involved in something very bad, is to *be* very bad. This leaves an indelible mark on many of these children that can continue into adulthood. For some it makes it easier for them to do "bad" things in the future, and for others, they can quietly keep it to themselves that they are bad on the inside (one of the root causes of the implosive dynamic discussed earlier).

Acceptance becomes critical for abused children. Inside, they believe that they are not really likable because of the bad things they have done. The list of bad things continues as they grow up to include ordinary mistakes as well as behavior that breaks the rules in various settings. It is not long before the weight of being bad has crushed the hope that they may have had to ever be a good person whom others could love.

In the context of children sure of their inherent unworthiness, families must attempt the difficult task of separating the child from the child's behavior. First this must occur in the mind of the parent, who must then work to instill this in the mind of the child. When we feel terrible about ourselves, our behavior shows the results either as children or as adults. When a child feels that she is a bad person, she often acts poorly, confirming her belief and perpetuating the cycle. Identifying the solution to this problem can be easy, but implementing the solution is very hard work. The parent must help the child learn that he can improve his behavior. Who he is inside goes beyond how he acts, and is not simply a sum total of the mistakes he has made and the "bad" things he has done.

In each situation, work to separate the behavior from the person. After Amber intentionally hurts the family dog, you might say, "Amber, what you did was wrong. I know you are capable of being gentle with Lassie; now show me that you can treat her in nice ways."

In most cases the child knows what she has done is wrong. Doing "bad" things is a way she confirms her inner self-perception; that is why many of these children constantly do what they are told not to do. This is often intentional behavior to let you know that inside she is "bad." Therefore, you must confront the problem behavior, and at the same time work to support the struggling positive person inside, who is buried in the rubble of negative self-talk and a strong belief in being worthless and unlovable. There is nothing easy about the persistence and endurance the parent must have to continually work with and support the child who is being a problem on purpose. But remember, at the point the child convinces you that he is bad, the child wins the battle and everyone begins to lose the war.

Most children are not good enough at being bad to maintain this all the time, although some come pretty close. This leaves room for the opportunity to catch the child in the act of doing something good. With a child who has frequent problem behaviors, try not to let any positive behavior go by unnoticed or unmentioned. Each time you comment on something good he has done, you are confronting the error in his thinking that he is inherently a bad person. You must realize that the child may attempt to change your mind by rewarding any compliments with some immediate negative behavior. Anticipate this, and don't let the child turn your positive statement into two negative ones.

41

I make accepting the child sound like a battle of wills, and I believe it is. The parent must win this battle by staying positive about the ability of the child to do better, and it will help greatly to catch her at it, particularly when she does not expect it.

Particularly for a child who has been through multiple homes, either with relatives, foster care or adoptive placements, he has likely faced many adults who have eventually agreed with the child's inner assessment that he is a negative, unpleasant and problematic child. This is understandable, because the child does act in these ways. What such a child needs is the patience and force of will of a parent to override his problematic behavior and teach him how to be positive and likable.

It may help your persistence to consider that the child's behavior is a direct result of his past. Essentially, what has occurred is that the abusive adult in his past has taught him to continue the abuse by acting in ways that invite negative responses from everyone around him. I have used the analogy before of having a negative computer chip in the brain, placed there by an abusive adult, so that long after the adult is absent from the picture the chip goes on working. With this dynamic, the child perpetuates the abuse until someone deactivates the chip.

Belonging

Where do children belong who have a belief that they are bad, unlovable, and do not deserve a successful life? The answer is that they do not belong anywhere, unless they can learn to *feel* differently, and then they have a chance to *act* differently. A brief comment about focusing on behavior: some parenting systems solely work with behaviors, saying that this is all that really matters in the long run. Behaviorist thinking says that only externally visible behavior is to be addressed.

Certainly all parenting must focus on behaviors, but I think it is a mistake to stop there.

Behaviors are not causes; they are effects. This means that we behave as we do because we think and feel in certain ways, not the opposite. With some children, it may be successful to just work with their behavior, but not for children with a traumatic past. If you are able to help them think and feel differently, the children's behavior cannot help but change. Only if you can help a child think and feel differently will the child be able to be positive without you around. You will then become the source of positive energy because the child may not have an interior source. My advice is to work with the whole child, not just with behavior, which is only a small aspect of the child.

Does a child with constant problems belong in your home? You thought so in the beginning, didn't you? Perhaps a good way of looking at this is to say that the child's behaviors do not belong in your home, but the child does. This places the focus where it belongs: how can we eliminate the behaviors and the energy that does not belong, and make room for the child to begin to feel like he or she belongs somewhere? This can be a significant challenge because the child does not even like herself; in a sense, she does not feel like she even belongs in her own skin. So how do we make room for such children in our homes? Here are a few suggestions:

♦ Verbally let the child know she belongs until she is sick of hearing it.

♦ Don't let him get you to reject him; what you will need to reject are the problem behaviors, not the child.

- Find ways the child fits, such as finding what he is good at and having his skill add something unique to the family.

- Use as much physical touch and affection as possible. To do this, you will need to learn the difference between complaining (which can be translated that they actually like it) and refusing (they are not ready for it). But do not do a lot of touching until the child has been in your home awhile. Particularly to a sexually abused child, touch can send the wrong message until she gets to know you.

- Make sure that both parents have one-on-one time with the child. This is what we all do with people we are interested in.

- Give her a meaningful role in the family. Forget taking out the trash and cleaning up after Bowser in the backyard; give her a role that is needed by the family and isn't something no one else wants to do.

There are hundreds of other ways that signal to the child that he or she belongs in your family. Your mission, if you choose to accept it, is to find ways in your family to have the child feel like he or she belongs.

Trust

The child must be safe and secure, both in reality and in his own experience. Unless he is accepted for who he is and he has a sense of belonging, the meaning of trust, and willingness to trust, will escape him. If trusting is to rely on someone else and to make yourself vulnerable by counting on them to come through for you, what idiot would want to trust? Isn't the goal in life to seek pleasure and avoid pain? Pain comes from other people hurting you, using you, getting in the way of your getting what you want, and nearly always letting you down. At least these are the general thoughts of people who have paid the price of relying on others with negative, and sometimes tragic, results. So trust is a concept that includes a fundamental shift in one's orientation to life -- finding the good things of life *with* others, not *despite* others.

Most people grow up with the experience of life as a social event. We receive life itself and nurturing from our families, and companionship from siblings, relatives and peers. We celebrate with the community we are a part of. We participate in various situations that are mini-extended families such as our classroom, sports team, scouting group, clubs, or a variety of other social groupings.

But for some children who did not get beyond parents providing them basic needs and nurturing, life has become a minefield of avoiding the reliance on, and vulnerability to, others. The child's world view is that others take rather than give, and hurt rather than help. For all these reasons, the fundamental building blocks of safety, security, acceptance, and belonging must be experienced by the child before the child will understand why anyone would want to do something as absurd as trusting another human being.

The tragic consequences of living a life without trust are seen in many of the people we consider casualties of our society. Socially isolated individuals, those looking for escape in drug and alcohol abuse, are people who neither have nor want a personal support system. Abused children have been initiated into a training program to be such members of our society. They have learned well that they will never really fit in, they will seldom contribute, and their own personal devastation is compounded with the pain that they will cause others, particularly those unlucky enough to love and be concerned for them.

I mention these unpleasant dimensions of the problem of living a life without trust just in case you needed more motivation to do all you can to help a child go in a different direction -- a social direction, one that includes family, friends, and community as positive elements of one's life. It is extremely difficult to learn trust as an adult, if it was not learned as it should have been in childhood. For the sake of the child, your family, and everyone who will come in contact with the child over his lifetime, invest now in teaching the child the essential value of trust, if he is to have any hope of a rich, fulfilling life.

How do you teach trust? The first step is to create a world that can be trusted. This requires the many elements we have discussed, such as the lack of fear of being hurt, knowing basic needs will be met, and being surrounded by a consistently predictable world. From there the child must be taught to rely on others. This does not often come from the child; it must come from the adults and the family.

Putting the child in situations where she must rely on others is the key. This can be family work projects, cooperative ventures such as the child earning half of the money for a new bike (he must rely on the parent for the other half), team sports, or a host of other situations in which the child cannot accomplish something she wants without others.

Of course, the child will try to avoid such situations. One of the standard traits of abused children is telling the people around them that they want nothing from anyone. These children want us to believe that nothing is motivating enough to be vulnerable to others for. I seldom have found this to be the case. Nearly all children have strong wants. Abused children may give the external appearance of not having things they want, but watch carefully when they do not know others are observing. Saying "you can't do anything to me or take anything from me because I don't care" is one of the abused child's strongest insulating factors. The problem is that it is very difficult not to want things, and most of the children who say this can not live it.

Trust is bred in an environment of respect. You must respect the child and demand respect in return. To do this, you primarily do not demand it verbally, but by your every action. Children respect strength, they respect power, they respect adults who cannot be manipulated.

I believe that for many abused children, respect starts with a very primitive form of recognizing that the adult is a factor to be reckoned with. This can include the parent setting firm rules, the parent maintaining control over the mood of the home and the child's own mood. Children learn respect from experiencing that adults are physically large and strong, particularly when this power is not used to hurt them, but to enforce the limits.

I believe that most children and certainly most abused children test adults and the family rules to find out if the adult is serious. The child needs to learn whether the parent will be able to enforce the rules, and to find out just who is in charge. Consider the look on the face of a very young child approaching mommy's favorite glass vase as she looks around to see if you will enforce the rule of not touching it. If the adult does not pass this test, everyone is in for a hard time.

As the primitive tests are passed, there are many other tests of the child's ability to trust you. These children will try to find your flaws to confirm the belief that you cannot be trusted. The child will look for inconsistencies, "lies," and hidden agendas. At times, it may help to reflect this back to him or her, for example, by saying, "I know you are wondering if I'm telling you the truth, so I want you to check with your teacher to find out," or "You may think that because it rained and we can't play in the park as promised that I will not keep my promise;

but when it stops raining today or tomorrow, you will find out that I keep my promises."

These children have had adults shield them from bad news, believing it somehow protects them. But the child interprets this as being deceitful and lying. Tell her the truth; if she can rely on you to hear bad news, there is a chance she can rely on you for good news.

In my opinion, only after the beginning of respect and trust can the foundation of being a successful social person happen -- which is the ability to develop and maintain relationships.

Relationships

Relationships are places where there is a mutual interchange that meets the needs of both parties and no one is used or abused. The foundation of a relationship is interdependence, trust and respect. The first relationships formed by abused children are pretty rough and tenuous. It is a frightening thing to open oneself to someone else, particularly when this is done on purpose.

Do not be surprised when an abused child withdraws frequently into her shell at the first sign of anxiety, much like a human hermit crab. The child will project negative motivations onto your words or actions, hoping you can prove her wrong. It is fine to offer verbal reassurance to these children, but remember that your actions, not your words, are what speak the loudest.

Do not put up with less than what you want from these children. They will frequently lapse into attempting to use or abuse you, or they will give you very little so you set lower expectations of them. Do not fall into this trap, for the benefit of both yourself and the child. Relationships are reciprocal, two sided, give and take. Anything less is just that -- less than a relationship.

You are the adult, and you are the one who knows how to have a relationship. So you must set the tone by being vulnerable, by relying on the child (for some things), and by setting the example of trusting first. If it sounds scary to you to trust and be vulnerable to Genghis Khan Jr., then consider what it is like for the child to trust anyone else. Grit your teeth and get ready to be disappointed, and get ready to give more than you receive in return.

All relationships have some element of love, because respect, vulnerability and reciprocity are the beginnings of love. When you teach a child the steps of a relationship, you are teaching him or her the beginning lessons of the most important skill for a successful life -- how to love.

Do not get in a hurry, particularly if you are seeing some signs of progress, even very small steps. Relationships take time. They grow one step at a time. If you skip any of the steps along the way, it will feel like a game of chutes and ladders, or should I say chutes and chutes? You will find yourself losing more ground than you feel like you have gained. If you are in a hurry, the child will sense that you want something from him, and he will instinctively resist anyone who wants something from him due to the his past experiences.

When you do begin to see some signs of movement in the child, or others tell you they do (sometimes we are too close to see the growth in our own children), do not overdo it by speeding up the process. Do not give large amounts of trust to the child before he can handle it. Do not rely on the child for anything major until you are both prepared to handle a less than successful outcome. I do suggest upping the ante, but do so gradually, and avoid huge leaps of faith. If you entrust the child with too much, you will both be disappointed if it does not turn out well. Small successes are much better than a perceived big failure.

Self Understanding

The next milestone on the journey to actualization, or becoming a complete person, is the ability to look at and

49

understand yourself. How do people learn to have self understanding? As you can see from many adults that you know, this process is not instinctual. We learn to understand ourselves by having a recognition of our inner thoughts and feelings, and then we use this reflection to consider our behavior. But there is an important step that comes before inward reflection, and it is interacting with others and seeing in them a reflection of what we are like.

We use mirrors each day to see what others see when they look at us. We use mirrors to clean, to groom, and to alter our reflection. We do the same with the reflection we receive from others around us. However, we give the greatest consideration to reflections of ourselves that come from people we trust and those whom we know care about us.

Abused children who never reach the level of forming relationships never trust and know that the other person cares for them, so they ignore the reflection or they see the other person's abusive intentions rather than seeing themselves. If we never look in a mirror, our appearance is not only unknown to us, it becomes internally irrelevant and ultimately pretty rough to others.

After children have learned to maintain at least some level of relationship, they can begin to look into the mirror and see themselves through the eyes of others for the first time. Initially, they may not like what they see, something like the rest of us peeking into the mirror first thing in the morning. These children will argue with the mirror (you) and say the mirror is wrong (ever say that about a scale you just weighed yourself on and didn't like the reflection back?). The children will externally assert that they actually look much better than your reflection, but internally they believe it is much worse than what you reflect. But arguing with the image is the first sign of progress, because children are in fact seeing an image of themselves, whether they like it or not.

Self discovery is both exciting and frightening. What if no one likes who I am? What if I don't like who I am? For abused children, these concerns have been answered; they know they are not liked by others and they know how unlikeable they are. So you are starting from a deficit. The good news is that for some abused children, their self image cannot get much worse, so there is only one way to go, and that is up.

When reflecting to these children, be sure to highlight some strengths. Find some traits or abilities that you find impressive or amazing. Be honest, but don't hold back from using a little emphasis when pointing out strengths: "You do such a great job at art; I bet you can become an artist if you want to."

For some time I worked with a child who was consistently negative, broke all the rules and quickly would get everyone to dislike him. No sooner would you compliment him on something than he was being unpleasant with renewed enthusiasm. Some of the other treatment staff felt the child was just downright unpleasant to be around.

As I worked with him, I looked for something that was special and unique about him with little success. Then I noticed that one of his favorite ways to get negative attention was to climb on things. He climbed trees, poles, walls -- all without permission, of course. It then occurred to me that his unique talent was his ability to climb. It may not be in high demand as a marketable skill for a profession (though I have always wondered who changes the blinking red lights on the top of radio towers), but you had to hand it to him, he was good at climbing.

After I convinced the program director to risk that he would not hurt himself, I got the green light to have this child do some climbing, and I was right there with my verbal amazement. I was being honest with my compliments of him; he could climb a telephone pole with his legs and arms, or go right up a tree without branches to stand on. Since he saw himself as a good climber, he let in my positive reflection of

51

him. It may not sound like much in the overall picture, but we began to reach this child by repeatedly reflecting his skills at climbing, and then used climbing as a metaphor and symbol of how he could approach other things.

An important aspect of self understanding is being able to see one's own motivations in an honest way, even when we are up to no good. Being able to accurately understand what is behind our own actions is the beginning to having a more realistic picture of the motivations of others. Abused children have notoriously poor skills in knowing why other people act the way they do. They are either culls, or worse, they believe that all problems and difficulties are specifically targeted at them by you and other unfair adults. It takes awhile to get there, but the journey to understanding others includes a stopover in understanding yourself.

The point of self understanding is to ask the age old question "Who am I?" Some of us adults are still asking forms of this question. It is a large part of the ongoing discovery of life. It will help abused children to understand this question for themselves if they have a sense of who you think they are. They have already heard plenty from adults, and it has usually been in response to some problematic behavior. If this is not who you want the child to see when he looks inward, then you must balance all the negative with as much positive as you can find.

A frequent statement in reports on children that I read is that the child lacks empathy. When I read this I wonder if the clinician realizes what he is really saying. Does the therapist consider this a personal deficit at age six, eight or even twelve? Empathy is one of the higher order concepts of moral reasoning, and a trait that is often lacking in adults. When I read that a child has been used and abused by others, I *expect* her to be on the lower rungs of the moral ladder in her ability to empathized with others.

But empathy is a very important aspect of long-term, successful relationships, so it deserves attention as the child matures. Self understanding can provide the beginning of empathy toward the self, because how can we give someone else a break if we cut ourselves no slack? The beginnings of empathy will come when the child realizes his faults and at the same time realizes that everyone has shortcomings. When the child begins to accept the fact that she falls short of the mark at times, then she can begin to accept others when they do the same.

From there, the child can branch out to caring how others feel, how others experience a difficult situation, and even to having a sense of what it is like for the other person when a commitment is broken, or when you hurt someone else physically or emotionally. Self understanding is the key that unlocks the door to all higher order human emotions and social skills.

Personal Worth

The highest level of the Building Blocks is personal worth. As I mentioned previously, reports often indicate that a child has no empathy, and poor self esteem and personal worth are often mentioned. It goes without saying that an abused child who struggles with emotional disturbances not only has low self esteem, but she actually has a deficit balance in her personal worth bank account. If you have been patient enough to stick with me on each step of the Building Blocks, then you will have a good idea of why this is the case. Without each of the other building blocks creating the foundation that supports personal worth, the child's belief in himself crumbles to very low levels.

There are many specific ways to teach personal worth, but the bottom line is that personal worth is not something you hear about, it is something you feel. You feel worthwhile because you succeed at something, you help someone, or you experience love from someone. Think about the things that make you feel your personal worth, and see if you can help the child feel his own worth. In order to be successful in all social situations, the child must learn to act right; she must also learn to perceive correctly what is going on and what is called for from her. In other words, the child needs to learn how to think right.

As soon as you can, let him in on one of life's most fundamental paradoxes -- we feel the best about ourselves when we think first of others and help someone else to feel better. Isn't that why you are still reading this, and why you will continue the thankless job of parenting your troubled child?

The cycle of feeling bad about oneself results in negative behavior, which results in problems with people around you and your environment, which invites you to feel even worse about yourself, and the beat goes on. It is only when this cycle begins to level off, and then head in a positive direction, that personal worth becomes a possibility for the child.

Fortunately, just as negative cycles have a tendency to repeat, so do positive cycles. In fact, the world is full of people who were able to fight off criminal behavior, drug abuse, gambling and many other negative spirals to start a positive spiral that is fed and can continue on an upward trend. For example, it is common over the centuries to find that some of the greatest religious figures were ungodly, so to speak, early on in their lives. Many inspirational speakers and figures have been in the depths and continue to feed their own positive spiral, not stopping along the way at mediocrity, or even being average. Help the abused child develop a positive cycle of behavior and see where he or she can end up!

Child therapists are taught that children communicate much better in ways other than words. Parents need to learn this same lesson. Children communicate their truth in symbols and in codes. Once you know the language of a specific child, the child will be basically unable to lie or deceive you except with words, and you will know better than to rely solely on the words of a child. The skill needed here is what I call translating. A child's actions, her energy, her nonverbal expressions, and her play all let adults know exactly what is going on with her. You simply need to be able to translate the code into a language you understand.

For example, in making statements, abused children are much like normal teenagers (if normal and teenager can be put in the same sentence). They often speak in opposites. Let's try some familiar statements: when a teen says "Mom, can I use the family car tonight, I won't go far, I won't go over the speed limit, and I promise to come home early," let's translate, "Mom, I need the car to help me cut loose tonight, and by being home early I mean early in the morning." OK, they are not all that bad; let's try another: "I wish you would just back off with all the rules." This often really means "I know you care when you set boundaries, but it isn't easy to follow them." How about "Yes, my school work is all caught up, so can I go camping this weekend with the guys?" This might really mean, "You'd better call the teacher if you want the facts; what do you think I'm going to say if you ask me if my work is all turned in?"

I must admit that teens are a little easier than troubled children, but try the same approach of considering the opposite of the words in such statements like "I hate this family," "I don't care if anyone likes me," or "I will just run away and it will be better for everyone." A closer meaning would probably be: "This family may be my last chance," "I don't know how to get people to like me," and "If I run away, will you promise to find me and let me know I belong here?"

Other Thoughts To Consider With Traumatized Children

Working with many parents, I have noticed an attitude among the parents who have been very successful parenting difficult children. I would have guessed that parents who did well might have previous parenting experience, have taken a parenting class or two, or have read a number of the many books that teach effective parenting skills. Although in some cases these factors were helpful, in some cases they were specifically unhelpful.

To explain the common factor that I found in parents who did well with troubled children, I will borrow a concept from Eastern spirituality -- "the beginner's mind." The beginner's mind is an orientation to parenting and to life. It is as if you are having an experience for the first time, and you are fully open to learning from it. This attitude eliminates prejudice, preconceptions that you know in advance what will happen (you often find what you are looking for), and too much reliance on past experience that may or may not be helpful in this situation. In fact, the beginner's mind avoids the belief that what has happened in the past will happen again.

With beginner's mind you go into the situation open to learning what this situation can teach. When you do not have a preconception of what the child will do, the child has more freedom to respond in a new way, and you have a better chance to notice small differences in her response. The beginner's mind is when we first and foremost want to learn from the child and the situations.

Parents who see parenting a challenging child as an excellent opportunity to learn completely change the game from dreading the next problem to actually looking forward to it. Instead of seeing the child as having one goal in life -- to make you miserable -- you accept the challenge to help the child see that he does not have to be miserable.

I have worked with thousands of parents, and the ones who viewed themselves as experts generally failed with disturbed children. I believe this is because the parents' methods were unsuccessful at changing the child to the level wanted by the parent.

Experienced adoptive parents who adopt a child with an emotional disturbance often struggle. I believe this happens because what worked in the past often falls short, despite the parents' belief that the child would eventually come around. I have also worked with parents with no experience, and I either find someone totally over their head or the "beginner's mind" -- learning quickly, not being sure what to do, but excited when something new is learned.

At first I believed that it was actually an advantage to have no parenting experience, so the parent was not comparing this child with others. But I have come to see that it is not the quality of experience, but the quality of the attitude that matters most. The attitude of the learner, the beginner's mind, can be very useful in the process of parenting the most challenging children who do not want to be parented.

This concept of beginner's mind also helps to avoid one of the most common problems among parents -- frustration. There are several reasons why you want to avoid frustration in parenting an abused child. First of all, frustration is my experience when I want things around me to be different than they are. I want traffic to move quicker, I want my boss to stop taking credit for what I actually did at work, or I want my child to learn the right way to act when I have taught him over and over. Frustration is the opposite of the beginner's mind. It says I know what I want and this is not it. We are not generally open to learning from frustration; we just want things to change in the direction that will please us.

Well, there are some serious pitfalls with frustration. I have already mentioned that it gets in the way of your learning from the situation. When I am frustrated, an insight might hit me in the face, but I am too busy wanting things my way to see it. Many of us have found that at times expressing frustration helps those around us modify their behavior by frustrating us less. However, an abused child will not respond positively to expressions of frustration. He will misread your message and believe that you are rejecting him. She might think you are about to hurt her or that you are getting ready to give up on her and send her away.

Also, the manipulative child, who studies you to find your weaknesses, will seldom miss your frustration. The child memorizes any signs of frustration to have more control over mom, or to find things to pull on dad to drive him to distraction. Frustration tells manipulative children, "All you have to do to get me off balance is to (fill in the blank)." Is that what you want to communicate to your manipulative child? Avoid frustration for all these reasons.

When to Get Help and From Whom

In the previous discussions of "coaching," I explained my value that outside help to a parent can be very useful. I would caution that you will feel much better about the whole process if you ask for the help before you really need it. It is almost always easier to fix a problem before it has become a crisis. You and the child will have much more workability if you are not at the end of your rope and the child has not declared total war on the household. If you would rather not get help until it is essential, then here are some signs that it is essential:

- ◆ You and your partner are fighting over how to handle the child.

- ◆ You have trouble sleeping, or have dreams of locking the child in a room and throwing the key into the river.

- ◆ The child is showing a serious interest in self-harm.

♦ You believe the child needs medication to stabilize the situation, or you believe he/she needs a different medication.

♦ You are showing signs of stress that you are not sure you can handle, or you would rather not handle.

♦ You are finding yourself avoiding the child, your home, or family events.

♦ With everything going on, you are not sure you can keep your cool if the status quo continues.

Getting help does not necessarily mean from a professional source; it may be a friend who helps keep you sane, or a minister or rabbi. Help can also come from a child professional. Professionals may have vast education and experience, but none of it may pertain to your situation. How do you find out? Ask. Don't be afraid to have a meeting with a professional as a type of job interview. If you are going to pay her for her services, find out if she has what you need. Ask the therapist about his education and training, but most of all ask him about his experience in coaching other parents who have a very difficult child at home who doesn't fit many of the molds into which children often fit. If the professional is defensive or shows any discomfort with your questions, you have your answer -- move on!

If the professional has an approach to sell you, something she has been well trained in and something she offers to everyone who comes to her, again I would say, "move on." Professionals who have one approach tend to see you through the lens of that approach, and the results too often turn into cookie-cutter solutions that may not be what you need.

One more time to use caution is when you run into a professional who insists on working with your child alone and claims that confidentiality prevents you from knowing what they talk about. This was actually a common occurrence years ago, and fortunately is more rare now. If a professional says, "Just drop off the child and pay your bill on time," politely excuse yourself. Parents who agree to this get what they deserve -- paying for another adult to have secrets with your child, an expensive lesson indeed.

Avoid promises of a "cure." Also avoid any short cuts or "intensive" methods that "speed up" the process. All of the above approaches by professionals may have a place, but in my opinion, their place is not in the treatment of abused children.

Chapter

3

Attachment

A quick overview of this publication will show that I have more to say on some issues with children, and less on others. For example, there will be many more suggestions for understanding and working with children with trauma and bonding problems than for those with learning disabilities or medical conditions. This is primarily due to my instructors, who have been the children themselves. I have worked more with populations that tend to be emotionally and behaviorally troubled due to abuse than with other populations of children.

With this in mind, this chapter on attachment should receive special attention. If you want the *Reader's Digest* condensed version of this entire volume, then read the chapter on trauma and then this chapter, and you will learn much of what I have to say. Because of the importance of this chapter, you will find it to be more detailed and somewhat more technical. With the foundation of the information in this chapter, much of the rest of this book will be easier to understand.

As parents, when we consider children who work against us, one of the early issues we must discuss is the process of attachment, or the lack of it, between the child and family members. The difficulty of some children to bond with others has been observed for at least the last 100 years, but has only been viewed as a treatable mental health problem for the last few decades. We are still learning a great deal about the quality of attachment between children and parents, and what to do when the connection is less than strong.

Understanding and Treating Attachment Problems in Children: What Went Wrong and How Problems Can Be Fixed

The study of psychology over the last hundred years can be compared to reading a novel by starting late into the book and reading progressively backwards to the beginning. Our understanding of the complex mind and psychological make-up of Homo Sapiens has begun with adults, moved to young adults, teens, adolescents, and toddlers, and finally, we are beginning to read with great interest the first chapters of life. As we have done this over the last thirty years, there have been continuous professional awakenings occurring as the antecedents of social, mental, and moral distress begin to tell their stories in very young children.

The purpose of this chapter is to collect the blinding flashes of insight, as well as the mundane aspects of research, in order to begin to tell the story of how the patterns and organization of a human personality are established in the way an infant enters the stage, and what happens early in the first act. The theme of a human being's story and, to a large extent, the fundamental success or failure of their entire life, is established in the early attachment and bonding between the child and the primary care providers.

We are just learning to understand very early childhood and the precursors to social and interpersonal success or failure. This is assisting us in beginning to see clearly how patterns of dysfunction in adulthood can be causally linked to the quality of very early attachment.

Attachment Problems--What Went Wrong

How important is a secure attachment in setting the stage for personality traits and patterns of interpersonal and social success? The following quote by Mary Slater Ainsworth sums it up well:

> Securely attached [infants] are later more cooperative with and effectively more positive as well as less aggressive and/or avoidant toward their mothers and other less familiar adults. Later on, they emerge as more competent and more sympathetic in interaction with peers. In free-play situations they have longer bouts of exploration and display more intense exploratory interest, and in problem-solving situations they are more enthusiastic, more persistent, and better able to elicit and accept their mothers' help. They are more curious, more self-directed, more ego-resilient--and they usually tend to achieve better scores on both developmental tests and measures of language development (Ainsworth, 1979).

Some of the most severe attachment disorders are found with abused and neglected children. The trauma of abuse produces formidable hurdles for these children to overcome. Neither the children nor society can afford for them to also have serious attachment deficits.

Attachment is defined by James as "a reciprocal, enduring, emotional, and physical affiliation between a child and a caregiver" (James, 1994). Research with primates has shown that the more advanced the species, the longer it takes to mature (Bowlby, 1982). The evolutionary message encoded in these phenomena is that Homo Sapiens not only do better in a social network, but survival itself requires sophisticated levels of social interaction for many years following birth.

The natural selective process has made humankind the most dependent of creatures on one another. The social survival network that is first and foremost in importance is the attachment bond with one or more primary care providers. To facilitate this, humans have instinctual patterns leading to survival that involve social mechanisms. Bowlby describes the role of instinct in the process of attachment as "a complex weave of survival and adaptability combined with fixed action patterns in a feedback loop with the environment" (Bowlby, 1982). Without attachment, survival is very much in doubt for one of nature's most helpless of creatures at birth.

Since Bowlby's early work on attachment starting in the fifties, it has been believed that attachment and bonding may well be among the essential keys to explaining the most fundamental psychological and social problems. We now have significant research to confirm the global belief that a person's basic psychological disposition can be established very early in life. The way a child begins to understand his or her surroundings, what Bowlby called "inner working models," has been found to influence a child's perceptions from early childhood on into adulthood (Sroufe, 1988). An abused child may develop a working model of distrusting all relationships, a topic that will be explained later in the chapter. Ainsworth's research on child abuse shows the impact abuse has on the development of a child far into the future (Ainsworth, 1978).

Studies have shown that infants whose relationships with their mothers are more secure are more competent as toddlers, preschoolers and public school students (Belsky, 1988). The belief that attachment may have a generational dimension was given credence in a study that found that the history of nurturing a mother experienced in her own childhood predicted the quality of the attachment she developed with her own infant (Lewis, 1984). Abusive mothers have been shown to be more emotionally sensitive to their infants than neglectful mothers, but less sensitive than non-abusive mothers (Crittenden, 1981).

It has also been found that socially withdrawn children are more likely to come from insensitive mothers, and social withdrawal from peers predicts future social problems (Rubin, 1988). Although the Rubin study focused on mothers who were insensitive due to a lack of awareness, there is perhaps a greater risk for the children of mothers who are aware of what the child needs and wants but do not respond.

Research has shown a link between attachment insecurity and later behavioral problems (Erickson, 1985). Foundations of social success were found in a study showing that secure attachments predicted more competence with peer relationships, a more positive disposition, higher levels of empathy, and having more friends as the child matured (Lewis, 1984). In yet another study, infants who were securely attached at eighteen months were more enthusiastic, persistent, cooperative, and effective (Matos, Arend, and Sroufe, 1978). The nature and quality of primary attachments have predicted socially meaningful characteristics in later life (Bates, 1988). The above are just a few samples of the significant research findings over the last twenty years in this area.

More specific to trauma and abuse, research has also shown that abused and neglected children are more likely to show avoidance of their mothers and resistance to the mother after even a brief separation (Belsky and Nezworski, 1988). Abused children have also been found to be more difficult to raise, while neglected children are more passive, and children in supportive environments are more cooperative (Crittenden, 1981). And finally, a study resulted in the ominous conclusion that antisocial children become adults with disproportionately high rates of alcoholism, accidents, chronic unemployment, divorce, physical and psychiatric illnesses, and welfare involvement--some of the definitional characteristics of societal casualties (Caspi, 1987).

In psychology, as in medicine, we are much quicker to identify a problem than the causes or the solutions to the problem. It is clear that our society has many dysfunctional members. There are over two million men and women in our jails and prisons, the highest rate of incarceration in the developed world. The majority of men and women in our correctional institutions were abused children, and many have lived a life of antisocial behavior beginning in childhood.

Our drug and alcohol programs are full with waiting lists; domestic violence, divorce and broken homes are at the highest levels in our history. Poverty, unemployment and hopelessness exist in abundance in modern America.

Although causative cultural phenomena can be identified, failure in our society is experienced one person at a time, and one life at a time. How do some people beat the odds, while others have the odds beat them? Some of the most exciting answers to this question are coming from the study of early dispositional patterns developed in childhood, or what can be called secure and insecure attachment. Bowlby addresses the importance of attachment in the following statement:

> A young child's experience of an encouraging, supportive and cooperative mother, and a little later father, gives him a sense of worth, a belief in the helpfulness of others, and a favorable model on which to build future relationships. Furthermore, by enabling him to explore his environment with confidence and to deal with it effectively, such experience also promotes his sense of competence. Thenceforward, provided family relationships continue favorably, not only do these early patterns of thought, feelings and behaviour persist, but the personality becomes increasingly structured to operate in

moderately controlled and resilient ways, and increasingly capable of continuing so despite adverse circumstances. Other types of early childhood and later experience have effects of other kinds, leading usually to personality structures of lowered resilience and defective control, vulnerable structures which also are apt to persist. Thereafter on how someone's personality has come to be structured turns his way of responding to subsequent adverse events, among which rejections, separations and losses are some of the most important (Bowlby, 1982).

Attachment Theory

It must be said from the outset that the following is an extremely brief treatment of traditional attachment theory, and can only touch on some of the major areas of a very complex topic.

What is being referred to here as traditional attachment theory was first advanced by an English psychiatrist, who was initially trained as a Freudian psychoanalyst. This psychiatrist, John Bowlby, had an initial goal in 1956 to explain in Freudian terms the behavior of very young children after a significant loss. From this beginning, research and clinical practice has steadily grown and in some ways is just now hitting its stride, forty years after its inception.

Initially, Bowlby, as well as other clinicians, had noticed in young children's responses to loss that there was a somewhat predictable sequence of behaviors: first, children protested with anger and rage; second, they became depressed and showed despair; and finally, the children became detached from people and the environment around them (Bowlby, 1982).

One of the first methods of understanding this behavior was research with primates. Researchers found that young primates gravitated to stimuli of a low, familiar, limited range of magnitude and avoided stimuli of a high, irregular, extensive range of magnitude. This indicated an organismic preference for the predictable and calming sensations over chaos.

When research animals were raised in extremely restricted environments, they would respond with two equally unproductive reactions--either approach all stimuli, or avoid all stimuli. It was consistently found that when primates were raised in an environment where their evolutionary adaptation did not fit the environment, they would develop bizarre and, at times, non-survival behaviors (Bowlby, 1982).

Primate research was subsequently replicated with humans with the same results. It was found that the attachment of humans had a lot to do with the infants experiencing their needs being met, as well as *how* these needs were met. For example, being given a bottle to feed is qualitatively different than the touch, warmth and comfort of breast feeding with the mother (Bowlby, 1982).

As Bowlby's discovery work on attachment proceeded, he found no simple explanations for human attachment, but instead a complex succession of increasingly sophisticated systems mediating attachment behavior. These included the following system components: instinct, physical, emotional and social systems.

The Role of Instinct

A major influence upon attachment is instinct. For Bowlby, attachment is an instinct, as are sexual behaviors and parenting behaviors. The first human instincts of primary importance are the instincts to survive, to be social, and to be adaptable to the environment. How these three instincts interact together is as important as how each functions independently.

Instincts are not restricted to infants; they also affect the mother. Although an infant appears to be predisposed or "wired" to the voice, smell and face of the mother, in a similar manner the mother is instinctively predisposed to respond in a protective and nurturing manner to the child. Mothers are wired to develop an ideal level of proximity to the infant. Studies with mothers have indicated that the young age of a mother and a low educational level signal risk factors in providing a nurturing environment (Sroufe, 1986). One specific example of the mother/child instinctive reciprocity is smiling, which in infants is reserved initially for a human face and voice. Smiling is one of the first vehicles of communication (Bowlby, 1982).

Despite the importance of instincts on attachment, these mechanisms are not tamper proof. Deviations in evolutionary adaptation, as Bowlby describes instinctive behaviors that don't achieve the desired results, can produce maladaptive behavior patterns. These patterns can include being at odds with the child's own best interests, or even working against survival itself.

Bowlby believed that instinctive behaviors can be thwarted, which could make them revert back to more primitive behavioral levels, or become cross wired with their inherent purpose to promote reciprocal social bonding (Bowlby, 1982). When this occurs, a negative cycle develops, with the child slipping further and further away from the instinctive goal of connection.

Physical, Emotional and Social Factors

The three important factors of attachment theory are the physical, the emotional and the social.

Physical factors influencing attachment involve aspects of human physiology, including hormones and the central nervous system. The slow development of the pre-frontal lobes of the brain may have infants acting primarily on the pleasure principle enhancing attachment with the mother (Bowlby, 1982). The importance of physical touch and other senses has already been mentioned.

Emotional bonds are developed (or not developed) rapidly in infants, and once established, they are long lasting. The apparent role of emotions in the attachment process appears to assist in appraisal of both the infant's internal organismic states and also of the external environment. Bowlby calls this affective appraisal "intuition."

Social reciprocity is the purpose of attachment. To facilitate social behavior, early responses to stimuli become more discriminating with age--for example, an infant may initially respond to a picture of a face, then to a real face, then to a specific real face.

Physical sensations combine with the infant's emotional/intuitive appraisal, producing behavior that is social or anti-social. Only if the child can accurately assess the affective state of another person can she productively participate in a social interchange (Bowlby, 1982).

Attachment Theory Behaviorally Defined

The theory of attachment coming primarily from Bowlby's work has historically been defined in behavioral terms and can be summarized in eight important steps: 1) Social responses are first elicited by a wide array of stimuli, then this gradually narrows and after several months becomes confined to one or more individuals, 2) A bias develops to respond more to certain kinds of stimuli than to others, 3) The more experiences of positive social interaction a child has with a person, the stronger the attachment becomes, 4) Exposure to human faces produces discrimination in the attachment figure, 5) The timing of attachment is critical and needs to develop during the sensitive period within the first year, 6) The sensitive phase begins sometime after six weeks (this position has subsequently been criticized), 7) At the end of the sensitive period, the infant responds to non-attachment figures with a fear response, making it difficult to attach after one year, and finally 8) Once a child becomes strongly attached, she prefers this person over all others despite separation (Bowlby, 1982).

Whether or not the above processes remains functional for attachment may depend on the final phase of four attachment processes in infants: a) preferences to look at certain patterns and movements, b) discrimination of one'stimuli over another, c) preference for the familiar, and d) resulting positive feedback continues approach behavior, while negative feedback results in diminished approach response, and then becomes withdrawal behavior (Bowlby, 1982).

Efficacious and Problematic Behaviors

Bowlby breaks attachment behaviors into minute details. He addresses the important roles of crying, smiling, clinging, feeding, signaling, approaching, greeting and maintaining proximity. All these can be used to observe a developing bond.

There are also disruptive behavior patterns that can develop which are contrary to the attachment process. The very early affective or intuitive appraisal of the environment develops standards, or "set points," by which situations are measured. When set points are maladapted due to early disruptions, parental bonding behaviors may be met with anxiety, alarm, and at times anger (Bowlby, 1982).

A variety of other behavior patterns can develop problems. Early negative experiences with hunger, illness, unhappiness and pain can produce disrupted bonding. If an infant's signaling behavior is not responded to in either sufficient quantity or quality, withdrawal can occur. Children have egocentrism, which means that after twelve months of age, they often construct their own internal world and can ignore exterior information that contradicts this internal world (Bowlby, 1982).

Infants have predictable responses to separation from the attachment figure. When separations are short, the reconnection period is usually rapid. However, longer separations can produce anything from distress to the child's rejecting the attachment figure (Bowlby, 1982).

When the focus turns to abused children, studies have found several important outcomes: abused children show significantly more frequent assaultive, harassing and threatening behaviors; they can respond to friendly overtures either by avoiding interaction or by mixed avoidance and approach; and they alienate and avoid adults who might help them, which can develop a self-perpetuating cycle (George and Main, 1979).

A New View of Attachment Theory Based on Trauma

Bowlby's theoretical treatment of attachment remains the most complete and influential viewpoint thirty years after it was first published. Few theories hold up over time without moderate to substantial modification and alteration. Bowlby's theory is somewhat of an exception, although initially it is not without flaws.

Perhaps the biggest flaw in traditional attachment theory is its exclusive emphasis on behavior. Attachment behavior was later to be recognized as the outgrowth of attachment and not the attachment itself. This realization has been recognized concerning behavioral approaches of all kinds--behavior is an effect, not a cause. Bowlby himself acknowledged this by pointing out his initial "failure in the first edition to make clear the distinction to be drawn between an attachment and attachment behaviour" (Bowlby, 1982).

Ainsworth goes a step further to point out that no behavior in and of itself can be called attachment behavior. Ainsworth has also offered three classifications of attachment behavior to more clearly define behavioral traits. These three classifications have received significant research attention: A) insecure avoidant, B) secure, and C) insecure resistant (Ainsworth, 1978). Crittenden later added three new classifications which are avoidant, ambivalent, and compulsive compliant (Crittenden, 1981).

Research with these classifications has revolved around the use of a procedure developed by Ainsworth called the "strange situation" (Ainsworth, Blehar, Waters, & Wall, 1978). Briefly explained, this involves putting the child in a controlled situation without the mother, then introducing a stranger and assessing the behavior. Although this procedure has been a research standard for many years, its value in clinical application is not without controversy (Greenspan and Lieberman).

Traditional attachment theory initially confused the dependence of human infants and how long they take to mature, with their ability to attach. It was initially believed that humans took longer to form attachments than less advanced primates. Bowlby originally stated that the period of time may be many months to one or two years before the infant can be said to have attached (Bowlby, 1982). Developmental psychology research has now shown that attachment usually begins at birth (Lieberman & Pawl, 1988) and some, including this author, would argue that it begins even before birth.

It is not surprising that attachment theory has needed revision; what is surprising is the degree to which it has been supported by research in much the same version as originally presented. With the intensive focus on child trauma over the last two decades and its influence on attachment, it is possible to take attachment theory a step farther.

Throughout Bowlby's descriptions of behavioral systems of attachment and bonding, there are hints of other important aspects of human attachment besides behavior. Restricting the discussion of attachment to behavior does not assist in identifying the causes of the behavior, and is of limited value in treating and rehabilitating attachment disorders.

Recent work on the origins of attachment has developed a need to find an explanation that is not limited to behavioral factors, but incorporates and weaves together instinct, intuition, learning, and the experiences the child has with the environment. In studying the processes and responses of children abused early in life, I define attachment in four principal areas: Spiritual, Inter-personal, Physical, and Affective. These are the four ways a child can experience attachment. All of these areas have behavioral manifestations, but they go much deeper than behavior and, in fact, can be said to cause the observable attachment behavior so clearly identified by Bowlby.

Spiritual--this can be described as the experience of oneness. In infants, this begins as a state of being one with the mother. Afterward, the child has experiences with the mother and others, progressing to an internal world that includes developing beliefs and eventually developing values. This core experience of feeling connected or belonging to an ever expanding network of "I Thou" relationships can be called the individual's primary orientation to a social world. If the spiritual attachment process is halted at any stage, the result in the individual is permanently arrested development of their social orientation unless there are specific and effective interventions, which will be discussed later.

Inter-personal--from before birth, infants are wired to receive pleasure from the attachment figure. In fact, initially there are no barriers between the self and the other person. As the experience gradually develops of establishing where the infant stops and the attachment figure and rest of the world starts, the infant experiences all interaction as inter-personal. At this level, instincts are in sync with the positive experiences of being inter-related with the other person. This produces a social disposition that can continue for life, or it can produce the opposite, a lifelong anti-social orientation.

Physical--the infant first operates on the pleasure/pain principle. What provides pleasure is pursued and what produces pain is avoided. Either the child's many needs are met or they are not. The child learns very quickly that to be social is either pleasurable or painful. A series of negative physical experiences, regardless of the cause, may produce disrupted set points that endure long after the pain is gone (such as child abuse and/or neglect).

Affective--the child's intuitive appraisal of the environment combines all of the above into an emotional response to the world. Fundamentally, it feels good and pleasurable to be attached, or it feels anxious, frustrating, and bad. The affective response stems from the first three areas and determines the strength of the behavior.

Understanding these four ways that children experience attachment, as well as the behavioral manifestations of each, begins to give a blueprint of how healthy attachment or attachment disorders develop. How these four components of attachment can be used to understand and to rehabilitate attachment and bonding, particularly in traumatized children, will now become our focus.

Ψ Attachment Problems and How to Recreate Attachment

In the first part of this chapter, the process of attachment has been considered in traditional behavioral terms, as well as adding affective, physical, inter-personal and spiritual states of connectedness. The goal thus far has been to describe how, when, and why attachment occurs. Now our focus turns to the clinical question of what we can do about attachments that have become disturbed, or that have never developed in any form.

This section begins with a discussion of assessment and moves to a brief review of the multiple issues that will likely be encountered in therapy for attachment problems. The remainder of the chapter presents a detailed model for treating attachment disturbances that the author has developed and used with good success in a residential treatment program that treats serious attachment problems in young children.

In Part I, attachment theory was explained in some detail to form the foundation for clinical attachment interventions. For all its strengths, the question that remains not fully answered in traditional attachment theory is, "What can be done about attachment problems?" This is not to downplay the contribution attachment theory has made to clinical work with this population, but as an explanatory theory, it provides few, if any, prescriptions for treatment. It also falls short of answering whether attachment can be developed later in life when none exists in the first months. The volume of cases where attachment problems are primary concerns has required the therapy world to ask these and many other important questions. Finding the answers has required clinicians to forge new ground.

The use of the term disorder comes from the diagnosis currently called reactive attachment disorder in the Diagnostic and Statistical Manual of Mental Disorders (American Psychiatric Association, 1994). The term disorder requires an explanation. The presence of a reactive attachment disorder in a child in most cases indicates dysfunction in the parent, not the child. The behaviors associated with this diagnosis are inherently adaptive and functional in the child's initial situation. For many children, avoiding attachment has been an aspect of the instinctive process of survival. Because of this, the clinical focus of all attachment work must principally be on the total environment, not solely on the child.

James has identified the roots of attachment in fundamental interactions such as crying/responding, proximity seeking, attention getting and distress/comfort. She goes on to set out the progressive mission of attachment--first, protection of the child, second, providing for the many needs of the child, and third, guiding the child in understanding and maneuvering in social interaction (James, 1994).

A number of factors can disrupt each of the above social transmissions, but few as massively as the trauma resulting from child abuse. One of the most damaging dimensions of abuse is the frequency that the abuser is a primary care provider. What is often called the "ultimate betrayal" (abuse by a parent) can now be understood in its devastating consequences. The person or persons the child must rely upon to survive and thrive have taken on the role of a threat, causing the adaptive response of avoidance. However, to further complicate the child's situation, if the primary care provider must be avoided, how can the child survive? Is it any wonder that traumatized children demonstrate odd and confusing affect and behavior?

Statistically the most frequent source of harm when all types of abuse are considered is the child's mother. The mission of attachment can be immediately thwarted in these cases when the child experiences neither protection nor provision for basic needs, much less the final step of guidance. It may not take long before the child's seeking proximity and signaling distress becomes the avoidance and manipulative control so often seen in children with trauma caused attachment disorders.

Ψ Assessing the Extent of Attachment Disorders

Before the focus turns to clinical solutions, it is important to determine the nature and extent of the attachment problem. A variety of methods have been used to assess attachment disorders including the often used "strange situation" described in Part I. Observational indices have been used by clinicians to examine the mother/child bond, including: 1) intensity of conflict, 2) duration of disturbance, 3) generalizability of dysfunction, 4) level of dysfunction in learning capacity, 5) existence of oppositional behavior, 6) negativism in response to requests, 7) passivity in interaction, 8) overly compliant behavior, and 9) ineffectiveness and lack of persistence in problem-solving behavior (Romer Witten, 1994). James goes on to say the following:

> The evaluator must assess the quality and nature of the child's trauma-related interaction patterns in order to adequately and accurately assess the quality and nature of a traumatized child's attachment behavior patterns...a partial set of questions that reflect these subtle but important distinctions include at least the following: Under what conditions is the child compliant? Who regulates the intensity of feelings in the interaction between adult and child? Does the adult help the child function more independently or dependently? How does the adult achieve this support? To what extent are the boundaries between adult behavior and child behavior maintained or blurred? How are these boundaries established? Under what condition does the child engage in exploration? Does the child use the adult to enhance her ability to explore? Does the adult take over and dictate what the

child should do? To what extent does the adult
coach the child regarding possible solutions to
problems? If the child has a high activity level,
under what observable conditions does this
activity level change? Does the child's behavior
regress during interactions with the adult? If
so, in what ways is this regression observable?
Is the regression appropriate to the situation?
Does the child show anxiety when the adult
must leave the room? If so, how? What is the
child's response to the adult's return? (James,
1994).

A variety of instruments and clinical methods have been
developed to assist in the assessment of attachment
disturbance, including this author's "Attachment Disorder
Assessment Scale" (Ziegler, 1990). Some methods use
observations of the child and mother, and some rely on
information provided by someone who knows the child well,
perhaps in addition to other clinical assessment instruments.

A brief comment must be made at this point concerning a
topic that is complex and needs more discussion than can be
provided here--the trauma bond. Some behaviors that appear
to be signs of attachment in children are actually seriously
confused interactions which reverse the purpose of healthy
attachment. These behaviors have been called trauma bonds,
and they have as their purpose the protection of the abuser by
the child. These displays of loyalty are bred upon fear and
perhaps even concern for survival on the part of the child. It is
clinically essential to distinguish between healthy attachment
and a trauma bond.

Ψ What Must Be Fixed

To identify clinical solutions, we must first identify
specific problems that develop from disrupted attachment.

The following quote from Herman effectively starts this discussion:

> The child trapped in an abusive environment is faced with formidable tasks of adaptation. She must find a way to preserve a sense of trust in people who are untrustworthy, safety in a situation that is unsafe, control in a situation that is terrifyingly unpredictable, power in a situation of helplessness. Unable to care for or protect herself, she must compensate for the failures of adult care and protection with the only means at her disposal, an immature system of psychological defenses (Herman, 1992).

One important point mentioned in the above is the adaptation of the child. To a large extent, most attachment disorders are adaptations to initially unresponsive, painful, or in some way unsuccessful attempts to attach. A serious clinical challenge arises when the child's adaptations become psychologically ingrained. When this occurs, the child is neither aware that he has made the adaptations, nor does he remember why he is acting the way he is. Nearly all attachment adaptations are pre-cognitive because they cannot be recalled, due to the age of onset, and they are pre-verbal as well. For this reason, the deepest levels of attachment issues are not available to insight or cognitive interventions.

James has identified a number of other therapeutic objectives of remediating attachment and bonding:

- When a child adapts by playing a role for the parent, the child loses himself in the role and has no sense of self.

- Actual or perceived trauma overwhelms the child's ability to cope with life.

♦ Regressed or even infantile behavior is common.

♦ Other issues include hypervigilance, heightened startle response, irritability, anxiety, hyperactivity and dissociation.

♦ Numbing and avoidance of affect are frequent.

♦ The alarm/numbing response produces arousal in the form of anxiety from the trauma and then numbing when the anxiety gets extreme.

♦ Understanding risks and the ability to solve problems are often poorly developed skills.

♦ The exploring and learning process is halted and the focus turns to safety, as well as needs and wants.

♦ Attachment problems may incorrectly be viewed as being hyperactivity, low IQ, oppositional defiance, or conduct disorder (James, 1994).

There is evidence that physiological systems of the child are being negatively influenced by the disruption of attachment. The child's brain may learn to organize around a stress response at a very early age (James, 1994; van der Kolk, 1996). The trauma arousal may even be neurologically addictive by activating production of endogenous opioids, which alleviate stress and may then intensify the trauma bond (van der Kolk, 1989). The unhealthy trauma bond becomes reinforced neurologically and the child's loyalty to the abuser becomes stronger as she views her survival in the hands of the abusive parent.

In this topsy turvy world, the child may learn to survive by developing a trauma bond with the abusive parent, but also learns that intimacy is to be avoided at all costs. The unavoidable results are degrees of symptoms such as ego deficiency, handicapped emotional relationships, connections with others based on needs, lack of emotional claim to a care provider, impaired intellectual functioning, and deficiency to regulate aggressive impulses as well as frustration and displeasure (Bates and Bayles, 1988).

Several other factors deserve at least brief mention. Parenting style requires clinical attention in cases where attachment is an issue. In a study of discipline, abused children had more problem behaviors and more oppositional responses to parents. Abusive parents were more punitive in discipline, more angry when disciplining, and punishment was not altered to fit the situation (Trickett and Kuczynski, 1985).

Social support for single parent mothers may be another important intervention. In a study of neglectful mothers, they reported less social support, and people in their environment viewed them as deviant and not wanting support (Polansky and Gaudin, 1985). The role of the parent was pivotal in a study of one-year-olds who showed more positive and less negative affect with happy signaling from the parent (Hershberg and Svejda, 1990).

The last three important areas where attachment must be remedied are: 1) the importance of developing a social rather than anti-social personality, 2) the regaining of childhood, and 3) the development of a conscience.

Much of what has been discussed refers to a social or anti-social orientation. But there is another loss. The process of survival, pleasing the parent, and constantly adapting to a harsh and unsafe environment will rob the child of his childhood. Successful clinical intervention requires giving the child a chance to once again have childhood experiences and to return to him a child-likeness.

An attachment disordered child will often have a poorly developed conscience. To develop a working conscience, the child must experience connectedness to others, which gives the child the ability to read others' emotions and to react with distress to the distress of others. The child then learns to attune first with the parent and then to others, thus planting the seeds of a conscience (Kochanska, 1993).

The parent plays an important role in conscience development, including discipline without an emphasis on power, thus appealing to a child's internal sense of wrongdoing. This results in more internalization and a developing conscience (Kochanska, 1991). Whether developing a social orientation comes first or a conscience comes first, is less relevant than the essential need for both to develop.

Ψ Factors That Influence Reattachment

There is not one scenario that the majority of attachment problems fits into, but several, which will be discussed in the next section. Regardless of the situation, the goal in clinical attachment work is to facilitate the reciprocal, enduring affiliation between parent and child, if this is possible. However, there are factors to be considered that may stand in the way of attachment. This does not mean that attachment therapy should not be initiated, but it does mean that we must recognize the stress factors and inhibitors in the child's life that are potentially working against the clinical goal.

The first factor is the attachment history of the child. In most cases, there are understandable and often logical reasons why attachment problems initially develop. In general, attachment problems are adaptations on the part of the child for survival and self-protection. It means little to the child who has distancing and avoidance behaviors that the threat, the abuse, and the pain of the past are long gone. To children who remember, it is like the abuse happened yesterday. To children too young to remember the abuse, their bodies, through neurological processes that store trauma memories independently, do the remembering for them (van der Kolk, 1989).

A child may be fortunate to start fresh in a loving and supportive environment, but traumatized children can never start totally fresh; their past is always with them. Without understanding the child's past, the clinician or parent cannot hope to understand the child's present. Because of the child's past experiences, expectancies develop that fit her working models of herself and others. Until the clinician knows this, he cannot know the child.

Trauma bonds have been briefly discussed. One of the best diagnostic indicators of a trauma bond is an intense loyalty to the abusive or neglectful parent. It appears at times that the strength of the loyalty is in direct proportion to the seriousness of the abuse. Loyalty is also one of the outgrowths of loss, which is a significant and complex topic in itself.

To many children, loss of the primary parent, regardless of the reason, is the loss of love, safety and protection (James, 1994). Where loyalty comes into play very directly is when the child perceives that any attachment, particularly if it is positive, will be a direct betrayal of the loyalty they feel for the abuser. Understanding why the child feels loyal is often because it is his "real mother" or "real father." Unless the child has never experienced any form of attachment, which is rare, loyalty will necessarily be a part of attachment therapy.

Other potentially influencing factors in a mother/child attachment are physical and/or psychiatric conditions with either the child or parent. A child cannot be accurately diagnosed with an attachment disorder if he is currently being abused. This must be one of the first investigative inquiries. Various psychiatric conditions with either the parent or child can substantially affect attachment.

Issues such as addiction of the parent, dissociation, schizophrenia, mood disorders and parental developmental delays or, at times, a low intelligence level, can create barriers and make the parent physically or emotionally unavailable.

The same result can come from the presence of these same psychiatric factors in the child.

Other health issues can also be important, such as serious or frequent illness. If the child perceives, correctly or incorrectly, that he is likely to lose the parent to illness, he may opt to withdraw and protect himself. This can be a major unspoken factor with children who have lost a primary attachment due to illness, suicide or even death by accidental means.

Ψ A Model for Treating Attachment Disturbances

The clinical complexity of attachment work can seem overwhelming. Already in Part II of this chapter, over four dozen important treatment issues have been mentioned. It is now time to outline a treatment process for attachment disorder therapy to handle this complex task.

James makes several general points that are useful when considering the treatment process: 1) individual therapy is inadequate to treat attachment problems, 2) a treatment milieu must be developed, 3) only after a relationship has been developed can treatment for trauma and loss be effective, 4) children should not be forced to explore their trauma or loss, 5) young children should not be asked to say good-bye to a loss without having something to take its place, 6) provide support, hope and guidance, 7) follow the child's pace with accepting a loss and 8) provide a nurturing environment where a relationship of safety, consistency and emotional closeness is possible (James, 1994).

James' above points are excellent and her clinical handbook on attachment problems, *Handbook for Treatment of Attachment-Trauma Problems in Children*, is highly recommended. She identifies five steps in the treatment of attachment disorders: a) teaching, b) self-identity work,

c) affect modulation d) relationship building and e) mastering behavior (James, 1994).

While each of the above is clearly important to treating attachment disorders, it is equally important *in what order* the process occurs. The building blocks of treating attachment disorders once again are helpful here (Figure 2). The building blocks can be viewed as a therapeutic staircase that begins with the bottom step and progressively moves upward.

The important aspect of the staircase analogy is that to be stable, stairs must be firmly established on the foundation of the step below.

Without *safety*, there is no attachment, no relationship, and no successful therapy that can occur. The stairs progress to *security*, which is provided by consistent and predictable structure. This progression continues upward to *acceptance* on the part of the environment of who the child actually is, not just what her potential may be. The child must experience a *belonging* to the source of a potential attachment, although she will seldom acknowledge this feeling. *Trust* can only come after these preceding steps, and only then can a true *relationship* be available. It is in relation to another that we learn *self-awareness*, and only with self-awareness can *personal worth* blossom. Personal worth is definitely a higher order state, but it is important for attachment as an adult. For even when a person has learned to attach and to love, if he does not feel that he is worthy of the love and attention of the beloved, they he push the beloved away because he believes the other person deserves better.

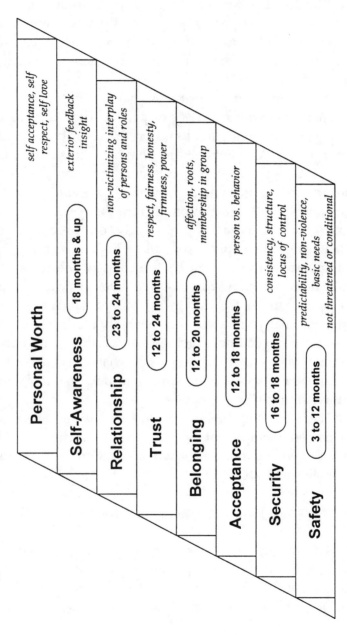

Figure 2. Building Blocks of Treating Emotional Disturbance

Building Block	Age	Description
Personal Worth		self acceptance, self respect, self love
Self-Awareness	18 months & up	exterior feedback insight
Relationship	23 to 24 months	non-victimizing interplay of persons and roles
Trust	12 to 24 months	respect, fairness, honesty, firmness, power
Belonging	12 to 20 months	affection, roots, membership in group
Acceptance	12 to 18 months	person vs. behavior
Security	16 to 18 months	consistency, structure, locus of control
Safety	3 to 12 months	predictability, non-violence, basic needs not threatened or conditional

These building blocks have been found to be an invaluable framework in the clinical practice of the author's work over the last decade. They can be used to determine how far the treatment has progressed, and what the next step should be. They can also be an important diagnostic tool to consider on what step children enter treatment and how far up the stairs they have been able to go.

It is important to mention that a child may be on a different step with a variety of people. They may be on the trust step with one parent and on the security step with the other parent. As mentioned in Chapter 2, it is also important to point out the most common misconception among inexperienced attachment therapists--believing they have a relationship with a child long before the essential steps have been climbed. What appears early on to be a working relationship inevitably turns out to be hollow mimicking or manipulation and control by the child of the therapist. If a child does not know that you are safe, that you accept her, that you can be trusted, then you may fool yourself into believing that you have a relationship with the child, but it is not yet the genuine article. Most of these children have become very good at pretense; what they need from a therapist is to spot this dynamic and help them experience a real relationship.

These building blocks do not take the complexity out of attachment therapy, but they can help immeasurably as a map to know where you are and identify the most direct route to your clinical destination.

Ψ Three Scenarios of Attachment Disorders

Attachment disorders fall into three categories: 1) disrupted attachment, 2) anxious attachment and 3) no attachment (Lieberman and Pawl, 1988). A disrupted attachment is when a child experiences a significant attachment and then loses it due to illness, death, separation, abuse or some other reason. An anxious attachment is one that was not sound in the beginning and remains unsound. No attachment is when a child has developed an attachment block due to the fact that no significant attachment has ever been achieved. Clinical interventions with these three scenarios are somewhat different in emphasis and in process.

Disrupted Attachment--The essential element of this scenario is that a successful attachment was developed when the child was very young and therefore the instinctive, neurological and pre-cognitive disposition still moves toward attachment. However, the child is not acting like he wants to bond or to get close to others. As with each of the three scenarios, there is good reason for the child's behavior, which in each case goes back to trauma. In a disrupted attachment, the bond initially worked as the child's natural dispositions intended, and then something in the attachment process was disrupted. Discovering what went wrong will assist the clinician to determine how to get attachment back on track. Figure 2 is a representation of what happens in disrupted attachment.

The four ways that humans experience attachment, which were discussed earlier, are shown in the figure--spiritual, inter-personal, physical and affective. With all sound attachments, the process proceeds in this order. The child first experiences spiritual attachment or oneness with the mother in the womb, and then in the close proximity of touch--cuddling, perhaps breast feeding, and warm skin-to-skin contact. It is not clear to the infant that she is separate from the mother. Then the child experiences some sense of separateness, but all contact with the world is inter-personal in nature. She pursues all experiences, explores all possibilities with no regard for protection. To a child, all experiences are interpersonal.

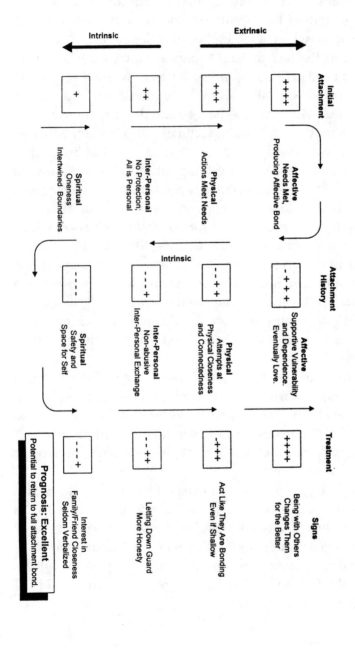

Figure 3. Foundations of Attachment
Disrupted Attachment
Attachment Sound / Then Broken

Children offer themselves without reservation and explore the other person with no sense of boundaries that separate.

Since children must interact with their world to survive, very quickly the task becomes letting their environment know when they are hungry, tired, needing touch or feeling pain. The interaction with their world becomes more and more a series of physical encounters where their needs are or are not met. Depending on the success of these interactions, the final bond is developed--the affective or emotional bond. Feelings are produced with all three of the previous experiences of attachment. This is the primary vehicle for the appraisal of the environment or intuitive process that Bowlby describes as "being experienced by the child as a feeling or being felt" (Bowlby, 1982).

To develop a successful attachment, all four areas must be experienced as positive by the child and parent, indicated by the pluses on the left side of Figure 2. The disruption in this scenario comes only after a successful attachment. The child first experiences a disruption when the interaction of affective experiences and physical experiences results in a negative appraisal (intuition) of the environment.

It is a chicken and egg issue whether the affect follows physical needs not being met, or whether children experience physical needs not being met because they feel unsafe, insecure or because other experiences produce the arousal of the alarm/numbing response (James, 1994). If this pattern continues to produce anxiety arousal in the child, the inter-personal nature of their disposition must change due to instinctive survival needs.

The more intense the arousal becomes, due to affective and physical appraisals by the child, the more serious the inter-personal disruption becomes. The level of damage to the inter-personal experience determines the disruption to the spiritual bond or the deepest core of the attachment experience. In Figure 2 the arrows indicate the flow of the disrupted process.

Disrupted Attachment Intervention--In extreme cases of disrupted attachment, the rehabilitative route begins with core experiences--spiritual and inter-personal. If the attachment has been completely disrupted, children will need to experience a spiritual or core safety as well as an intuitive experience of there being space in the environment for who they are. This is neither a cognitive nor verbal experience. This is why it means nothing to a traumatized child to tell her she is safe, you will take care of her, or, in the case of an adoption, that you will be her family from now on. Words mean less than nothing to a child with no spiritual experience of attachment. What must happen is a day-to-day experience of safety. This not only means an environment free from external danger, but also one where children are loved for who they are.

This points out the complexity of the beginning levels of the rehabilitative attachment process. The child by this time may be acting in extremely negative ways to drive everyone away (stealing, lying, cheating, etc.), but must experience that who he is, is accepted and wanted (step three on the building blocks). These children have learned very effective ways to keep everyone at a distance. The closer someone comes, the more negative the child will become.

A typical personality trait of children with an attachment problem is control. The children will go to great lengths to put every possible aspect of the environment under their control. They experience control as comfort and security; when the parent is in control, they initially experience anxiety and fear. However, unless they can hand over the control to a trusted parent, they cannot regain their childhood, which is a major clinical objective.

As any parent of an attachment disordered child knows, it is easier said than done to accept a child who is trying to get you to reject him, and it can take a very long time. The time required for a child to re-experience a spiritual bond is one of the reasons that techniques such as rage reduction, coercive holding, marathon flooding and other so called rapid therapies have no real chance of lasting success. Another serious flaw in any quick physically or emotionally coercive approach is the likelihood of developing or reinforcing a trauma bond rather than a healthy attachment, thus leaving the child in worse shape than when he started the treatment.

The process of rehabilitation of a disrupted attachment moves from the spiritual to inter-personal (non-abusive inter-personal interchange) to a physical experience of beginning to accept levels of physical closeness and connection. This is facilitated by the experience of physical needs being met, and finally beginning to feel supported, safe, cared for, and willing to risk dependence and vulnerability once again to another person. Depending on the level of disrupted attachment, this process can take from a year or two (notice the number of months listed on the steps in Figure 1), to as much as five to seven years, which is a length of treatment more consistent with scenarios two and three.

Anxious Attachment--This second scenario comes from an initially disrupted attachment where only a partially successful bond has been experienced by the child. She may have initially experienced the connectedness and oneness at birth, but very early in infancy came the alarm/numbing response when environmental appraisals produced anxiety for her safety and security. This is first experienced in moving from a spiritual bond to having no self-protection in interpersonal situations, only to have painful or negative results. This immediately signals internal and even instinctive mechanisms of adaptation for survival, and results in an unsound attachment out of necessity.

The process of the disrupted attachment is reinforced each time physical needs are not met, such as crying and not being comforted, or feeling hungry and not being fed. The result of the unsuccessful inter-personal and physical bonding is a withdrawal and distancing affect that will become an ingrained automatic disposition for life without external intervention. It is not difficult to identify adults with this affective pattern which constantly works against their meeting a very basic human need of being attached and close to a significant other.

The anxious attachment process can get worse with time, and a negative spiral can result. This includes the infant withdrawing from the insecure parent who gets anxious and frustrated because the child rejects her. Thus the cycle spirals in a negative direction until whatever initial spiritual bond that had been established is no longer apparent in the child.

Anxious Attachment Intervention--The process of rehabilitation for anxious attachments moves in the same fashion as disrupted attachment (see Figure 3). This is because there was an initial bond, although it was limited. The child must again experience safety and a predictable environment that makes room for him as he experiences himself.

Another complexity of the treatment process is that the family must enable the child to experience acceptance at the same time that negative adaptive behaviors such as violence, withdrawal, and other behaviors designed to distance are confronted as unacceptable. The answer to this problem most often rests in the teamwork of the knowledgeable and experienced therapist coaching the open and aware family in how to accomplish this challenging step.

There is little doubt that essentially all rehabilitative attachment therapy occurs in a family; it does not occur in the clinician's office. An analogy may be drawn that the plays may come from the coach on the sidelines, but the game is played, as well as won or lost, on the field.

Again, the process is for the child to then move to experiencing success over time in inter-personal contact. This

Figure 4. Foundations of Attachment
Anxious Attachment
Attachment Unsound / Remains Unsound

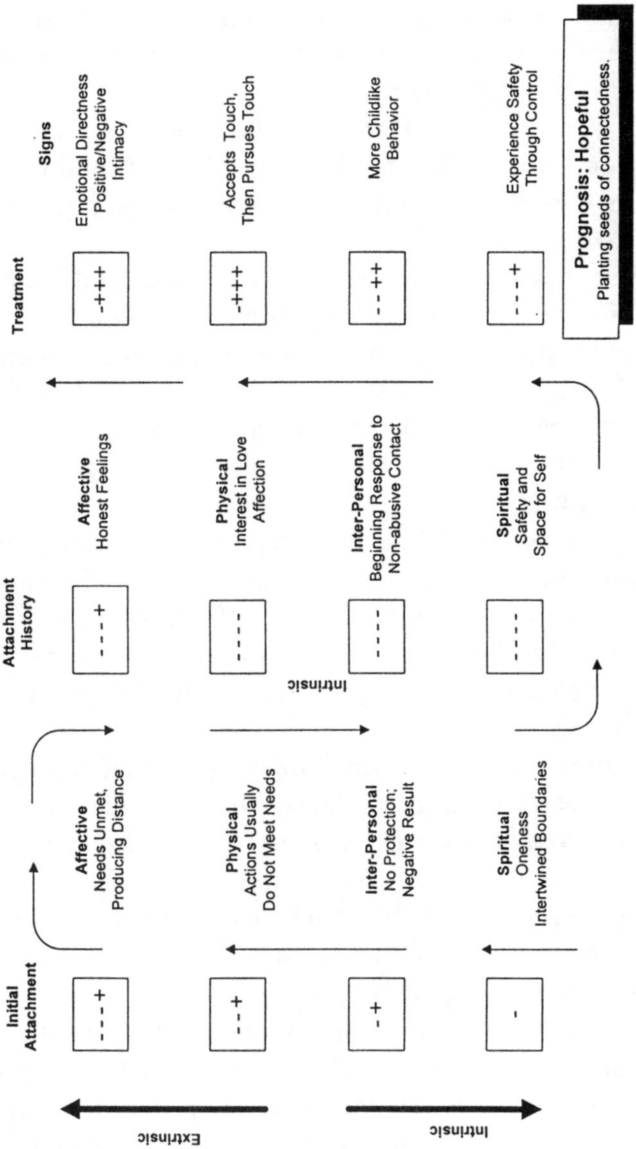

Initial Attachment		Attachment History		Treatment	Signs
Affective Needs Unmet, Producing Distance	- - - +	**Affective** Honest Feelings	- - - +	-+++	Emotional Directness Positive/Negative Intimacy
Physical Actions Usually Do Not Meet Needs	- - +	**Physical** Interest in Love Affection	- - -	-+++	Accepts Touch, Then Pursues Touch
Inter-Personal No Protection; Negative Result	- +	**Inter-Personal** Beginning Response to Non-abusive Contact	- - -	- - ++	More Childlike Behavior
Spiritual Oneness Intertwined Boundaries	-	**Spiritual** Safety and Space for Self	- - -	- - - +	Experience Safety Through Control

Extrinsic

Intrinsic

Intrinsic

Prognosis: Hopeful
Planting seeds of connectedness.

95

means learning to respond to an environment that predictably and unconditionally meets his basic needs. Slowly the child may be persuaded to accept human touch and even move to pursuing touch. At the top of Figure 3 is the rehabilitated affective experience.

In the case of anxious attachment, the best that can be hoped for during childhood may be that children share honest feelings. This usually means there will be much more negative than positive affect.

It is critical for parents to realize that honest negative affect is intimacy coming from these children. This can be hard to accept when you are on the receiving end day after day of anger or hostility. However, a child with an anxious attachment disorder could not express honest feelings in an unsafe home, so negative intimacy is an important step forward.

Some of these children will not develop an affective attachment as children. It may take the combination of the experience of wanting a partner, combined with some capacity of personal self-awareness and personal insight, to complete the affective attachment. It is also possible that many of the children with an anxious attachment may become adults who never reach a full range of affective attachment.

No Attachment--Certainly the most difficult of the three scenarios is the lack of any level of attachment in the early years of the child. This is the true attachment disorder, as opposed to the traumatized attachment, attachment problems, or attachment issues of most of the children who receive an attachment diagnosis.

Fortunately, the child with no attachment is somewhat rare in the population of children but not in the population of treatment programs for traumatized children. The process of the developing problem (see Figure 4) is identical to disrupted and anxious attachments. However, with no attachment, the process is immediately derailed either very soon after birth or even prenatally.

Earlier a reference was made to attachment beginning before birth. The child has feelings and sensations that are either physically pleasant or unpleasant in the womb. The proliferating use of alcohol and illegal drugs during pregnancy is the main source of prenatal causes of no spiritual connection. In this case, the baby may be on the chemical roller coaster in the womb each time the mother ingests the drug. In many cases, the unborn child has negative sensations and a negative experience of life before he is born. This may continue with their first task after birth of detoxing from heroine, cocaine, alcohol or other such drugs, an experience that can bring adults to their knees.

A variety of other causes can produce no attachment. The child may lose her mother to death or abandonment at childbirth, and not find a substitute primary attachment figure. Whatever the cause, the steps are the same--no spiritual connection leads to unsuccessful development of the necessary building blocks in Figure 1 from inter-personal experiences. This results in routine failure to communicate needs to the environment and therefore not having physical needs met. The failure of developing a spiritual, inter-personal and physical bond is cemented in no level of affective bond with anyone.

No Attachment Intervention--Due to the fact that there is essentially nothing to build upon in this scenario, the process cannot be called rehabilitation because the child was never *habilitated* with an attachment in the first place. This requires the process to proceed in the reverse direction from the first two scenarios (see Figure 4). One reason for this is that the child has never experienced any real level of spiritual attachment to anyone. Without an initial spiritual bond, it is uncertain whether a spiritual attachment can ever be developed in childhood. The initial experience of oneness is

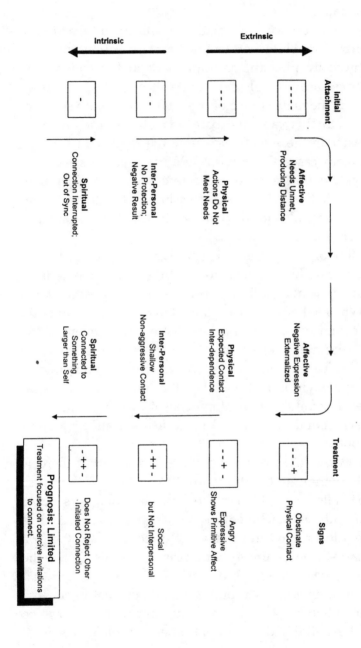

Figure 5. Foundations of Attachment
No Attachment Bond

critical for the child in the first chapter of life. If the seeds of spiritual attachment are not planted in time, there can be no harvest in childhood, but this does not rule out adulthood, which will be discussed in the next section.

The route to having a child experience sufficient attachment and to produce the many essential steps to social success as a human being outlined earlier, is to go in the reverse order of the other two interventions. The process starts with affect. Children with no attachment have no real sense of self or self-understanding, due in part to the inability to climb the stairs of Figure 1. Even as teens or adults, they cannot tell the therapist why they do what they do or what it gets them. They cannot explain what they themselves do not understand. They are functioning on auto pilot, which is wired to avoid social risk and vulnerability, at times more intensely than avoiding risk of danger and harm, which these children and adults do not necessarily avoid.

These children may not be able to tell you why they do what they do, but they can generally tell you what they want. Truly attachment disordered children want a great deal, mostly having to do with gratification (money, food, toys, sex, power, or control). They are actually rather easily motivated by gratification, although they will often tell you, "There is nothing you have that I want, and you can do anything to me but you can't hurt me." This is seldom the truth, although it is standard verbiage from these children.

Although they can often be easily motivated by physical gratification, they don't care what the cost of their getting what they want is to you or others. Insight, conscience, or social awareness are simply not capacities they have, and each of these will need to be taught. What they can do is to express themselves. This expression is almost entirely negative, but it is expression, and expression is the start of communicating and social interaction. It is better that a child scream "I hate you" than ignore you, although over time, parents may wonder if it isn't less painful to be ignored. The child must be encouraged to express what he feels inside.

The second step is to focus on the child's gratification system and his physical experience of attachment, which is accomplished by inter-personal dynamics. The gratification system is usually strong because these children usually have highly developed survival systems that are built upon gratification. The interplay here is the child wants something and so does the parent. The child wants gratification from things, and the parent wants connection with the child. Stated briefly, the strategy for the parent becomes "you get some of what you want, when I get some of what I want." This requires sophistication on the part of the parent. The parent can't say, "Give me a hug and tell me you love me or you don't get dinner." But it may look like, "If you will take a ten minute walk with dad, you can have ten minutes of Nintendo before dinner."

It may sound unpleasant, but the process of habilitating an attachment with an unattached child is inter-personally coercive. At the same time, it is important to differentiate this from the physical and emotional coerciveness of "holding therapies." Physical and affective coercion cannot be implemented without the child experiencing sensations they define as pain and abuse. This is neurologically processed with past abuse and, at best, a trauma bond is developed. It can be compared with spanking and physical discipline--it may appear effective in the short run, but in the long run, it produces many more problems than it solves.

These same negative results do not occur with inter-personal coerciveness, which is a function of social interaction, not physical or emotional pain. The reason treatment is inter-personally coercive is that if you wait for these children to come to the realization that they need connection with you, it may never happen. From the perspective of their internal intuition and "set points"

(Bowlby, 1982), the last thing in the world the child believes they will ever need is connection with you. They are personally, neurologically and socially prepared to live their life with no closeness to anyone. This is exactly what will happen if effective interventions do not alter this direction.

The constant interplay of treatment becomes: 1) in the context of a safe and secure setting, 2) the child is cared for and his basic needs are unconditionally met, 3) constant invitations are extended to the child to take the next step on the building blocks in Figure 1, and 4) on this playing field, the child learns the tough love condition that to get gratification of his many wants, he must socially pay for it with interaction, negotiation and mutual interplay where no one is used or abused.

Treatment consists of the interaction each time the unattached child wants something and the parent says what it will cost. This teaches the nature of social interaction that is ingrained in children with some level of healthy attachment. It also sets out a process of a) an environment accepting the child's expressed affect (even though it is negative), in which b) physical wants are for the most part obtainable with c) inter-personal contact. Whether the unattached child will ever reach a spiritual or core connection is uncertain, but it will be the last aspect to develop with children who have no early attachment experience.

At best, the preceding discussion of the attachment process is a road map. Taking the trip and not heading the wrong way is the challenging part. It is naive to believe that unattached children will improve with treatment in the therapist's office alone. There is very little children want from the therapist. Their most frequent desire is to manipulate the therapist, and they often do a remarkable job. There is seldom time to counter the manipulation, much less develop the coercive process where their wants are met when the therapist gets something in return.

It is a total environment that effectively treats attachment disorders. These therapeutic environments include biological families, adoptive families, treatment foster care families, and the environmental milieu of residential treatment centers (the latter is often the most effective response to the truly unattached child).

A Realistic Look at Prognosis

With dozens of serious treatment concerns, as well as biological, historic, psychological and behavioral factors, working against the treatment process at every step, is it realistic to hope for positive results in a parent's lifetime? The qualified answer to this question is "yes, it is realistic." The qualification is that it has taken time to create the attachment disorder and there are no effective shortcuts to taking the time to create an attachment in its place.

As noted above, not all attachment problems are the same. The three general scenarios described earlier all have a somewhat different prognosis. With disrupted attachment, the likelihood of successful bonding is excellent. The length of time the process of rehabilitation takes will depend on the level of disruption and a variety of factors already discussed. With anxious attachment, the prognosis must be downgraded to hopeful. One of the many reasons for this is the real possibility that an affective attachment may well be out of reach, at least during childhood. When a child has experienced no attachment during early years, the chances for a successful outcome are more limited, but there is a chance. The prognosis and length of time it may require of a professional working with a family will depend on the specific case. It can be from months to years. One thing is clear: the inventors of managed care and brief therapies were not experienced attachment disorder therapists.

The greatest concern for prognosis must rest with children with no attachment. In general, the prognosis for these children is limited. It is limited in part because there is the likelihood that a spiritual bond may be temporarily or permanently out of reach. Spiritual or core attachment is an intrinsic experience and not one that is necessarily available to cognitive or behavioral discovery.

Affective attachment is also extremely problematic for these children. The nature of loving human contact is that there are equal parts of pleasure and pain. As good as it feels to be loved, at some point the beloved will undoubtedly disappoint and cause pain. The unattached child does not experience connection as pleasure, and is so focused on impending pain that when it comes, this reinforces the need to avoid vulnerability to anyone. Can this be overcome? Realistically, the answer is "perhaps"; it has the best chance of success in adulthood.

For unattached children, the process of professional coaching and specific daily treatment interventions may take five to seven years to show major results. This is a far cry from the claims of a variety of quick attachment approaches. Those who shudder at seven years of treatment may do well to ask how long it takes a healthy attached child to learn responsibility and to develop an informed, functioning conscience. It takes a human being many years to be physically self-sufficient, so why would anyone be surprised that it would take equally long to be socially and morally well developed? It may not take years of individual art therapy, play therapy or even professional coaching in family therapy, but it will take years for healthy attachment patterns to form in the day-to-day environment the child is in if initial attachment was disrupted, partially developed, or absent entirely.

For parents and therapists who interact with these children, the personal demands are high and the rewards are often meager. As in any long and arduous journey (and this fits working with attachment disordered children), possibly the most important characteristic of the weary traveler who eventually reaches the destination is endurance.

The fabric of our social system is dependent upon healthy attachments in children. The future success of our social institutions may well rest in our ability to counter the rampant anti-social consequences of needy children, teens, and adults who have grown up in trauma, having never developed a conscience, and who now have a score to settle with society.

Part II

Behavioral Disturbances

There Is More

Than Meets the Eye

Chapter

4

Antisocial Behavior in Children

The first chapters of this book have addressed issues related to trauma for a reason. Based on my experience, I believe trauma is a fundamental causal factor of antisocial behavior and many other serious problems with children. As mentioned previously, these are the explosive children, the ones who relieve their internal pressure in an external way at anyone or anything in their path. However, it is not rare for an explosive child to also have implosive symptoms; for the most part antisocial children are self-centered and are more interested in getting what they want than in being hurtful to themselves or others -- that is, unless hurting others is what they want at the moment.

There are four categories of problem behaviors that will be discussed in the next three chapters. The first three are diagnoses: Oppositional Defiant Disorder, Conduct Disorder, and Attention Deficit Hyperactive Disorder. The fourth area of antisocial behavior includes three serious symptomatic behaviors: manipulation, fire setting, and violence.

Oppositional Defiant Disorder (ODD)

If there were an Olympics for children who refused to be raised, a child with ODD would carry the flag into the stadium -- or more likely, would refuse to carry the flag. This statement has an important element within it which is a key to understanding these children. A child with oppositional issues does not only want the world to conform to his desires, he will also oppose parental direction just to be oppositional. Just as a mountain climber reaches for the summit because it is there, these children refuse directions just because the rules or directions are there. At times there is some logic in oppositional behavior. For example, a child refuses to go to school because he does not like school. But do not look for logic in oppositionality in general; you probably won't find it. At times a child will refuse to do something she likes to do because being oppositional has become a habit.

The ODD child will sometimes surprise a parent or adult by doing the opposite of what she wants to do simply because she senses that someone wants her to do it. So if "getting their way" is not the primary goal, then what is the goal?

The first problem with determining the child's goal is that having a goal and working to achieve it is fundamentally a logical process. As with traumatized children, the child with oppositional issues is not often logical or thoughtful in his behavior or energy. Hidden in this pattern is a clue to how one might work with oppositionality -- it is relatively easy to anticipate oppositional behavior once you know how the child thinks.

One of the ways to work with these children is to help them become more thought-based rather than reactive. In other words, the goal is to change the way the child reacts by adding thoughtfulness to the process. A typical pattern of being oppositional begins with an adult wanting something from the child and the child reacting to this by refusing. This pattern can be so blatant that when cake and ice cream are served at the birthday party, and the child is told to wait until everyone is served, an ODD child may refuse to eat if he has to wait. Who is hurt by this? The child does not stop to think about this question. Through this pattern of reactivity, the child finds success by being oppositional. Since being oppositional will not be successful in life, oppositional patterns must be altered. Of course, another reason to change this pattern is that these children drive adults crazy with their refusals.

What are these children refusing? I believe the bottom line is that the child senses being lead in a direction, and he reacts to being lead rather than to the direction. Knowing this dynamic will come in handy in developing some strategies to work with oppositionality. But not all children impulsively react to adult direction. Some know what they want and ignore whatever (usually an adult) gets between them and what they want. I will discuss this dynamic primarily under the topic of manipulation.

For these children, being oppositional is a means to an end. Said differently, it is a way to manipulate the environment for the child's own purposes. In general, the older the child, the more thought out oppositionality is. But this is not always the case. Some children are so reactive that this pattern continues well into the teen years, and they refuse to go along with what is being asked or expected just because the children sense that someone wants something from them.

Children with oppositional behavior and attitudes are extremely taxing on parents because this issue strikes at the core of the role of the parent: to lead the child in directions that keeps him or her safe, to teach skills, and to help integrate the child into the social community in a variety of ways. If the child reacts to being lead regardless of the direction, the situation quickly can become a standoff.

Causes of Oppositionality

At this point in our understanding of the brain and its effect on behavior, it appears that oppositionality is caused by environmental conditions combined with individual

107

differences in the personalities and experiences of children. We may someday find an oppositional gene or an area of the brain that gets too much (or too little) oxygen. However, at this point, an organic cause appears unlikely. Unlike some other problems, trauma is not always present, but many times is. Entrenched oppositional behavior will more often than not have trauma as one of its root causes. For this reason, it is recommended parents refer back to the trauma.

When a child has been lead by an adult to places that are degrading, painful, frightening or all of the above, it is not hard to understand why he resists when he senses being lead anywhere by anybody. This helps to explain why children will give up things and opportunities they like by refusing to cooperate to get them. Although she liked the ice cream that was one aspect of being groomed for sexual abuse, she found out quickly that the reward was not worth the cost.

Although trauma can be a root cause of oppositionality, trauma is not a requirement of this disorder. When the foundation steps of the Building Blocks of Treating Emotional Disturbances (See Figure 1 on page 15) have not been present to a child at times in his life, the result can be anxiety and stress that comes out as oppositional behavior. It is helpful to consider the child's need for security.

The most basic security for a young child is being in a safe and nurturing family. For this reason, and because the likelihood of trauma is greater among foster children, the prevalence of oppositional behavior is much more frequent among foster children than among those in their own homes. This makes sense due to the instability the child has felt in leaving her own home and often having multiple homes in the foster care system.

When children feel unstable they become very sensitive to the messages of the environment. For example, they will hear "promises" when none were made. "This afternoon we might be able to go to the store" becomes a broken promise if it does not happen. As most foster parents know, a broken promise is serious business to a foster child. It is not only about going to the store. It can quickly escalate, and become about the child's ability to count on all the promises that have been made about his safety and security in a setting that he perceives has let him down. He has been let down before and he knows where that road leads.

Although you cannot avoid breaking a promise you never made, it is helpful to clearly distinguish between a possibility and a promise. When possible do not make a promise about anything that is not critical. There are too many things that could prevent you from fulfilling your commitment, and for these children, it is like they are in Las Vegas betting all they have on each poker hand.

Another cause of oppositionality is poor parenting. I could find more flowery terms that are easier to take, such as insufficient structure and discipline, but they mean the same thing. A fundamental job of the parent is to provide the child with the safety and security that come from structure. Discipline, which comes from the Greek word "to teach," is what is needed when the structure is not yet internalized by the child.

The most successful parents outline the structure and teach the child to internalize the aspects that she will need the rest of her life: proper nutrition, self care, personal space and boundaries, meeting one's own needs while respecting the needs of others, and all the other aspects of the internal structure of a successful human being. This aspect of parenting is so potent that children carry though life unhelpful as well as helpful socialization. For example, in my childhood I was taught to eat everything on my plate. As an adult I find myself doing this even when I don't like what I am eating, or when I have had enough. Again, some aspects of parenting can become a default setting for the child; it always happens first unless overridden by the child's thought process.

Some children learn to be oppositional when the structure is insufficient to provide them with the discipline (teaching) to internalize. In this situation the child has learned that he may not get his way on the first refusal, but he has learned from experience that he can wear down most adults with persistent obnoxious energy until he prevails. Most children can be taught to lack internal structure by having poor external structure when they are growing up. Children who frequently behave in the following ways provide a clue that structure has been missing at important times in their lives: incessant whining, constant pestering of adults, throwing tantrums when limits are placed, and pushing the limits until they find how far they are allowed to push.

The best strategy for demanding children is to help them find the limits quickly and firmly. You will have increased negative energy in the short run, but it will be much easier on everyone in the long run, and the child will experience the basic need of structure.

One of the most oppositional children I have worked with came to our program with the strong recommendation of the previous behavioral treatment center to avoid saying "no." When this child was told "no," he would rage and become violent for hours. The program said that it just wasn't worth it to the staff or to the child. My immediate thought was about the future. Would the world make the accommodations this program had been making? I felt that what the child could not afford was to stay in a place where the adults were trained by him rather than the other way around. So from day one, he was told "no" repeatedly. True to form, he raged and his tantrums would last hours. By the second week tantrums lasted half as long. After a month the tantrums were one quarter strength, and soon tantrums became brief episodes. At last the environment was training the child, rather than the reverse. Was it more work in the short term? For sure! But this was a lesson he would easier learn as a young child than later in life. For years this child was on my list of "most likely to spend time behind bars." Now he is a stubborn adult, but any dire predictions have not borne out. Would this have been the case if we carefully avoided telling him no?

Ψ What's a Therapist to Do?

It is the job of the professional to consider an important question before comparing the child's behavior to the DSM-IV clinical criteria, "Is there a legitimate reason to explain why the child objects to being lead by adults?" Active abuse is one of the most common explanations for this behavior. Using the concept of translating the behavior and energy of the child with oppositionality, at times children act in exaggerated ways to signal that something is very wrong. The abuse may not be in the home. It might come from a source least expected as has tragically occurred in church groups, schools, locker rooms, scouts or other youth groups.

Some children live in situations where the direction of adults has lead to very unpleasant consequences. For example, some children in foster care have grown up with adults who have serious mental health problems. One child comes to mind who after six months of treatment shared that his mother, who suffered from psychosis, would awakened him in the night to hide in the closet from terrorists. On one occasion, while hiding the whole family in the attic during the winter, she built a fire to stay warm. This child was so weary of adults that he said "no" first, before even thinking. Do your best to determine if the child is sending up a flare by his behavior before looking at him as having an oppositional disorder.

As previously mentioned, I believe the job of the therapist for reactively oppositional children (as opposed to manipulatively oppositional children) is to help the child bring more thought to his or her behavior. This may be a slow process because the child is likely to be just as oppositional to the lead of the therapist as the parent. It is also quite possible that being successful at bringing more thought to the child's behavior may move him or her into the other category of manipulative oppositional behavior. But I see this as a step in the right direction. He may not be any more workable but he has learned a basic and essential aspect of pro-social behavior -- it is mediated by a cognitive process. At the point he begins to bring thought to his behavior, you can now begin to work with what he is thinking. If little thought goes into behavior, there is little access to the internal process that determines the behavior.

Strategies for Treating Oppositionality

The first goal of any therapy is to know the individual you are treating. Several causes of oppositional behavior have been briefly addressed. What is behind the behavior of this child? Are there clues to why she acts the way she does? If you were in his shoes, would you reject the lead of adults in your life? If there are no apparent reasons for the behavior, become a detective and unravel the mystery of this child. In other words, get to know this child and do not let your experience with other children get in the way even if other children initially seem very similar. There is no question that there are similarities among children, but the key to this particular child might be unique to him or her.

Since more often than not a child with intractable oppositionality has a history of trauma, my suggestion is to treat the trauma first. In the process of addressing his or her pain, the symptomatic behavior may improve on its own. If the behavior does not improve, you will know a great deal more about the child and the way she processes her experience to be able to address her problem behaviors. My personal preference is to add group treatment to individual work when possible for young children (under twelve) who have been traumatized.

In the section on trauma, the building blocks of treating emotional disturbance were outlined. Because this process leads to the needs the child has before she can trust and form a relationship with you, proceed with a focus on advancing through these various stages.

Because these children react to the lead of adults, do your best to lead by modeling. For example, if you want the child to calm down, make sure you are calm. If you want her to hear you, be sure you are letting her know you are interested in listening to her. Children know that the language of adults relies on words. A two-year-old learns the magic of words by saying "no" (which every two year old knows is the most powerful word in the world) to everyone and everything. The child says "no" and waits for the predictable adult reaction. Oppositional children are often more interested in your reaction than the content of the refusal. Stay away from words that are easy for the child to refuse by using words. Use your actions and set the tone you want.

Again, since these children react to being lead, either avoid leading them or make sure you are one step ahead. Being a step ahead is to quickly consider how the child could or likely will refuse what you want from him, and consider how to first sidestep the opposition, or to have your next move in mind. Knowing that he objects when you suggest he do some art, tell him that he has the choice in this session to work in the sand tray or play with the farm animals, but art takes too long. The child may resist the two options available and choose the one unavailable.

This is an example of providing choices rather than giving only one alternative which he will likely reject. With choices it is harder for the child to know which direction you want him

113

to go, so he has more difficulty refusing. If you do want her to go in a certain way, either set it up so that she has no idea what you want from her, or have her believe you would rather she not do precisely what you would like from her.

Predictions are sometimes effective. Telling the child beforehand that you expect him to refuse things, may well prompt him to take another course to prove you are wrong. He might do this to refuse to do what you think he will do, putting his oppositionality in a double-bind (this is good).

I like to use double-binds with oppositional children. Some of the most difficult oppositionality is when the child gets very loud and verbally abusive. An example of helping the parent set up a double bind is to suggest the following: tell the child that you want him to be as loud as possible to "get out all his negative energy." If he continues to be loud he is complying with your directive, and you can tell him it is good to see him being cooperative (this will frost him and often shut him up in a hurry). If he does not continue to be loud, he is beginning to act in a more appropriate manner. Either way the child can't win.

Paradoxical interventions can be highly effective since the child is trying to figure out what you want and then oppose you. If he can't determine what you want, then he will be confused and have trouble being successfully oppositional.

Another approach can be to intensify oppositionality to make the dynamic very obvious to the child. Doing this alone without other interventions will likely be ineffective since the child believes that refusing the direction of adults makes great sense. Predicting the behavior and intensifying the refusals can be effective when it is set up so that the child loses what she would normally want. This can work by helping the child understand that she is being ruled by her own refusals, rather than her goals.

The essential element of being oppositional is to oppose or refuse something. Without something to fight against, it is difficult to fight. One way to reduce this behavior is to offer the child less of a target at which to shoot. Keeping the child off guard helps, as well as not being obvious about what you want from the child. However, reducing the behavior in your office is not necessarily the goal, it is to reduce the behavior at home. Your office can be a lab to test approaches that can be communicated to the family.

A frequent dynamic from parents is that they have put up with a child resisting their efforts to be parents so often they have begun to take the child's behavior personally. You can be of great help in demonstrating that it is not them but the dynamic of refusing direction that is generally going on. You can do this by pointing out the behavior from the child in other settings where adults are in charge, and by showing that the child also is oppositional to you.

With this in mind, it may be counterproductive to give the parent the message that the child is not oppositional in your office, because this may increase the amount they personalize the behavior. Many parents take a child to see a counselor and then they feel worse when things go well in the therapist's office. If it is true that the child does not act inappropriately in your office, talk to the parent about the approaches you suggest they try at home to get a similar result.

Be careful of a dynamic in family therapy where the child is oppositional to the parent, and you act in ways that the parents believe you are siding with the child. It may be more effective if you have the child be oppositional to you, and in this way the parents see the dynamic. It is better for the child to refuse your directions than the parents', and the parents can see how you work with the behavior. Therefore, what you might do in individual work (reduce oppositionality) you might do otherwise in family therapy (increase oppositionality toward the therapist).

The analogy was made earlier to the "terrible twos" dynamic of the child learning the word "no" and using it at every opportunity. Another way that children with oppositional patterns are similar to very young children is that they can often be rather easily distracted while they are trying to stay focused on being a problem. Once confused, they often lose track of what they were trying to do in the first place.

To briefly restate the issues to avoid in therapy:

♦ Avoid siding with the child while working with the whole family.

♦ Don't lower your expectations of the child or let the parents do so.

♦ Don't be too consistent with these children; you will be a huge target.

♦ Don't work toward a cure, work to teach the parents how to systematically reduce oppositional behavior gradually over time.

♦ Don't focus therapy solely on oppositionality; the causes and issues producing this behavior may be the source of improvement once you find them.

Parenting a Child Who Does Not Want Parenting

Most parents would agree that parenting is difficult enough without having a child who battles with you every step of the way. But this is exactly what happens with children who have been diagnosed with Oppositional Defiant Disorder. This problem is more than simply being obstinate, which most children (and adults) are at times. ODD pits the child against the parent, preventing the teamwork needed to have the child learn and grow into a successful adult. Most of the parent's energy can go into dealing with the child's reactivity rather than teaching and modeling the skills the child needs.

What makes this even more taxing is that the energy demanded of the adult is essentially wasted energy, because in the end, you have little to show for your effort other than a headache and a wish that someone would develop year-round summer camps.

The previous section has addressed therapists. Make sure you read over this section if you have a child in your home whose behavior fits the description of ODD. Take the information in this previous section and make adjustments to fit your home setting. Parents and therapists are both adult targets of oppositional energy from these children. In addition to the points previously raised for therapists, there are several issues that may be helpful to you as a parent of one of these challenging children.

One of the most important goals for parents is to work toward gradually decreasing the amount of oppositional energy from the child. You know there are no pills (including Ritalin) to give them and have them wake up the next day inquisitive and cooperative about all you have to teach them. Improvement is a gradual process that takes more patience than most of us have. In order to sustain gradual improvement, you need to be able to see small signs of progress. Therefore, be looking for how often the child acts in certain ways to be able to see if this behavior is increasing or decreasing. It is very possible that you may be headed in the right direction by obtaining a decrease in the oppositionality of the child, but still have the behavior beyond what you can stand in the family. This is one reason it is important to have an outside observer, such as the family therapist or coach, to help you see that despite how difficult the child is, there are real signs of progress, and therefore good reason to continue what you are doing in hopes of more improvement.

Just as with therapists, parents need to consider how you present an easy target to a child who wants to refuse your lead. Parents who are forever telling their children what to do in both important and non-important situations, make themselves a huge target for the child to simply say, "No, I won't do it." A general suggestion is to minimize the situations that can turn into a power struggle where the child can win simply by doing nothing. It is very easy to do nothing. Avoid letting the child get the upper hand by doing nothing.

For example, at dinner the child is eating his spaghetti with his fingers. You could say, "Use your fork," and the child could ignore you or say, "No, it's too hard." As an alternative, you could minimize his ability to easily object by saying "You know how to eat spaghetti correctly, so if you do it right you can eat with the family; or you can wait until we are finished so you can eat the way you want and we don't have to watch." Once the child chooses, hold him accountable. For example, he ignores you and continues to eat with his fingers. You pick up his plate and tell him it will be returned when the family is done eating. Once you have given the child a choice, make sure you follow through on the consequences. After the child has had consequences, the next time he may be more likely to take you very seriously. In this example, the child can still refuse, but you have set it up so that refusing is a choice. Doing nothing is not a way he can win in the situation.

In the section for therapists, they were told to help you see oppositional behavior as a problem the child is having, and not for you to take it personally. But it *is* personal you say? Only if you let it be. For the child, it is no fun if he doesn't both get his way and upset you at the same time. A great way to do this is to attack you in personal ways while being oppositional. In the previous example, he might say "I have to eat the spaghetti with my hands because you are such a bad cook." This only works to rile you if you let it. Whenever you see such a blatant attempt to upset you, I suggest you smile knowingly or even laugh, which is the opposite of what the child is trying to get from you.

To prevent this tactic from working for the child, deflect any personal comments she makes and reflect back to her what she is choosing to do, while ignoring what she is saying. Keep in mind that it is not personal; if anyone else were trying to parent this child, they would be having the same struggle, you just happen to be playing the part of the parent in this melodrama.

The concept of creative inconsistency was briefly mentioned earlier. This approach can be very useful for children who oppose your parenting. Creative inconsistency is not being so predictable that the child knows just what you are likely to do, so she can beat you at your own game. In the game of chess, if your opponent is very predictable you can get the upper hand easily by anticipating her next move. Oppositional children look for patterns in your responses so they can get the upper hand. But you may ask, "Isn't predictability important in raising children?" The answer is yes, but not in every situation. The predictability that children with ODD need is to understand that no matter how much they refuse to go along with you, this approach will predictably fail; and they will not get what they want. In this way the parent is in charge, which is essential for all children to know, if they are going to feel safe and secure.

At times you need to be able to keep the obstinate and manipulative child off balance and not sure what you are likely to do next. Given that you set the rules and you are able to vary your responses when you choose, you should always be able to gain the upper hand with the child. Work with your coach to get better and better at this. I mean this sincerely, it can even be fun to become so proficient at keeping these children off balance with oppositional behavior that the child is not sure what to object to, and can't quite figure out what you are up to. OK, it may be a little jaded to enjoy the fact that the child is confused, but if you have one of these children in your home, I think you can appreciate what I am saying!

The parenting skill that is needed in several of these mentioned areas is to be a step ahead of the child's plan to be a problem. For example, it is time for the child's bath and you expect a battle, as usual. You go to the child early in the evening and tell her you will need to have enough time for the typical hassle of taking a bath. Unfortunately, this will mean she will miss a favorite TV program. The child objects to missing the program (more than the bath). You point out that the bath would need to be done early in the evening to be able to still see the program. The child has to ask herself if this battle is worth missing the show. It may be, if so, you have a "Plan B." The child does not take the bath in time and misses the program. You tell her that it is getting too late for the bath anyway tonight, and you will get her up early in the morning for the bath. The child objects and wants it tonight rather than in the morning. You say OK but only this once and only if it happens immediately. Are you getting a sense of how this works?

One of the principles that helps with oppositional behavior is to define and require the child to take a stand when he or she refuses to go along. In the previous section for therapists, an example of bathing was used. Another example where children can be powerful by doing nothing is to be consistently late in being ready to leave the house. Typically parents tell the child when to be ready, they check in with the child frequently to find she is not ready. Sure enough, it is time to leave, and she has done very little except whine about her favorite dress being in the dirty clothes, and she can't find her shoes (do you ever hear this in your house?).

This pattern can be altered in a hurry with a couple adjustments used to show the child that her refusal to cooperate is a choice she will have to live with. The altered scenario is the parent tells the child when she needs to be ready to go shopping. The parent does not check in the with the child and ignores the academy award nominated routine about the dirty dress and inability to find shoes. The time comes, the parent checks with the child and finds her not ready to get in the car. The parent then leaves her at home and drives off.

The above scenario can only happen if someone else is home if she needs supervision. If she has to go with you, the parent can check with the child when it is time to go, upon finding her not ready, matter-of-factly state that in five minutes she will need to leave the house in whatever shape she is in. Anticipating in advance, the parent can have a less desirable change of clothes in a bag in the car. When the five minute deadline is met, the child is assisted into the car, shoeless and in her pajamas and surprised that her refusals to dress have not sent you into a "tizzy." As you pull out of the driveway with your shocked child, you hand her the bag of clothes and say she might want to put on appropriate clothing if she doesn't want to go through the mall in PJs. The parent may then want to point out that since the child was not ready the first time, there will not be enough time to stop for a snack at the ice cream place, so maybe next time she may want to choose to be ready on time.

Can you see that winning these power contests can be fun? A number of years ago, I watched and liked the movie "Uncle Buck." It was certainly not the acting that I appreciated most, it was the fact that John Candy's character came out on top in a power game with an adolescent girl. It was typical Hollywood "over the top," but this character stood his ground, did not give up, and prevailed. It was sweet to watch!

Household rules are meant to first of all make the household run smoothly. Secondly, rules provide an external structure for children. Children who have oppositional behavior tend to use the household rules against you. The way they do this is to require you to always be consistent with the rules when it puts you at a disadvantage. For example, if you let him know the consequences of misbehavior in advance, such as "Either the lawn is mowed by 10 am or you will be grounded for the weekend," the lawn does not get mowed and the youngster begins to ask to go places requiring you to say no over and over for the rest of the weekend.

When the family is ready to go to church on Sunday morning, Bill comes out in his grubby clothes and with a smile says, "I'm grounded, I can't leave the house." With this kind of energy, the child must learn by experience that the parent sets the rules, and the rules can change when the parent decides. Do not fall into the trap of having the child pull the string and you jump each time, just because you told him what you would do if he misbehaved. The child may be more interested in controlling your behavior than avoiding the consequence. When you see this pattern emerge, change the rules or consequences to fit the situation. When the child says, "But you said..." you just say, "I changed my mind."

With the goal to gradually decrease the oppositional behavior, it is sometimes important not to verbally comment on the child's progress or verbally guess what he or she will do? Can you see why? Right, they might intentionally increase the oppositional behavior because you want them to reduce it. If you see progress, great, keep it to yourself, or call a friend and brag to them about your skill as a parent. You have seen bumper stickers that say, "The proud parent of an honor roll student," so yours can say, "The skilled parent of a child with ODD who is improving."

Chapter

5

Conduct Disorders

Because psychology is not an exact science, categories of problem areas in individuals change and will continue to change. The Diagnostic and Statistical Manual (DSM) is less a definitive explanation of psychiatric and psychological disturbance than it is a tool that describes the current belief about categories of mental health problems and provides defining criteria.

In a very real sense the DSM provides a common language used by professionals. The DSM breaks problem areas into general categories such as developmental disorders, mood disorders, and personality disorders to name a few. One of the general categories is behavior disorders. Within this category is found the diagnosis of conduct disorder. When the psychiatric profession is not sure how to specifically categorize a problem area, but it is clear that a problem exists, the DSM refers to it as NOS or "not otherwise specified." This is a fancy way of saying the problem seems like this disorder but does not meet the specific criteria. As the field progresses, more is learned about certain disturbances and there may then become a more specific diagnosis. In my view, conduct disorder is one of these general diagnoses where we know there is a problem, but it is hard to be more specific about what it is other than observable symptomatic behavior.

We have individuals who have serious behaviors that do not fit in with a well ordered society, and the guidelines it must establish to minimize chaos when people live in proximity to each other. Ghandi called civilization the art of voluntary renunciation. We know that we could easily run the red light but we voluntarily give up this expression of our freedom and individuality for the higher good of safe and predictable highways. But at the same time we expect others to renounce their ability to run red lights as well, and this is why we tend to fund law enforcement as a top social priority. We know that without social order, which requires both rules and enforcement of rules, human beings can make life exceedingly difficult for themselves and others.

Individuals with conduct disorders either have not reached the higher levels of moral development to understand voluntarily renouncing their own freedom to act in antisocial ways, or they know what they are doing and have an internal mindset that allows the behavior to continue.

The difficulty with the diagnosis of conduct disorder is that the name infers too simplistic a problem. There is no question that there is a serious problem with the behavior of some individuals in society, but the problem is neither restricted to their behavior, nor is it necessarily best referenced as primarily a behavior problem. Behavior happens to be what we see. What we do not see is what produces the behavior. It may be that in the future we will refer to this diagnostic area as a moral reasoning disorder or as a symptom of narcissism. It would not be surprising in the future for the diagnosis of conduct disorder to be further broken down into types such as the two just mentioned or other categories as well. All this is to say that conduct disorders are much more than disorders of conduct, and with all due respect to treatment approaches that are strictly behavioral, if the treatment does not holistically treat more than behavior alone, it is likely to fail or be less effective than it could be.

The Causes of Conduct Disorders

For the most part conduct disorders arise from rather predictable causes. When children are raised in a moral vacuum, the ability of a child to set internal limits is impaired. I once worked with a ten year old female who was a compulsive liar. It seemed she looked at words not as a communication tool to tell the truth, but as a means to obtain her self-interest. Looking into her background, I found a startling fact -- she was taught to deceive others as a young child by her mother who survived by lies and deceit. By age five this child was stealing mail from mailboxes on days that welfare checks were delivered in their poor section of town. Right and wrong were self-serving concepts in this family. Something was right if it worked for you, and wrong if it did not. It is extremely hard to override this early training because in this way of thinking, someone would be a fool to not lie and steal when there is a likelihood they could get something they wanted and avoid something they did not want (like getting caught).

America's jails and prisons are bulging at capacity with more than two million individuals. There are commonalities among individuals in jail, and right and wrong viewed in an egocentric way (is it right for me) is one of these commonalities. For these individuals it is not their criminal behavior that is bad; getting caught is bad. This is why there is so little remorse among criminals. To the criminal mind, the problem in a free society is all the rules that get in the way of you getting your share or what is "owed you." Another problem for the criminal mind is the judicial system that enforces all these laws or hindrances to your freedom. This way of looking at the world is very personal and egocentric. Ghandi's voluntary renunciation is for "do gooders" or idiots who are too weak to take what they want. Those very familiar with the penal system can predict the advent of remorse after being found guilty and before sentencing, or upon appearing before the parole board. But there is much less remorse on the cell blocks, just individuals viewing rules, bars and cops that are in the way between them and the good life.

Criminal thinking is not the result of physical injury; it is learned. Although we do not like to think about it, there is criminal thinking in our grade schools as well as our prisons. The typical progression of conduct disorders begins young and follows a somewhat predictable pattern or life trajectory. I once read that the new administrator of the department of corrections for a large Northeastern state was called to the state legislature and given an assignment. He was told to estimate the number of prison beds that would be needed in the next fifteen to twenty years so the state was not always chronically short of prison space. Within a short time, the new director returned to the legislative committee and gave specific numbers and projections. When asked how he had arrived with such specific projections into the future, the committee was shocked at his approach. He had randomly contacted second grade teachers throughout the state and asked them how many future criminals were in their elementary school classrooms. When the committee members objected to calling second grade children future criminals, the director countered with irrefutable logic, "Where do you think the criminals of tomorrow are today?" I think he makes an excellent point.

Today's misbehavior could well be tomorrow's crime. When children are young we tend to go easy on them so they will learn. What we sometimes forget is that some children know well what is expected of them, and they also learn quickly how much they can get away with. When we go easy on them, what they often learn is either our expectations are actually lower than what we say and/or they can get away with more than they knew. When we lower our expectations the child, the parent and the community all lose.

126

I think it must be acknowledged that the seeds of criminal behavior are seen in the schools, on the playgrounds and even in second grade classrooms. It appears that for some individuals criminality is primarily a behavior problem, but I believe that more often this is really an outgrowth of criminal thinking. We would be wise to work with both the behavior and thought process manifested in the behavior of our children and teens, in order to make an impact on the fact that our nation has more incarcerated individuals than any society on the planet.

According to the DSM-IV, a conduct disorder is a serious disregard for the rules and social order as well as the individual rights of others. These behaviors are very easy to spot in children, so why don't we do a better job of preventing long term problems? I think there are several answers to this question. Unlike many societies, America has been founded not on a collective consciousness, but on an individual consciousness. In part this comes from being founded by individuals who had paid the price for conformity by being stripped of individuality. Our constitution is not about how important it is to have a strong government; it is about limiting the power of government and protecting the individual.

Our society values getting ahead, individual success, and individual advancement, as well as setting and meeting personal goals. We honor winners who rise above the pack and distinguish themselves from the rest. We respect the wealthy who have more than the rest of us, and we admire those who are more physically beautiful than us common folk. Fewer and fewer individuals in our society work at one company for their career.

The dynamic of individualism can be seen when considering gender in our culture. In the past women have been restricted in being individuals. A few decades ago a female who was seriously interested in athletics was suspect, and viewed as trying to be like a man. Women were to focus on the family not on themselves. We have not yet completely adjusted to the aggressive female executive with career aspirations of reaching the top in her field. But as long as our society pressured females to serve the larger good rather than being free to strive for individual needs and wants, the crime rate among females was a very small fraction of males. But as opportunity for individualism for women has grown, so has the female crime rate and the incarceration of females. I am not suggesting that women would be better off without being able to vote and staying home barefoot and pregnant. I am saying that a society that values individualism, personal attainment over communal attainment, will have a greater difficulty with egocentric "what's in it for me" thinking. When you consider the question "what's in it for me" only from a self-centered perspective, why would someone choose to be a parent, a police officer, or even a law abiding citizen? Only when we consider others do these choices make sense.

In the United States, we clearly have a society of individualism. This is why John Kennedy's words were so striking, "Ask not what your country can do for you, but what you can do for your country." America's collective individualism is in stark contrast to the more collective attitudes of other cultures and countries. If Kennedy had said these words in Japan, China or many other communally conscious cultures, people would have wondered why he needed to say something so obvious.

There can be great rewards for the individual in a culture like America, but at the same time, it is not hard to see that the more emphasis a society puts on individuality, the higher level of focus on "me" rather than "us" and, therefore, the higher crime rate.

There is much more that could be said about the connection between criminal thinking and the reinforcement of individualism in a culture. But I will mention one more point. We are in a society that holds winning as "not the best thing, it is the only thing." Everywhere you look there are winners and losers. But one of the problems with the focus on competition and getting ahead in our culture is that when eight children run a race, one wins and the rest are often considered losers. It is much easier to lose in our culture than to win, and the odds are often stacked against you particularly if you are a female, a minority member, physically disabled, mentally or emotionally disabled, young, old, a minority religion, gay, short, poor, overweight, of poor health, physically unattractive, etc. In other words the deck is stacked against most of us if the goal is to win, meaning to come out ahead of others. If only winners can have the good life, then most of us will miss the boat, or believe that we have. Within the context of this type of social thinking, children quickly learn that it is better to win than to lose. When winning is difficult or inaccessible for one reason or the other, some will actually try harder, but more will give up or become enterprising and cheat. If winning is good, then cheating is simply a means to a good end, and criminal thinking is born.

Let's return to the question of why don't we spot and modify conduct disorders in childhood when it is easier, rather than waiting until the behavior turns serious or criminal. Since our current understanding is that conduct disorders are primarily environmental in causation, I see several ways we miss the mark with young children:

1. We see a problem but we don't see the beginning of serious behavior -- just as the state legislators could not see criminals among second graders, we often have trouble seeing the serious progression that may start with misbehavior in young children.

2. We minimize the seriousness of the behavior among young children. Even when parents sense there is something wrong, they cannot bring themselves to see the full impact, so they find ways to minimize the level of the problems. "Boys will be boys," "It's a phase he will grow out of," "He doesn't do that when I'm around," "He just doesn't like his teacher," or a

host of other excuses that downplay the level of seriousness of the problem.

3. Particularly for males, and increasingly for females, we reinforce aggressiveness in children. We have a society that rewards winners, those first in line, and those who show personal initiative to get ahead in life. In other words we reward assertive behavior that often is closer to aggressiveness. Without parental discipline, the child acts to meet personal needs and desires while ignoring the needs of others. In our culture, we not so subtly reinforce males for being tough, outspoken, strong, and aggressive. In an effort to level the playing field, females are now reinforced in some of the same ways. As a result, more females are becoming discipline problems, becoming juvenile delinquents and being incarcerated for criminal activity, than ever before.

4. Parents are too involved with their own struggles to notice the pattern developing with the child -- the curse of being a modern parent is lacking the time to live two lives, one as a parent and family man or woman, and the other pursuing a career, perhaps involving more than one job, and perhaps some level of a personal social life. Noticing and working with behavior problems in young children takes the time and attention that is difficult for many parents. Telling yourself that this problem is just a phase the child is going through may be more of a statement of your hope than the reality. There is no shortcut for having the time with children to be a good parent. Many parents either don't have or don't make the time to be the parent the child needs.

Poor parenting accounts for all of the above as well as poor modeling, poor limits, inconsistent discipline and structure, and poorly enforced consequences for misbehavior. There are many ways to reinforce misbehavior and the seeds of conduct disorder, rather than to eliminate it. Children naturally want things and usually do not consider the consequences or the effect of their actions on others. If they do not learn social skills and principles as well as develop moral reasoning, they may continue to mature in age, size and sophistication in getting what they want, but not mature in their understanding of how their actions affect others, or the serious consequences that breaking societal rules can bring. The root cause of the vast majority of conduct disorders can be traced to important gaps in the learning, discipline, and parenting the child needed along the developmental path leading them to where they are.

Conduct disorder can also have trauma as one of the root causes. Trauma can cause the anger and rage that fuels the flames of serious behavior. As such, trauma is more of an indirect than direct cause of conduct disorder. Studies have frequently found that the majority of incarcerated criminals have a history of child abuse and neglect. Child abuse may be a common experience of criminals, but it does not directly cause their criminality, because the vast majority of abused individuals do not end up as criminals. However, a history of trauma along with some of the environmental factors listed above increase the chances of this problem.

Research has thrown a wrench into the works concerning the causes of criminality. There are preliminary data that indicate that there may be a nature versus nurture link to criminality. It may turn out that there is a genetic link to conduct disorders. This has come from studies that find that children of incarcerated criminals, particularly for violent crimes, are more likely to show similar behavior even when not raised by the criminal parent. It is too early to really know what this means because of the correlation versus causation issues, but it is an intriguing finding indeed. Could there in fact be the "bad seed" that has been dismissed long ago as an old husband's tale (something with even less validity than an old wive's tale)?

While we await the definitive explanation of the root causes of criminality, we may want to focus on what we can do about it. If we were to turn the tables and ask how we can help prevent conduct disorders, the list would look like good ol' solid parenting:

♦ A stable and safe environment.

♦ Clear structure, boundaries and rules.

♦ Consequences and discipline to help the child learn external and internal limits.

♦ Teaching the child to consider the needs of others along with other social skills.

♦ Liberal doses of parental modeling of all of the above.

Only after all these steps have not prevented the problem would I begin to consider a cause other than the environment.

Ψ Thoughts for Therapists

There is often special urgency in treating children with conduct disorders because of the seriousness of the situations their behavior presents. Another factor that can cause the therapist stress is that generally, a child diagnosed with this issue has been a problem for years and often without receiving professional help. Now it is up to you, and a retroactive cure would be most appreciated by the family, the caseworker, the probation officer, the school principal, and the community at large. The first thing to tell everyone is that the child's behavior may get worse before it gets better. Now that you have lowered everyone's expectations you can breathe easier. Just kidding! The real reason to say this is that it is often true.

As with PTSD, sometimes getting to the underlying issues (rage, abandonment, isolation, and trauma) is much like surgery to remove a serious splinter -- it hurts, it looks worse after it is removed, and it is a little bloody, but the healing only begins when you get to the source of the problem. The plan of attack is to first work to understand the client and look for and treat the causes, while working with the family and the school to address the symptomatic behaviors.

The first step of any therapy is to get to know the child. Do not assume that the child has been correctly diagnosed with this or any other disorder. Use your own professional judgment concerning the best diagnosis. Some children are called conduct disordered when it is more appropriately oppositional defiant or even an adjustment disorder, either acute or chronic.

The child is the one who will lead you, as well as information from the parents who live with the child each day. It is always helpful to receive information from each part of the child's life -- home, school, community interactions such as church, scouts, grandparents and other snapshots of the child. It is frequently the case that a child is a serious problem in one setting and not as serious in others. This may provide important clues to the problem. Do not assume that the place where the child is most seriously acting out is the source of the problem. The opposite may be true. The child may be reacting in angry ways in the one place where expectations are clear, and consequences are firm and consistent.

Spend some time with the child, as well as with the family, and be sure to talk to other adults involved in the case before settling on a treatment direction. As mentioned earlier, this may need to take place within the atmosphere of urgency on everyone's part. The best thing you can do in this case is to have everyone calm down and take one step at a time. If you get in a hurry yourself, you risk the following problems: a) you may indicate that there is a quick cure, b) you may intensify everyone's anxiety, and c) you may be buying into the belief that the child needs to be fixed rather than considering all aspects of the child's environment, which may be reinforcing some of the problem behaviors.

As you learn all about the child and the particular case, be ever vigilant for aspects of the child's world that need adjusting. Like most other problems, the adults may just want the child to be different, but the key to addressing serious conduct problems will likely be environmental interventions. Look for where the child gets support, who has obtained the child's respect and how, and where the weak links are in setting limits for the child.

I believe in tough love for children with conduct disorders. For parents who are too tough -- they will need to learn the support and inward belief in the child that comes from love. For loving parents who have cared so much that the child has been given chance after chance -- they will need to learn how to toughen up. The balance of the two can be a real challenge given serious behaviors. Parents can be hypersensitive when their child seriously acts out. Any reference to adjusting what they are doing can be interpreted as judgment and faultfinding.

Knowing the proper balance of believing in the child and taking a firm stance with the child's behavior can be difficult without an outside coach to get an objective view. Environmental interventions will generally require the parents to act in ways that are very uncomfortable for most parents. For example, my advice with serious behavior is to call the police. Parents often want to shield the child from contact with the system for fear of starting them on the road to delinquency. Many parents do not want to involve the criminal justice system because they don't want the child to "get a record." The fear of the child having a juvenile record that travels with the child throughout life is greatly exaggerated when you learn how the system really works; just ask anyone who works with the juvenile court.

It is not always clear what will impress upon the child the message that rules are important and will be enforced. For some children it is being questioned by the police, perhaps being arrested, or even spending some time in the slammer.

Because of the way our systems have changed, I spent a good deal of time the first ten years of my career trying to keep status offenders out of juvenile detention centers (jail). For the last fifteen years, I have worked hard to have violent and dangerous children spend more or even some time behind bars for their protection, and for the protection of others. Although the school shootings over the last few years have loosened up the system somewhat to consider holding children who pose a threat to others, the pendulum had already swung much too far, making it extremely difficult for a child to be detained even for very serious law violations. In addition to safety issues, the message sent to the child can be very unfortunate -- the legal system has no real teeth. When they hit mid-teen years and commit the same crime, they may find themselves being tried as an adult and staring at mandatory sentence guidelines of five to ten years in jail. A middle ground must be found between these extremes.

One of the most difficult things for parents to do is to separate who they are and their own self esteem from the behavior of their children. At least this is a trait of caring parents who take their parenting role seriously. Occasionally poorly performing parents raise a child who is successful in life, and it is certainly true that excellent parents have raised children who go in a negative direction in life. But more often poor parents often disavow the behavior of their children or blame the child for the family's many problems.

Although it is a trait of conscientious parents to blame themselves for their child's problems, many parents find it difficult to separate their parenting and the child's response to their parenting. However, it is important that parents are able to separate their effort and the result of their effort. To do this, many parents of conduct disordered children will need your help. Irresponsible children do come from good homes and very responsible parents. Conversely, very successful and functional children can come from neglectful and/or dysfunctional homes.

Although there is clearly a correlation between the quality of the parenting and the child's social growth, there are many factors that enter the picture that also play a role in the outcomes. One of these factors is that many of the emotionally disturbed children discussed in these pages were initially raised by a parent (or parents) who is no longer in the picture. The child learned much of the problematic behavior from a previous environment. Whether this is the case, or if the parents are doing their very best and the child is still not responding well, it is important for the therapist to have the parents separate their role of providing the structure and discipline, from the child's role in taking responsibility for the choices he or she makes. The parent cannot decide for the child, and therefore cannot take credit for the child's choices whether they are bad or good.

Many parents who care very much about their child tend to get trapped in extremes in the face of serious behavior by the child. Some parents will work very hard and long to help the child do a better job, and then snap at some point, and wash their hands of the situation. Other parents will see the importance of hanging in with their child no matter what, and they continue to support and at times defend the child at all costs. As a therapist, help parents avoid extremes like these. Support the child, but avoid defending him or insulating him from the consequences of his behavior.

The experiences of living are often the best opportunities for children to learn. If the parent softens the blow of the consequences that come from the extended family, from school, or from the court system, the parent may be robbing the child of important lessons that arise from the poor choices she makes. Help the parent see this, as well as the importance of identifying anything that will intensify and emphasize the lessons that come from consequences of behavior.

As with most therapy, the relationship building process is very important with conduct disordered children. As a therapist you may have special access to the child because you may be one of the few adults who is not upset with him, reactive to him, or fearful of his next poor decision. You have the chance to be with him with one major purpose -- to hear him, support him and assist him to understand the choices he has. Few other adults can or wish to spend this kind of time with children who have seriously inappropriate behavior. Use the time to everyone's advantage.

As the professional in the picture, one of your roles is to continue to monitor the progress of your work and the improvement of the child. Along the way it may be left to you to determine that, despite the many adjustments and attempts everyone has made, the results are less than adequate. This may mean that a referral is in order, or that more intensive treatment is needed.

Some professionals paint themselves into a therapeutic corner by believing that their approach or the service they provide is the best available. These therapists are potentially setting themselves up for a big fall. No matter how good you are or how effective your approach is, it is quite possible someone else or some other approach could be as effective or even more effective.

Avoid believing that you are the last and only hope for the child and family. This type of thinking may be a strong motivation for you, but it may decrease your effectiveness and send the family a message of desperation. When you are seeing minimal or no progress in the case, first consult, look for ways you can alter your approach (if a technique was not successful the last fifteen times you used it, why would you be hopeful the sixteenth time), and then consider more intensive intervention such as seeing the child more often, looking for a day treatment setting, or considering the total treatment environment of residential care.

In the earlier section on attachment problems, I expressed my belief that attachment specific work was not effective during adolescent years for a variety of reasons. Beyond the ages of twelve or thirteen (with allowances for individual differences in children), the treatment of attachment problems is essentially the same as the treatment of conduct disorders. There is one slight difference in tone and that is more emphasis is placed on reciprocity with attachment work, something most non-attachment disordered children already understand at least intellectually.

How Does One Parent Such a Child?

If you have read the section to the therapists working with children with conduct disorder, you have a good idea what I want to say to you as a parent. If you have not read the previous section go back now and read it. There is no way around the pain, exasperation, and the continuing concern that a parent feels for a child who is heading in the wrong direction in life. However, there are some things you can do to help, and there are things you can do that can unknowingly make the situation worse.

Starting when children are very young, it is important not to minimize serious behavior. How serious any behavior is depends on the developmental age and maturity of the child. At times a "normal" action at one age can be a concern when the child is a little older. Many parents of children who get into trouble with drugs or with the law say that they saw some problems developing with the child, but they had no idea it had gotten so bad. Don't be one of these parents who have been out of the loop in their own child's world. When you see a problem at any age, address it, work on it, and if it doesn't get better, get help.

I have mentioned a number of times that the best way to understand the child is to learn to translate the child's behavior. This is very true for children with serious behavior problems. Although the behavior is the most obvious aspect of the problem, the inner fire fueling the behavior is coming from somewhere. You will be ahead of the game if you can find out what is eating at your child.

In eastern religions the seeker is given a "mantra" by the teacher to say over and over again in order to fully understand the message. The mantra of the parent with a seriously acting out child is "hold him or her accountable." Say it to yourself over and over until it comes to mind with every action and every choice the child makes.

A child with a conduct disorder will need your support or he will alienate himself from everyone. This is particularly important since he is busy burning his bridges between his friends and adults who may at some point have liked him, or tried to befriend him. If this happens the child declares war on the world (few win this battle), and he can even decide to declare war on himself through alcohol, drugs, suicide attempts or other risky and dangerous behavior. The battle cry of these children is "Who cares?" Your answer must be that you do. In the midst of your support you must also confront the behavior. It must be clear that you will stand behind your child, but you will not accept nor defend poor choices he or she has made.

With the thought in mind of confronting serious behavior, the answer to the next question is "yes." The question is, "should I call the police on my own child?" The worst thing that can happen to the child is not that he or she gets in trouble with the legal system. The worst thing they can learn is that our society has few, if any, serious consequences for serious behavior. If you know of illegal behavior by your child, calling the police is one way to intensify the consequences that she needs to feel if she is to think more clearly about the results of her actions.

At this point it goes without saying that as a parent, you should not ease up on structure because the child is flaunting or resisting the structure. Back to the rule of opposites, when a child is doing a poor job living with the current structure, he needs more rather than less structure. Every child will say the opposite, but he speaks loudest by his behavior. However, when he is doing well with your structure, this is often an indication that he may be developing an internal structure of his own, which means you might be able to gradually loosen up on your end. If he is doing poorly, he is saying he needs more not less structure.

Parenting is a team sport; all parents need help at all stages of the child's development. When you are angry, frustrated or feel lost in how to respond or help your child, get help sooner rather than later. In fact, it is good to have made contact with someone who could be of help to you before you have the crisis where the help is essential. Ask around for someone who is good with children and helpful to parents. Make some calls, ask several therapists who the best professionals are in town (in addition to themselves) and see who comes up on several lists.

Three Behaviors Associated with Conduct Disorder

There are a host of problem behaviors that come under the banner of conduct disorder. Three of these deserve special attention here -- setting fires, violence, and the triad of lying/ stealing/manipulation.

Fire Setting

Perhaps the most chilling problematic behavior to a parent and the community is fire setting. This behavior is covert, often unpredictable, impossible to ignore, and exceedingly dangerous, all of which put this problem at the top of the list of serious behaviors. In fact, it is common to have not only foster homes but even intensive residential treatment programs refuse to accept children who start fires into their program. There are other aspects of fire setting that compound the concerns it raises.

It is very easy to set a fire, and the means to do so are available everywhere. There is a universal fascination of human beings with fire (one of the only things more mesmerizing than television is a campfire at night, or a fireplace in a dark room). The fascination with fire is even more intense among children who set fires. Some of these children are curious, some are seeking attention, and some are angry and seeking revenge on someone or everyone. In terms of sheer destructive ability, nothing rivals the damage a child can do by setting a fire.

It is a myth that there is a certain type of child who sets fires. Fire setting is a behavior not a classification of children. In fact, fires are set for many reasons by a wide variety of children. It is likely that most of you reading this played with matches and set a fire when you were not supposed to as a child. The curiosity motivation surrounding fire setting should be handled by instructions for parents, information from schools, and supervision by adults to prevent the damage a fire can cause.

The most disturbing fire setting behavior is the child who intentionally acts to gain negative attention or worse, to cause harm to people or property. With the help of fire and life safety professionals, we are much better able to assess the tendencies of a child to determine the risk of future fire setting behavior. Every community has professionals who can help with this. If not, contact your state fire marshal for a referral. If there are any questions about the seriousness or potential of repeated fire setting, get the child in for an assessment specific to fire setting. The results of the assessment will help determine if education, therapy, or incarceration are indicated. Clearly this problem is not something to be taken lightly.

As with other conduct disorders, fire setting behavior must be accurately translated to know what the message is from the child. This is an ideal attention getting behavior for some children. Just a "flick of a bic" in a field or dumpster and literally, it is red light and siren time. It can be a very powerful feeling for a child to put so many adults into action, and then to stand back and watch the excitement. If the motivation behind the behavior is attention, it is best to hear the child's cry the first time. At this point the problem can be addressed. It is not about being violent; fire just happens to be an effective means to an end. Again, if in doubt as to what the behavior is saying, get a professional trained in this area to assess the situation.

A comment to professionals and treatment programs: children who start fires are very treatable. With attention to the risks (close supervision and preventing access to fire starting devices), treatment of these children can be straightforward and effective. These children and their families deserve to have treatment resources available. If you do not know much about treating fire starting behavior, find out more.

Violent Behavior

Perhaps second only to fire setting in level of concern are violent children. Only in the last few decades have we become vigilant concerning violence toward children, and now we have to work with violence from children. There is little question that violence is becoming more prominent among children in our society. There is more violence from children in school, in foster care, in community recreation programs, and on the streets. Violent crimes among adults have actually been going down over the last decade in our society as a whole, but the opposite is true for young people. The many school shootings have drawn international attention to the fact that our society, including our schools and our children, is armed and ready for violence.

Regardless of what we see all around us, our culture proceeds into the twilight as the most violent society to ever populate the planet. There are enough guns in private homes in America for every adult to have at least one. We argue whether guns should have safety locks. We debate whether assault weapons should be available. And yet we continue to have a major segment of our culture proclaiming their stance on bumper stickers such as "Guns don't commit school violence, children do." Children are always the barometer of a family and of a culture. If we cannot learn a lesson from the violence in our streets, our crime rates, violence in professional sports, and even what we call entertainment (Hollywood movies, professional wrestling, video games and much more), then at some point we will need to learn from the violence that we see in the eyes and in the behavior of our children.

Let's get one thing straight right off the bat: television is an important factor in the discussion on violence in our society. The excessive amount of time the average American child spends watching TV (the most recent research indicates on average seven hours per day!) is eclipsed only by the absurdity of what children are watching.

A family friend recently gained international attention for a research study of Hollywood animated children's movies. Dr. Kim Thompson found a high level of violence in G-rated children's movies and some violent acts or violent themes in 100% of what has formally been rated as appropriate for children to watch. Every night on prime time TV it is possible for children to see dozens of adults modeling violence as a way to disagree, to get what one wants, and even to express affection. This isn't including the less than wholesome offerings on cable networks.

Although the networks and major studios in Hollywood attempt to dance around the issue of the effects of violence (like tobacco companies dance around the truth about the effects of the product they sell as well), the fact is that violence in the media produces more violence in the children who watch it. This topic has been frequently researched with very clear results. Violence in the media also gives a message that minimizes the consequences of violent acts both physically and legally. Children, TV and violence are not a positive combination.

Causes of Violence

There appear to be at least four different sources of violence: environmental, organic, genetic and intrapersonal. Of the four, it appears the environmental causes account for the vast majority of violent behavior. Environmental causes of violence include adult or peer modeling, and poor parenting (such as poor limit setting, poor initiation in moral development, abuse, living in unsafe surroundings, lack of supervision, and reinforcement of violent behavior). Organic causes are internal to the brain and include brain trauma, insult or brain injury of any type that can result in impulsive, unpredictable and/or violent acts. Organic causes require a more detailed look into how the child's brain is processing the stimulation it receives, and then how he or she responds. ADHD could be an example of an organic cause of violence, although this is not true in all cases. Frontal lobe damage to the brain in both children and adults can cause behavioral and personality changes including violence.

The third area, genetics, we know the least about. At this point a genetic cause of violence is a theory with some preliminary evidence to support it. We are increasing in the sophistication necessary to understand both the brain and its functioning. Through our growing knowledge of our genetic coding, we will be learning more about organic and possibly genetic predisposition to violence, such as how violent tendencies may be passed on to a child from the parents. Of course we may also find out that what we thought was a genetic link is actually something entirely different. The study of the brain promises to be one of the most important aspects of science as we begin a new millennium.

We can not always blame the environment for the poor choices made by individuals. It may be that a child received every important aspect of effective parenting and still acts in violent ways. So we must also mention the fourth or intrapersonal cause of violence. Some children enjoy the power and control they feel when they act violently. We must be careful when considering intrapersonal causes of violence because some children "choose" violent behavior which stimulates endogenous opiates in the brain (much like the body's own dispensary of pain killers producing feelings like "runner's high"). While the child may act in a violent way intentionally, the cause of this pattern is generally rooted in childhood trauma and thus is an environmental cause. It is possible that an individual could choose violent behavior when it would not be considered appropriate (when one is not in a situation of threat), without the presence of other causes of this choice of violence, but this is quite rare.

It may be quite some time before we know enough about a genetic link with violence to be of practical help to families. Organic causes of violence will need professional consultation, particularly medical assistance. The primary causes of violence at present that we can impact with the greatest results are environmental causes. Attention has been given to how to address violence prevention, and there are now effective prevention programs that are available in schools. For parents the following suggestions are offered:

◆ Translate the behavior and the energy - As with other problems, take the time to understand the meaning of what the child is doing. What is he saying by his behavior? Consider a number of possibilities before settling on one you believe is close. You are much better equipped to respond to the child if you understand her message.

♦ Start with firmness when children are young - There is no substitute for structure and limit setting in preventing violence. Violent behaviors (that does not actually protect the individual) is acts that go beyond acceptable limits. Children do not set limits for themselves; they must have them established from outside before they begin to internalize limits.

♦ Take decisive action - Violence at any age is not to be tolerated. The message must be given clearly and plainly to the child that he or she has stepped over the line, and this is a rule that will be enforced.

♦ Zero tolerance for violence - As a part of setting limits, you will need to know where the situation is serious enough for you to draw the line of zero tolerance. The suggestion here is that the more you are concerned about the violent themes of a child, the sooner you need to draw the line.

♦ Involve law enforcement and the courts sooner rather than later - Part of enforcing the rule of no violence and taking decisive action is to initiate the systems our society has set in place for serious behavior, and those are our law enforcement and court systems.

♦ The issue of physical holding - There has been an interesting debate in the last few years about physical interventions with children when they become violent. This is a whole topic in itself. Young children expect adults to protect them and if a child becomes violent to him/herself or to others, it is the responsibility of the adult to protect the child, and this may mean in a physical way. There are numerous training programs available for parents and professionals covering how to safely handle unsafe behavior from children. When decisive physical action is needed, do what it takes to protect everyone.

♦   If your efforts are unsuccessful, get maximum help while the child is as young as possible -- thinking the child is just 'going through a phase' or that the situation will get better on its own can be a serious mistake. Violent behavior should always be a serious warning sign. When the fire alarm goes off, drop what you are doing and take action. Violence is an alarm that signals that something is not right. Do not ignore violence hoping it will go away. It will most likely escalate until the needed action is taken. Get the help you need from the right source. You may need to do some detective work to find the right help, but do it sooner rather than later.

Lying, Stealing and Manipulation

So why lump these three obnoxious behaviors together? The reason is that these are all forms of deception, and they are often combined by children to meet an egocentric purpose. A common issue that arises in the response of adults to all three of these behaviors is morality. Across the board my recommendation to serious cases of deception is to save morality for later work with the child because you will likely be wasting your breath.

Another reason to focus on the morality of deception after the child progresses in moral stages of development is that: the parent will find it very difficult to climb inside the child's frame of reference if the moral lens is what the parent is looking through. The reality is that deceiving others is not a moral issue to emotionally disturbed children when they are young. In fact, when the child appears to understand that it is wrong to lie and cheat, this is a clear step in the right direction.

147

Deceptive behaviors are used initially for one reason -- they advance the agenda of the child. Said differently, deception helps her get what she wants. This is not always getting something "good." It may be to get "bad" attention, or to get the parent so angry the adult might lash out at the child. But in each case, the child tries to keep the adult in the dark as she continues to do what she wants. By putting the morality issue down the road in working on these issues, the point is not that morality is somehow less important. The moral issue is the ultimate issue in deception -- a person should not lie because it is wrong. But to a deceptive child, morality is a foreign language which gets in the way of what she wants. The beginning step is to teach right and wrong, and only then is there a chance to have the child see lying, stealing and other deceptions as wrong, even when they get the child what he wants.

The starting place in handling these behaviors is that you want to extinguish them. If you can extricate your mind from thinking about the right and wrong of some behaviors of young children, you can learn to moderate your response in a way to avoid unknowingly reinforcing the very behaviors you want to eliminate. If this is not clear, an example may help. The young child goes into the parent's room and helps herself to mommy's jewelry. The initial motivation may have been curiosity or to have such nice things for herself. The young child thinks this is good, to have good things. But mommy is furious and feels invaded by the child. The young girl may have unpleasant consequences, but she cannot ignore how much energy mommy has hidden in this drawer with the jewels. It would be unlikely if she did not pursue this energy as much as the jewelry, and the behavior may get worse rather than better. The alternative is for mommy to express to someone other than the child how she feels about the invasion, and to take the necessary steps to stop this behavior in the child with as little reinforcing energy as possible.

Lying

Adults are much more focused on the "truth" of verbal statements than children. Children frequently mix external reality (one answer to Pontius Pilate's eternal question, "What is truth?") with the child's own reality (often very different than the reality of others) when they tell stories and communicate with adults and peers. This is not a lie to the child; this is communication. While writing this, a young child came to tell me to come out in the street to see a white horse on the neighbor's roof. Not really wanting to go out, I knew there was no such thing. At the insistence of the child, I went out and looked down the rural road to see a building in the foreground and a small hill behind it where a horse was grazing. But looking at this scene as the child did, the horse in fact was right above the house and visually looked like it was standing on it. It was my adult mind that said that the house is closer than the hill where the horse grazed. Looking at the child, I said, "I now see the horse on the house. Thanks for showing it to me." He seemed pleased and let me go back to writing. Factually accurate? Not exactly, but it was true. Start with understanding the situation from the child's point of view. As in this case, it may not be deception (although some adults might have scolded the child and said, "Don't tell such tall tales," without checking it out).

What children experience may be different than those around them, and the meaning of words can also be quite different to different children. Adults use words mainly to describe reality, while young children tend to use words to alter or have an effect on reality. For example, the young child who just had dessert is asked by his dad if he has had dessert yet, while holding some very tasty cookies in his outstretched hand. At that moment, the young child does not have a moral dilemma. In good and bad terms, he knows what good is, and there are chocolate chips in them. The child's dilemma is how to respond to dad's question and end up with the cookies.

"No" should work he thinks to himself, and that is what dad gets. The child gets cookies and the world is right, until mom comes back into the room. Was this a lie? Yes, but this deception was clearly focused on getting a good thing. The parent can best talk to the child about telling the truth so that a practical result is achieved -- mommy can believe you. At young ages, start with the practical implications that the child can understand and leave the moral implications to when these can be understood.

A general suggestion for situations where many children are likely not to tell you the objective truth, is to ignore the words and focus on the eyes, face, behavior and energy. Very few children can lie to an adult who knows the child, when the adult considers these factors more than the child's words. Some adults say, "What do I do when I know he is lying but I don't have proof?" My answer is that this is not a court of law, the standard of proof is a preponderance of evidence to the adult. If you are pretty sure, act accordingly. The few times you are wrong, you can apologize (this is good modeling) and tell the child that this is an example of how important it is to always tell the truth so adults can believe the child's words.

There are two kinds of lying that deserve some focus: habitual lying and crazy lying. Habitual lying can quite easily become a pattern for children with emotional disturbances. There are many reasons for this behavior such as: the child thinks adults don't believe him, the child says whatever it takes to get his or her way or avoid trouble, the child is more used to lies than the truth, lying can change the reality more to the child's liking, lying is often easier, lying helps avoid responsibility, lying helps keep the adult off balance and in the dark, and lying drives some adults crazy and that is always a good thing for a manipulative child. There are more reasons, but you get the picture. Lying has become such a habit that telling the truth can seem out of character for the child.

The second type of lying is crazy lying. You know that kind -- there appears to be no reason to deceive and you get a lie anyway. Sometimes crazy lying is meant to deceive, but other times it simply has no purpose. For example, the child is not to touch the freshly baked cookies until dinner. One disappears, and the child has chocolate on her hands and face with a full mouth as she mumbles that she did not eat the cookie. Some adults when confronted with this may think, or actually say, "Excuse me, do you think I have lost my marbles?" No, the child does not think this will work, it is just lying that makes no sense. Other crazy lies happen when a child is not in trouble, but lies for no particular reason.

Habitual lying can be handled by first focusing on the practical aspect of the need for the truth, and second, by implementing the "reality check plan." This plan says that I have learned from this child that if it is important, I must check it out before coming to my own conclusion.

"Billy's mom said I can spend the night," and mom says, "What is Billy's phone number so I can talk to his mom?" To be effective, the reality check plan must be implemented across the board. "Susie, is the TV on?" "No, Dad." You go in to check. Susie looks up and says, "Did you think I was lying?" You say, "Remember until we work this out, I have to check on the things you tell me." This approach is particularly effective when the child tells the truth and wants something, but must wait until the words are checked. The frustration in the child confronts the behavior to deceive adults periodically.

My suggestion for crazy lying is to ignore it. It is not done for a reason, it makes no sense, it is not worth your energy. If it happens often, you might have a reality check plan, but this may be more effort than it is worth. Crazy lying happens to be one odd symptom of many children with problems. If you feel better, you can walk away from a crazy lie and mumble to yourself, "Yep, she still has some problems." But you already knew that.

Stealing

You finally fulfill your dream to be a Jeopardy contestant. The board comes up with the clue: "stealing" is all it says. You go for the buzzer and say, "What do emotionally disturbed children do to make sure you notice them?" Alex says, "You are partially right," and he gives you credit. The rest of the answer is that children also steal to do the following: get things, anger you, retaliate, exert power, get you to dislike them, prove he/she is bad, and a hundred other possibilities. How do you know what the message is? You translate the likely possibilities and go with the one that seems to fit the situation best.

As with lying, there are various kinds of stealing: impulsive, compulsive, symbolic, or attention getting. As with lying, don't jump too quickly for the moral lesson. If the child is young, start with the practical reasons why stealing does not work for anyone. Impulsive theft is when the hands have the gum in the store and the feet are headed for the exit before the brain has time to ask how much it costs (or "Who has been watching me?"). Impulsive stealing is often opportunistic behavior; the opportunity presents itself and the motto the child lives by is "carpe juiceyfruitum" (seize the gum).

Compulsive stealing is a very strong habit where the habit tells the person what to do. This child doesn't feel like herself if she hasn't stolen something today. As with all compulsions, there is an element of stress release that comes from the behavior.

Symbolic stealing is essentially a message to anyone around who is listening. The behavior is often not designed to get some tangible object. It is often to let an adult know something about the child, but the message is in code. Stealing food when there is plenty available says "I am insecure," or stealing the pencil of the smartest child in the class says "this is the only way to even the playing field."

Attention getting stealing also has little to do with obtaining something; it is all about being noticed. These children are sure that being themselves is insufficient to gain the focus of anyone's attention. Negative behaviors in the past have been considerably more successful at being noticed, and stealing is generally very successful at getting real energy from adults.

The best ways to handle these different types of stealing are very similar. As always, translate the behavior. If the behavior is meant to send a message, let the child know the message was received so he doesn't have to send it several more times. If he is seeking your undivided attention, watch out. If you give him the attention he wants because he stole your car keys, it worked, and there will be more important things missing around the house.

Think action, not reaction. Action comes from caring about the child and the things that are important in the child's world. Action is having a plan to understand the child while decreasing the stealing behavior. Reacting is going along until you get hit with a brick (the child steals from you), you say "ouch" and tell the child to never steal again. However, the child either hears "she didn't hear my message," or "I sure got mom's attention that time." Parents do not have to speak or act in code. They can go to the child and say "I know you took some food from the kitchen because you have not always had enough to eat when you were young. Since you feel more secure knowing there is food hidden somewhere, we will give you your own place in the pantry to put food when you feel this way." To the child this constitutes "Message received."

Sometimes stealing is not as complex as mentioned above. The child knows it is wrong and does it to do "something bad." The usual message here is, "I want you to know that I am a bad person," or "You need to know that I have a dark evil place inside me like people have always told me, or else I wouldn't do these bad things." Some adults oblige the child

153

by confirming that he either has bad behavior, or he has a bad streak in him. This confirmation will not decrease negative behavior. If you want a child to stop acting in negative ways, you will need to address the negative internal view that other adults have reinforced. In some cases it may be difficult to find enough positive aspects in the child to reinforce, but without doing so, the negative spiral will continue and perhaps intensify.

Manipulation

Manipulation is not a universally negative concept, nor is it always negative with children. The physical therapist manipulates the sore muscle, and the Federal Reserve Board carefully manipulates the US economy. These are not bad things; they can be very positive. Manipulation of people indicates an action against their will or attempt to restrict their choices in some way. This sounds much less positive, but we need to realize that manipulation, both good and bad, happens all the time among people. In fact, this book could be considered all about manipulating your child toward a successful adulthood (I like the sound of that). Part of the judgment of good or bad is the intended result of the manipulation. Is the desired result good or bad for the targeted person? The belief that all manipulation is negative should be reconsidered. A great deal of manipulation from children is negative, but not all.

How could manipulation from a child be positive? Actually there are many ways. Often times manipulation comes from someone who would like to establish greater influence and power over the target of the manipulation. Dustin does not want to get dressed for school so you say, "If you go like this, I think the girls in your class will enjoy seeing you in your pajamas." You are attempting to have influence over how the child dresses by saying something that has a different meaning than its face value. Positive aspects of manipulation from children are quite different than this.

Children need to test their surroundings and they need to test you. Just like the National Emergency Broadcasting System, you cannot wait until the crisis to see if communication works. So sometimes the child manipulates you to see if your limits are real. Will you stand by them, and will you enforce limits in a safe way? The child needs to know how you will handle a real problem by creating a test problem. You will not hear from the child, "Dad, the preceding has been a test and only a test, if this had been a real emergency you..." You will have to spot testing behavior when you encounter it. Testing behavior is positive, but I do not know any adults who like it. Testing can be very important for a child to find the limits of his or her surroundings.

The strength of the walls and fences not only keeps someone in, but also keeps bad people out. The child needs to feel your personal power. Therefore it is important particularly in the early stages of a child coming to a new environment that he feels the strength and power of the protective adult. Of course the way the child does this is disguised. When the child first arrives and either verbally or behaviorally announces that she does not plan to obey the household rules, this is a manipulation, a test to see how much influence she will have in the home. She is finding out who is in charge and she is testing your mettle. Do not be fooled by her words or actions of protest. She really wants *you* to be in charge. Children do not want to be in the frightening position of facing the world alone without the protection of a strong adult, despite what they say. The children who say the loudest, "I don't need you or anyone," are the most frightened inside, which is why they make such an issue on the outside. Remember the rule of opposites mentioned previously (try the opposite and see if it fits better).

While some manipulation from children can have positive aspects behind it, there is one general thought to keep in mind -- do not let manipulation work. This needs to be explained. While it is true that children speak in codes, it will be best for everyone when they can learn to directly communicate personal needs and wants so the adults don't have to retranslate the communication. If a child challenges your authority or rules by covert behavior, make sure it is not successful, or you will get more of it. At that point the child has learned that he is more powerful in this environment than he should be. If a child tries to influence you in inappropriate ways, do not let it work or she will not sense power from you. If this happens her respect for you will be shaken, and her sense of safety will be decreased. Remember that "what works," in the opinion of the child, will be repeated. If you want constant manipulation from your child, then just let the manipulation work and you will get more.

As with its other cousins of deception -- lying and stealing -- don't give manipulation a lot of external energy. Be firm, and read the child's energy to understand what he or she is up to. It is often good to verbalize to the child what she is doing. It will generally make her externally angry, but she will know that her deeper message was received.

Just as there are some positive aspects to manipulation, there are some very negative ones as well. There is something that is deeply upsetting to many adults about having a child who is often covert and manipulative. Parents will say that they can't trust the child. They may use the same yard stick that they use with other adults and say they don't like dealing with someone who isn't "honest, forthright, truthful or trustworthy." These are very big words for a child who does not internally understand the issues in the same way adults understand them. Do not use the same standards of directness with your adopted child that you use to select a business partner. The negative aspects of manipulation can have a strong influence on an adult's response to the child. Many adults react and often feel like they need to be on guard. Violence may be more of a concern to parents, but constant manipulation will wear down a parent quicker than most other obnoxious behaviors.

To avoid having the child successfully drive you away, there are some effective approaches to a constantly manipulative child. The first is humor. Humor is a wonderful tool to combat manipulation for many reasons. Nothing is more infuriating to someone who is trying to control another person than to have the person say something humorous or chuckle at the attempt. This is a very quick way to signal to the child that her attempt did not work. Humor indicates that you see what is happening, you understand what is happening, and you are not at all about to fall for it. Humor also lets you as the adult feel more powerful, which is what needs to happen with manipulative children. Humor gives you an internal signal that you are in charge of your energy and therefore of the situation. Humor also lightens up a potentially heavy situation, and if someone is going to lighten up the energy it must be the adult.

Let's consider an example of the use of humor. The family is going somewhere and your little bundle of manipulative joy has been in the habit of selecting hideous clothes to wear in order to drive you up the wall. You and your partner anticipate this and dress hideously yourselves. The two of you walk into the room and are greeted by a shocked child who was bettered at her own game. At this point you break into laughter perhaps joined by the child, perhaps not. As a group you all decide to change into clothes that you would want to be seen in public with, or you go for it and perhaps go to a less public place for the picnic. Your playfulness in this situation says that you are sure of yourself enough to act silly. Remember, rigid adults are easy targets for these children.

Some adults mistakenly call this type of humor sarcasm, and all parenting books say to stay away from sarcasm. However, sarcasm is often misunderstood. Sarcasm goes beyond humor, and is defined as using humor for the goal of being hurtful to the other person. Using humor with manipulative children is designed to help, not hurt. When you receive sarcasm from someone, the intent is for you to feel worse about yourself. The use of humor with these children is designed to have them get beyond the games so they can fit in better, as well as feel better about themselves. Avoiding sarcasm is important, but being pointedly humorous or playful can be very effective and is not sarcasm.

For someone to manipulate you, the other person must have a good sense of your predictable reactions and responses. It is good to be less predictable when dealing with constantly manipulative children. Mix up your responses. This makes you a much more difficult target to hit for the child. For example, the child could attempt to offend or anger you. You quickly spot this and say, "What a good idea, I never would have thought to do that." The child walks away scratching his head and wondering what that was about. However, you walk away having once again beaten him at the manipulation game. The odds are very good that you will not get that behavior again (because it did not work), and over time you will get fewer attempts to influence you (manipulative behavior) if the attempts simply do not work. The concept defined in previous pages for this principle of mixing up your predictability was called creative inconsistency. Although this appears to be contrary to the principle that children need a predictable environment, creative inconsistency helps to provide predictability when power and control of the household cannot be easily taken from the parents.

In the same way that lying in young children is not a predictive sign of a morally bankrupt individual in later years, manipulative behavior is not a good prediction of future criminality. Certainly it is possible for the child to grow up continuing to manipulate everyone and everything, and end up running into the concrete wall of the criminal justice system that knows something about manipulative people. However, manipulation is actually a sign that the child is learning some rather complex aspects of human communication and interaction.

To manipulate others you must be able to predict their behavior, to read them, to plan a course of action, to implement your plan, and to gauge the results of your work. All this can be very successful in business or in politics (speaking of manipulation) if these skills can be aimed in the right direction. Sometimes it is difficult to tell the difference between the methods of a manipulative criminal and the public servant, other than the former is motivated by self interest and (we hope) the latter is driven by community interest. Don't see Mike as a little criminal waiting to grow up. Work on his behaviors one situation at a time. You can make a big difference over time.

Chapter

6

Attention Deficit Hyperactive Disorder and Bipolar Disorder

These two disorders have been combined in this chapter because they share many similarities. In fact, the same symptoms in a child might receive either or both diagnoses. Both of these disorders also appear to have causes in part due to brain functioning. However, these disorders have defining differences as well as similarities. I will begin with the more frequently occurring disorder -- ADHD.

Attention Deficit Hyperactive Disorder

No other mental health issues related to children have captured the national debate in the way Attention Deficit Hyperactive Disorder has done. As with other diagnoses, as it became more widely identified, it seemed that throughout the country there was an epidemic of hyperactive children in our homes and particularly in our schools. What helped the spread of this diagnosis was the availability of the magic bullet medication to treat the problem. Having this tool to help the problem brought both positive as well as negative impacts on children. Soon parents were going to their pediatricians for Ritalin in numbers that would rival Prozac for adults some years later. Of course, the problem that always arises with new diagnoses and new treatments is that many children are swept along in the parade. The polarization and backlash were inevitable.

Organizations sprang up to promote the stimulant wonder drugs for ADHD or to object to the widest use of drug therapy for children ever seen in our culture. To many, the concern was that we would be raising a whole generation of robots dependent on drugs who would likely become drug addicts when they grew up. This debate was everywhere in the media in the 80s and 90s with no victory coming on either side. If victory could be measured in numbers, the pro-drug group definitely has the upper hand because more children are on stimulant medications today than at any time over the last three decades. Like the presence of child abuse in our culture, this debate about children and stimulant drugs periodically gains media attention and then the media loses interest for awhile, only to "rediscover" the problem all over again.

Today the ADHD debate continues, sometimes subdued, sometimes not. You can still find pamphlets with warnings of the evil of drugs like Ritalin. However, gradually the numbers of children on medications has continued to increase. Controversy is likely to continue, in part because there are likely more changes on the horizon for this disorder, which is the most frequently diagnosed mental health disorder among young children.

As a society we know that very active children do not have a mental health disorder, they are just enthusiastic about being children. The percentage of children in our schools who are identified as ADHD and come to school with their medication has continued to grow since the late eighties. Fifteen years ago, I consulted with one school for children with special education issues that had a full 80% of the children on stimulant medications for ADHD. When I questioned this large number, the staff was proud that they were ahead of other programs at spotting and treating this problem. Their view was that if a child had a positive response to stimulants in the academic setting, the child deserved to have them. To me this sounded like saying that if Olympic athletes could improve their performance by using stimulants, then they deserve to have them. Fortunately, in my opinion, over the last ten years more attention has been given to holistic ways to look at overactivity or attention problems, but stimulants remain the most frequent response.

The changes I alluded to and the next potential uproar with this disorder is the consideration that this is not one disorder at all but two quite different problems that require very different solutions. I will also touch on a new theory that ADHD has been misunderstood and is not a disorder of attention. It is no secret that ADHD was carefully debated in the committee that drafted the DSM-IV. The arising opinion was leading to splitting this disorder into two distinct disorders -- the hyperactive impulsive disorder and the underactive unfocused disorder. The political decision that emerged was that the professional community (not to mention schools and families) was not quite ready to accept and adjust to this change.

There was one other compelling reason to delay major changes in the view of ADHD until the next DSM edition, and that was how little we actually know about the second disorder, including the important question of how to treat it. It is therefore very likely that in five years we will be looking back on the days when these two disorders were incorrectly lumped together and perhaps misunderstood altogether, and wondering why so much stimulant medication was used for children who did not need it nor show much improvement with its use.

For now, let's use the common view of ADHD, while acknowledging that we might not yet have a full understanding of this disorder. Hyperactivity is the easier of the two disorders to diagnose and to treat. We have substantial experience and research on this problem. We know that this disorder is not just behavior that is busy and bothersome to the parent or teacher, it is a disorder with roots in the brain's ability (or inability) to discriminate among stimuli and to modulate the body's response. This disorder has been called a disinhibition disorder, meaning that the problem is more the child's inability to turn off some of the brain's impulses and reactions in order to focus on others.

A quick lesson (or review) of the way neurons act in the brain may help here. Stated simplistically, the brain is made up of several trillion stand-alone neurons that have one ability -- to receive chemical and electric impulses from other neurons and to pass them on to another neuron.

In a sense the brain works much like the crowd at the Super Bowl as it does the "wave." When the person next to you stands with arms extended, the message gets to you that it is time for you to stand as well. It may take several minutes to go around the stadium, but in your brain this is infinitely quicker.

For example, when you are in your kitchen and turn around and touch a hot skillet with your elbow, the billions of nerve endings send the signal "ouch" up the arm and to the brain which decides that "ouch" is not what is wanted, and the signals are returned to the arm to move away immediately. You know how quickly this happens, so the efficiency of the billions of involved neurons shows that the nervous system is truly a wonder.

In the above process, the nerve cells do not have a volume control. As was previously mentioned, they do only one thing, and that is to receive and send a signal. The receiving of a signal requires the strength of the signal to be sufficient enough to reach the minimal threshold. At this point, the neuron fires and sends the electrical charge and the chemical message to the next cell. The firing of the cell is always at the same strength. Other functions of the brain can tell the difference between warm water and scalding water. I mention this "all or nothing" aspect of nerve firings as an analogy for hyperactive children. The brain of an ADHD affected child has difficulty in assessing the strength of the stimuli, and seems to respond at the same strength regardless of the situation.

Clinically hyperactive children often wake up in high gear. The stimulation of the alarm clock might as well be the smoke detector saying that there is a fire and death is imminent unless jumping out of bed is immediate. I swear that I have awakened some of these children from a dead sleep and they are up and on their feet in one bound. If I did that, I would undoubtedly snap something vital. At times these children go to sleep in a similar fashion. They go from being loud and moving around, to nearly dropping on the spot into delta wave sleep. When I watch what children do when they are high on the hyperactive scale, it is clear to me that this is not the child deciding this, this is the way the child's brain runs his body, and it is not like other children.

The brief behavior descriptions above are a bit on the extreme end of hyperactivity. More common are children who cannot maintain their attention on anything for more than a few minutes. These are children who touch, grab, or smell something almost without knowing they are doing it. These children jump to the front of the line and sometimes they have to climb over others to get there. Sitting, reading, and studying are all difficult to the point of painful activities (therefore the trouble that arises in school, where they need to do these very things for many hours each day). One of the ways to know an active child from a hyperactive child is whether the child has the ability to slow himself down. Whether he has the interest to do so is another matter. Children who are hyperactive feel better moving. The process of activity is a tension release.

The problems created by hyperactivity are substantial. Mention has been made of impulsivity -- the child being pushy and aggressive to get what he or she wants. These children act like they need constant stimulation and then overreact to the stimulation they get. This can make them needy and either seeking constant attention or demanding it of any adults who supervise them. Tantrums are frequent due to the overreaction to things that happen around them that are not on the list of wants. These children have excessive emotionality; nearly everything can be an issue.

The results of the taxing behaviors of ADHD begins with worn out and irritated parents. It is possible for even the best of parents to become frustrated to the point of overreacting to the behaviors of the child, and potentially even physically abusing the youngster. This is one of the reasons why hyperactive children will be more frequently physically abused than other children. They will also sustain more injuries, broken bones, and trips to the emergency room due to reckless, impulsive behavior.

Other frequent results of hyperactivity are that the child is shunned and avoided by others -- peers, siblings, your relatives and your neighbors. These are the children your family dog will sense and stay away from. The social isolation of the child due to feeling a lack of interest by others can further heighten his/her demands for attention. Given all the unfortunate results of this disorder, it is unlikely that the child is overlooked or the problem not noticed. Hyperactivity is one of the few mental health problems that is more likely to be over-diagnosed than under-diagnosed.

The second aspect of ADHD and likely at some point to become its own separate diagnosis is attention deficit, and may in the future be called something altogether different. Looking at the symptoms of these children is almost looking at the polar opposite of the hyperactive child. These children are often slow, they can seem under stimulated rather than over stimulated. It is as if they do not find enough interest in things to stick with anything for very long. These children daydream, and it takes more energy than they can find to maintain interest in a topic, an activity, or a discussion.

At this point you may be saying to yourself, "This sounds like Bill at work." In fact, both attention problems and hyperactive problems do follow children into teen years and adulthood. The common belief in the past was that puberty saw the final stages of these issues, but in fact, the majority of diagnosed children still have the same themes as adults and must either use medications or make accommodations for these problem areas. It may be that Bill at work has struggled since childhood with attention deficit.

I will say less about attention deficit because we know less about it. Professional research is only recently studying this issue as opposed to decades of research on hyperactivity. In regard to the treatment of attention issues it appears that so little has been documented in research that we do not know just what does work. It appears at this point that stimulants are not the answer, although many professionals and educators swear by them. In the absence of research, I believe we can make some good clinical estimations of what will help these children by understanding the struggles they face. Some ideas will appear in the following sections.

The New Thinking about ADHD

I have already mentioned that in the future psychiatry/psychology may separate ADHD into separate disorders. However, even more fundamental change in our view of this disorder has been proposed by Russell Barkley, who is a psychologist and an expert on the issue. Dr. Barkley has made ADHD the major focus of his career and has played a major role in shaping the professional discussion for a number of years. For anyone who is primarily interested in ADHD, Barkley's book *ADHD And The Nature Of Self- Control* is recommended. Filled with theory and research, this book may answer more questions than you are asking, and may be more than you ever wanted to know. However, a new theory is proposed in the book that merits consideration.

Barkley's new theory is that we have been focused on the wrong issue with ADHD, namely attention. What is presented is that ADHD is in fact not an attention disorder but a disorder of the developmental process of personal inhibition and self-regulation. Where this is most obvious in these children is how self-regulation affects executive functioning. Yet another way to view this disorder is to consider it a chemical/electrical disorder of the prefrontal lobes of the brain to develop psychologically meaningful understandings of time. In other words, these children are unable to make sense of the past and how it affects the present, or to consider the future and determine how the present relates to what is likely to come next. ADHD then becomes a disorder of time -- recognition, meaning, and understanding of anything other than now. Let's break this down to consider the practical significance of this new view.

The theory first says that ADHD relates to attention but that this is not the fundamental issue -- rather, it is a peripheral symptom. Through research, it appears that by far the most effective treatment of the disorder is medication. This would tend to point to a problem located in the chemistry of the brain. If attention is not the fundamental issue of the disorder, then how does the theory explain children who flit from one activity or experience to another? The answer is that something has gone wrong in the brain's development of its capacity to inhibit and self-regulate focus, attention, awareness, and activity. Looking at the child in this way would indicate that Mike goes rapidly from one thing to the next primarily because his brain has difficulty shutting out some stimuli while allowing in others. In a sense, this is the opposite of inattention; it in fact is too much attention to too many things. Said differently, the child is attending to everything and therefore not attending to any one thing long enough to function successfully in the environment. According to this new theory, this disorder impacts the exercise of personal will and volition. In this sense, ADHD is more of a prison than actually being placed behind bars.

The term "executive functioning" was mentioned earlier. A brief look at what is meant by this term is very important in the understanding of the behavior of children with ADHD. Barkley identifies eight skills that comprise the most relevant executive functions affected by this disorder:

1. Working or representational memory -- History books will commonly point out that if we do not understand history we are destined to repeat it. This is exactly the case with ADHD children. Since their available information from the past does not enter into decisions they make, they will repeat history and mistakes ad nauseum. They also lack the ability to generalize either deductively, going from the general to the specific, or inductively, going from the specific to the general. In other words, if he is reckless on his bike and crashes, he may conclude it was the bike and another reckless ride with another bike might not result in the same scrapes and bruises. In the same way, if she has been rude and used foul language with her two teachers and ended up with a school suspension, there is no reason to refrain from such language with a different teacher.

2. Internalization of speech -- For speech to have meaning it must have a clear representational meaning, not only to others who are the recipients of the message but also to the individual sending the message. This is also true in reverse; the recipient must form internal meaning from speech or it will be like hearing a foreign language. Verbal exchanges are only communication when the representation of the sender comes through to the receiver. Poor executive functioning may produce a lack of the representational understanding of received speech and/or sent speech.

3. Psychological sense of time -- This returns us to the issue of ADHD being a disorder of understanding and working with time. This is related to working memory in that it is important to be able to draw meaning and conclusions from the past and to carry these understandings into the present. It is also important to be able to understand how what is happening in the present may affect the future. It is as if these children are in a time warp where they are stuck in the now, but without learning from the past.

4. Internal representation of information for goal directed behavior -- Even with a relatively immediate reward for specific behavior, the child can stay motivated for only a matter of a few minutes. We must be able to put our experiences into some meaningful form to have them be useful. These children go through experiences in life but lack an ability to make meaning of what has occurred. Because of this, goals or future focus are beyond the child's reach.

5. Private internal emoting and self-motivating -- If he is sad, he cries. If she is angry, she screams. Most of us have learned to feel internally, which comes in handy with a boss we detest, or getting a ticket from a police officer. We also need to be able to keep ourselves on task, on target, and sticking to a preordained direction. But ADHD interferes with internalized skills such as emoting or internal personal support and self encouragement.

6. Capacity to imitate complex behaviors -- This may include difficulty with simple behaviors as well. Recently I have been working with a child in our program who has difficulty with getting himself clothed each morning. It appears that he has no routine or game plan -- pants first, then shirt, then socks, etc. His serious ADHD appears to require him to begin anew each day with the task of doing this series of behaviors that for other children are routine. He has no economy of motion or activity and appears to use many times the energy to accomplish the same task as other children. Even

more pronounced is the inability to copy complex behaviors. Social interactions between people are some of the most complex of behaviors because of the importance of awareness and reading the reaction of others and altering your behavior accordingly. All of these complex abilities are an extreme challenge or out of reach for many ADHD children.

7. Internal over external processing -- This is another way of saying what you see is what you get, quite literally. The lack of the ability to internalize meaning from memory, emotions and their meaning, plans, deductions, assessing the situation, and using reasoning to alter your behavior are all affected to some degree by ADHD.

8. Goal directed activity -- Mentioned in several of the above points, these children want, demand, grab, feel, express and live now, and waiting five minutes for something is not "getting what I want right now." Goal directed activity requires a desire that is understood to be in the future, having a plan to move in a certain direction, and staying the course until the goal is achieved or the original goal evolves into a new goal. If you are stuck in the now, goals are of no use and have no useful meaning.

Knowing the specific deficits ADHD children contend with may help explain how simple tasks and routine events are anything but simple and routine for some children.

The Causes of ADHD

The causes of ADHD are difficult to identify, particularly since we are probably looking at two quite different disorders. It appears that the main physiological cause of hyperactivity is the inability of the brain to assess and control stimulation and resulting responses. What is affected is the neural substrate in the prefrontal region of the child's brain. Another way to look at the problem is as a disorder of the ability to inhibit some stimuli to intentionally focus on other stimuli. This is why it is considered a disorder of self-regulation. Due to the physiological aspect of this problem, the only method that has shown consistent results has been -- yes, stimulants.

Stimulants are effective in a paradoxical way. The stimulant speeds up the brain in order to slow the body down. Simply stated, the stimulant helps the brain speed up to catch up with the very rapid processing of information, and helps the brain discriminate and respond more intentionally and less automatically. On stimulants the clinically hyperactive child has a better chance to see something he wants, and to decide if grabbing it is the best way to handle the situation. Overall he may be more focused and look and act slower, although the same stimulant would speed up someone who does not have this disorder. This is one way to help in the diagnosis of hyperactivity. With the caution that you can not tell from just one medication trial (there are a number of stimulants that act differently), if the child becomes more irritable, anxious and hyper, either he has the wrong stimulant or his brain does not need a stimulant in the first place.

The question can be asked, "What causes the brain to act differently with these children?" The answer is not fully known, but ADHD symptoms can often occur from some form of brain insult, or injury. This can be caused by damage to the brain from an accident or more likely from drug or alcohol exposure while the child is young and the brain is still developing. The brain is an amazing organ of the body that takes a very long time to fully develop (a two-year-old's brain is only 25% developed). If the brain is subjected to internal or external damaging influences, this can alter its ability to continue to develop at the usual pace. It also appears that there are critical periods of development such as the prenatal period, where damage such as drug and alcohol exposure can do the most damage. Another example of a critical period is around 30 months of age during the period of the most rapid development of speech and language.

I believe there are other causes that result in very similar symptoms of hyperactivity and attention problems. Emotional trauma is one of those causes. The hypervigilance, anxiety and lack of sound judgment and reasoning brought on by child abuse can look very similar in symptoms to the "organic" hyperactivity discussed earlier. Some children also come from very disorganized and chaotic environments that do not promote an inner discipline nor reinforce the child's reasoned responses to stimulation around them. Many of these children are medicated and after psychological treatment for the many environmental causes of the symptoms, they no longer are helped by medications and can successfully be removed from them. The majority of children in our residential treatment program who have come to us on stimulant medication have successfully discontinued their use during treatment.

What Helps?

As with other disorders discussed in these pages, understanding the problem of ADHD goes a long way to knowing what will help the child. If this is primarily a disorder of self-regulation, then it would make intuitive sense that the child's environment will have to provide external structure for what is seriously lacking in the child's internal structure. This turns out to be right on the money. In the same way, if the psychological sense of time is adversely affected, as well as understanding the world and one's own experience in a temporal way, then the environment will have to compensate for this problem. To help here, the past and the future need to be brought into the present for the child in a salient or impactful way. For example, these children will make the same mistake dozens of times because they have difficulty making use of the past. If an adult steps in to help the child see that overeating may feel good at the time but will end up feeling unpleasant later, there is a chance you can help him or her learn from past experience.

The above points out the overall theme of working successfully with ADHD children: external structure helps with gaps in internal structure. This includes tight consequences as well as immediate responses to positive and negative behavior. There is little advantage to therapy for these children in a therapist's office, except for other issues the child may have such as PTSD. Life, as translated by a knowledgeable parent, is the best teacher. It generally helps to eliminate distractions, and then give strong and even exaggerated strength to external structure by using auditory and visual cues, prompts, reminders, props and additional aids that help remind the children of what needs to happen.

Ψ Therapists

It is very common in my experience to misdiagnose ADHD because some of the problem behaviors are also involved with several other diagnostic categories such as PTSD, ODD, and Reactive Attachment to name a few. One of the first jobs of the clinician is to consider if there is another diagnosis that better fits the situation. Many times the child will come into your office already diagnosed by teachers, parents, relatives, neighbors and perhaps a pediatrician. The allure of an ADHD diagnosis is it "explains" the problematic symptoms and has a silver bullet cure (stimulants). I have had parents get upset when they do not get the diagnosis they want, but your job is to carefully consider the big picture which may require you to defer a diagnosis for some time to gain additional information.

As you are probably aware, there are four primary medications that are used to treat children who have hyperactivity. Their common names are Ritalin, Cylert, Dexadrine and Aderol. There can be significant differences in the effect of these four on a child. Some children may react negatively and even violently to one medication but be helped substantially by another. For this reason, it is important to take the time necessary to find the right prescription and the right dose and regimen.

It goes without saying that this requires a physician. It is easy to write a script for a stimulant, but it takes time and work to understand the child enough to develop a comprehensive plan that may include a stimulant, but goes much further. Although most stimulants used to treat hyperactivity come from pediatricians, my preference is to work with a child psychiatrist who is a specialist rather than a generalist. There are advantages and disadvantages to stimulant drugs that can be explained by the prescribing physician. It is unethical for a psychologist to prescribe medication, but the professional is an important part of the treatment team, and in fact may be the one who provides the majority of the information, together with the parents, used by the physician to determine the medication amounts and protocol.

I briefly mentioned the controversy that continues to surround the use of stimulant medication with children. There are adamant adults who believe stimulants are evil, mind controlling substances that make children become robots or lunatics. Some stimulant detectives even believe the rash of school shootings can be traced to psychotropic drugs. At the same time there are equally adamant adults who believe many more children deserve the help of stimulants than currently are on them. I do not see this as a moral issue or a "one cure fits all."

My own view is to use medications wisely, and if there are other less chemically intrusive approaches, to try them. Once it is clear that a stimulant may be helpful to the child, medicate to reach a therapeutic dosage (until it produces the desired results or demonstrates that it can not produce positive benefits), rather than under-medicate to be conservative or careful.

Several non-medication approaches are available. Depending on your point of view, if the current research is correct that nothing is even close to the therapeutic value of stimulants, then an effective non-stimulant approach may tell you that the problem is not hyperactivity. Or, if you believe that medications are not the only route, then other approaches are at least worth consideration. Non-medication approaches attempt to either address the child's inability to modulate his or her attention and behavior through the child's self control, or these approaches focus on the brain's ability to do this through an approach such as altering the child's diet. Teaching the child focus and self-control is the basis for approaches such as concentration and meditation, biofeedback, and physically active intervention such as running or martial arts. Each of these approaches attempts to help the children to increase internal awareness and to bring more voluntary control to their experience. From my own experience with these approaches, which has been substantial, each provides children with an opportunity to improve his or her ability to self regulate.

I believe one of the reasons medication is the most effective treatment of ADHD is the appeal of putting the white pill in the child's mouth with no further effort needed. It remains true that the value of any plan is in its implementation. Medications are a quick and easy plan. In our own program, numerous hyperactive children have been helped with aerobic running, but it takes work on the part of the child and an adult who needs to model and help motivate the child to stick with it until she begins to internally feel the benefits. In a society that looks for the quick, easy, and foolproof cure for everything, I am not surprised that medication is the most successful intervention.

Diet deserves to be mentioned. Diet has not always fared well in research studies. I mentioned my caveats about research at the beginning of this volume. I always ask the question, who is doing the research, and do they have an agenda (J.R. Reynolds funded research to see if tobacco is harmful)? There is very good research that indicates that diets strongly affect children. Haven't you experienced that for yourself? Why would these children be different? It does not make sense to rely solely on diet, but it does not make good sense to assume that what we eat does not affect us, or affect hyperactive children. It does appear that the conventional wisdom (I call these old husband's tales) of associations between hyperactivity and sugar are completely unsupported by science. It appears more likely that the chemical influence of food preservatives and additives may have an effect on the brain and play some role in hyperactivity.

Diet is a topic that is hard to reach any consensus on because we all literally have our own tastes and preferences. To some people, diet is just short of a religion, with elaborate rituals and observances. All cultures also have some form of traditional healing remedies that seem to work as often as they don't, either because of the placebo effect (30% of people get better because they think they will) or because of legitimate curative powers of either eye of newt, or my grandmother's favorite, vinegar and honey. Even medical science has to admit that one of the strongest curative agents there is comes from the patient's belief in the cure.

Making decisions solely on research is difficult if not ill advised (i.e., eggs are bad, no eggs are good, a glass of wine at dinner is good or is it bad, aspirin is to be avoided or is it a life saving daily regimen, etc.) Although I have read the weak findings in some research between diet and hyperactivity, I have also read the opposite. When I run into differences such as this, I fall back on common sense, and my sense is that what we eat affects how we act (does that really seem hard to believe?). In our programs we do take diet seriously, and the adage that "you are what you eat" is important in our selection of the diet for the children.

Ψ The Therapist's Role

As with other disorders, a major role of the therapist is to support the parents in providing a therapeutic setting in which the child can best improve. In no other disorder is support more important than for the parents of hyperactive children. Parents can get to the point of believing that something is wrong with them when they get to their breaking point several times per week, if not per day. Parents feel guilty when they try to get a break from the constant vigilance required of supervising the child.

Perhaps the greatest struggle for parents is in the area of the use of stimulants. Parents are not insensitive to the national debate on "using drugs to control children." They may get intense pressure either one way or another from friends or relatives. It is not uncommon that the air becomes instantly charged in my office when I bring up the question of medication. When a parent comes out of their chair my keen intuitive sense tells me that this is not the first time they have considered the subject. As pediatricians will tell you, some parents just want a prescription for the child, while others will avoid it fiercely. Either energy could be other than what the child needs. The conflict that parents can feel makes perfect sense. They are being asked to put a chemical into their child's brain without knowing in advance if it will makes things better or worse. As a professional, one of your jobs in supporting the parents is to help them weigh the issues with medication. It will be important that parents trust you and your judgment, so talking about medications on the first visit may be ill-advised unless parents bring it up first. Form a team with the parents, school, and the physician to make the best decision and develop the most effective interventions, with or without stimulants.

Parents

Let's start at the top. Are you, as a parent, tired of being blamed by everyone for your child's behavior? More than even politics and religion, everyone has an opinion on how children should be raised. Regardless of people's parenting beliefs, most people look to you as the parent to keep your child in line. That is great and I am sure you would not have a problem with that if it were possible. When we covered conduct disorder in children, I made the point that you are not your child's behavior, and this needs to be repeated here. In the vast majority of cases, you are not the cause of the hyperactive behavior of your child. People who think you are the problem are generally ignorant and do not deserve your attention. More informed adults have some understanding of how hard it is to raise a child with hyperactive behaviors. If your neighbors, friends and/or relatives give you grief about your child's behavior, go to the nearest mirror and in your most supportive voice say to yourself, "Some opinions are more valuable than others."

Now let's tackle medications head on. Whether you want this to be true or not, stimulant medications are by far the most effective treatment of hyperactivity, and nothing else is even a close second. I know how some parents do not like to hear this, because I don't either. I want there to be some less intrusive and natural intervention that does not have side effects. We can all be disappointed together, and now, let's take a hard look at stimulant medications.

You probably knew before you starting reading this book how stimulants work on hyperactivity, and if not, go back and read the previous section. The bottom line is that in clinical hyperactivity, the child's brain is not functioning in a way to promote improved self management and self control. After knowing all the facts, you can still decide not to use stimulants with your child; but for the child's sake, the issue deserves serious consideration.

Some of the reasons I don't like stimulant medications to treat hyperactivity are the common side effects: increased weight loss, mild to moderate increases in anxiety, changes in sleep patterns, and changes in facial appearance. However, my biggest problem with these medications is the message they can send to the child -- you are somehow broken and this little pill can help make you whole. Of course, this is not what we want our medicated children thinking. I would rather put the emphasis on what the child can do himself to increase internal control without the reliance on an external drug. However, with all our preferences and opinions out on the table, the fact remains that if your child has clinical hyperactivity, the best known intervention is stimulant medication.

I have mentioned some of the negatives of medications. Let's look at the positive side of these potentially helpful drugs. If the right stimulant is used at the right therapeutic dosage with the right regimen (this may be saying a lot in some cases), the effects of the drug can be nothing short of a miracle. Children who formerly spent much of the day in an endless cycle of reacting to anything and everything in the environment, now can slow down and smell the roses. Children who were constantly at odds with others in their world can now fit into social situations and begin to hear positive comments from others. Children who in the past were shunned and avoided by peers begin to make friends and get invited to spend the night or go to a party.

Some of this may sound melodramatic, but in some cases I have seen the results of medication even go beyond these comments. If stimulants are effective they make the child's brain more like everyone else's, and the child has a much better chance of doing well in all the things he does. Even children who don't like taking medication for hyperactivity have told me that they will continue to do so because of how helpful it is to them. What if a stimulant can improve your child's concentration, improve his/her ability to process stimulation? What if a pill can help the child's responses catch up with external reactions? What if your child could do significantly better at school, at church and in your neighborhood because you are helping him follow an effective medication regimen? Does he then deserve to have this help?

But wait. What about the concern that these children will gravitate to drugs to solve other problems in their lives? The good news is that solid research studies over the last thirty years do not support an increase in drug or alcohol use and abuse among individuals who took stimulants for hyperactivity as children. For sure there are many issues to consider in the question of: to medicate, or not to medicate. Your answer must be your own. I have found my own comfort level with stimulants, in taking advantage of their positive elements while working to prevent any negative elements, and focusing on what the child can do to learn self regulation at an increased pace with the help of the medication. You will have to find the answer for your child and your situation.

If you are a parent who was sold on medications from the beginning, I would caution against giving the child a stimulant and leaving it there. Although the medication may be the strongest aspect of the short term solution, the child will still need practice at internal regulation that could be assisted with a focus on solutions in addition to medication.

A potentially difficult task of the parent is to discriminate between willful activities on the part of the child and hyperactive behavior that, for the most part, is the child on autopilot. Many parents attribute willfulness incorrectly in many situations, and find themselves punishing the child, increasing the child's anger and stress, and making the situation worse. You know your child best. Take the time to consider if the child is doing this on purpose, or if he is struggling to be able to control his behavior.

By now, you know that I am an advocate of having a professional coach to help parents. An additional advantage of a professional in the picture when working with hyperactivity is to help with your communication with your child's school and others in contact with your child. If the school, and your relatives for that matter, know that you are getting some help for the problem, they are much more likely to be understanding than judgmental toward you. Bringing a therapist to the individual education plan meeting or other school conferences can be an important step in having good communication between home and school. Some teachers and principals are wonderful, and without a therapist involved, some may question whether you are doing all you can. In many situations you will be treated differently when your coach is with you. This is just another reason to have a good, experienced and supportive coach on your team.

Do I have to convince you that you need a break from your child on frequent occasions? It is not so much if, as how, you say. No one can be a parent twenty-four hours a day and continue to do well at it. Parents need to be something other than a parent during some times. They need to be a student, a volunteer, a painter, a bowler, or whatever renews personal energy. Parenting a hyperactive child is generally a one way transaction -- energy withdrawals come out of your personal account. If you do not find a way to make energy deposits, your account will quickly become overdrawn and everyone will suffer. It may not be easy to find or arrange for respite for yourself and your child (yes, he needs a break from you at times also), but I can guarantee that you will not find respite without looking for and asking for it. For everyone's sake, take a break frequently from being a caring, responsible, hypervigilant and overworked parent.

Avoid the temptation of letting the child lower your expectations of his or her behavior. Yes, it is difficult to have him responsible for a job around the house that requires you to supervise him. There is no question that, at times, it is easier for you to do it yourself than struggle with the child doing a chore. But when you throw up your hands and do it yourself, your child has trained you to expect less and that is what you will get -- less. At times when it is difficult for the child, it is all the more important that she learn to stick with the task and learn the feeling of accomplishing something difficult.

If the child senses from you that he can be successful, he may feel more internal confidence as well. The other aspect of not lowering expectations is that even though these children are very active, that does not mean that they are actively helpful. At times they are downright lazy when it comes to expending effort that is productive and useful. Help him to focus his energy by providing him with external structure.

Children with ADHD need to have an environment that sends calming signals. Take a look at the various aspects of the child's life at home. How much violent and over stimulating TV does the child watch? Does the child listen to loud music with a driving beat that makes you want to break something? Just think what the music must do to the child's brain. So far I have avoided even mentioning video games. If the child likes video games, does he play any that calm him down? (I doubt it). If you want to develop a holistic intervention for an over stimulated child, take a look at everything in the environment.

Even if you have done your very best to build in some sanity in raising your child who is hyperactive, it is still an extremely difficult job. As with other difficult jobs, pace yourself -- do not get in a hurry. Look for the small steps that indicate progress in your child and in yourself. From a spiritual point of view, few life experiences will teach you as much about patience as this parenting challenge. Take advantage of this and train for the Olympic patience team. And one more thing -- be patient with yourself. You will make mistakes and you will get overheated at times. Give yourself a break. After all, you are doing more than can be realistically asked of any parent. At least recognize this within yourself.

It is important for both parents and therapists to recognize that there are no cures for ADHD. The only effective method to help the child is long term, continual management of the many symptoms of the disorder. Even with the best inter- ventions, involving token systems with immediate rewards, tight structure, and all the right external cues, the child will still need all of these as much next week and he does today. His need for this help will not go away, although it may lessen over the years. As with many other disorders in children, learn to pace yourself, because there is a very long road in front of you as a care provider, and there is even a longer road in front of the child.

Bipolar Disorder in Children

In a much briefer way than ADHD, I will mention Manic Depression, or Bipolar Disorder, in children. Bipolar Disorder is not one diagnosis but nine specific coded diagnoses that are generally separated into three areas: 1) Bipolar I, which includes depression and mania, 2) Bipolar II, which includes depression and hypomania and 3) Bipolar Disorder not otherwise specified, which does not meet the clinical criteria of either I or II. Many other psychiatric disorders appear to be related to Bipolar or perhaps the reverse.

The DSM-IV does not mention preadolescent children in any of the diagnoses in this category other than Bipolar NOS or Cyclothymic Disorder, which is a chronic and less severe disturbance than a Bipolar Disorder, and can indicate a predisposition to a more serious mood disorder in the future. Because children are not specifically mentioned, some have said this was an oversight by the psychiatrists who authored the DSM-IV. I think it is more likely that Bipolar Disorder is currently defined and generally thought of as a disorder primarily among adults or adolescents who are soon to be of adult age. The DSM indicates that Bipolar II has an early onset which it defines as adolescence or early adulthood. This appears to confirm that the DSM-IV views early onset not generally younger than adolescence.

It is possible for a young child to receive a diagnosis of Bipolar when there is a clear pattern of depression and manic or hypomanic symptoms. The most likely diagnosis would be Bipolar NOS, due to the fact that few children will meet the duration criteria for the clinically required periods of depression or mania. However, this diagnosis is, to the objection of some professionals and parents, rarely given to children for many reasons.

Children are by their nature changeable and inconsistent in their behavior and moods. It is not unusual for a child, as well as an adult, to have many ups and downs in a day. Because many children are more expressive than adults, they are often more honest in expressing exactly what they feel. If they hate you, they are more likely to tell you; if they play a game with you, they may say out loud, "I want to win and I want you to lose," or adults may just think this. I remember a child when she was five in the hospital with a serious case of the mumps. I bent over and said, "I'm sorry you feel so bad." She looked up and said, "I wish you had this rather than me." I had no doubt at the moment that she meant it, but to say it to me was the bold honestly of a child. Children tend to be more vocal or demonstrative than adults when they are feeling good, and even more so when they are feeling bad.

The cycling of moods is common for children. I believe that all people have moods that "cycle" in ups and downs. Our society does not expect very young children to be particularly good at managing the ups and downs of emotions. However, by adolescence and early adulthood, we do expect individuals to be very skilled at managing highs and lows, particularly when at their job, driving a car, while hunting, or when using power tools or machinery. The older the individual, the less we expect to see significant cycles of highs and lows. Therefore, we are more likely to view significant mood swings with adults as a problem than with children. To meet the duration requirement of a Bipolar Disorder the highs and lows must last days or weeks. It is much more common that an adult will get stuck in a mood state for multiple days than a child. Keep in mind that "being moody" is not a mental disorder. To have cycling moods become a psychiatric disorder requires that the pattern is extreme and is something that seriously impairs daily functioning. For a child this would be impairment in functioning at home, at school and in the community, or mood swings much more serious than normal fluctuations.

Children are just beginning to understand themselves and their strong feelings, which can be one of the more difficult lessons of life. Remember your first romantic crush as a child? I do; her name was Jane. I didn't understand why, but my body felt and acted differently when Jane was around. My feelings felt controlled by Jane. When Jane smiled at me, it meant more than getting an "A" on the math test. But when Jane moved to another state at the end of second grade, I was devastated and my life was ruined. I didn't understand the ups, and I really didn't understand the downs. I have had many more ups and downs with relationships, but I can remember vividly the joy and the sadness of this first experiment in understanding my feelings.

As I have grown older, I have gradually put more and more restrictions on what I let myself feel. In some spiritual traditions, they don't say someone gradually grows up, they say we all slowly learn to grow dead, because we deaden ourselves from unpleasant or unacceptable feelings that we "shouldn't" have. Often adults need to become more childlike and fully experience the world as a child. This is one of the ways that children in our lives help us stay young. Adults (such as grandparents) much more easily laugh, play, sing or even dance with a toddler than with another adult. They are being childlike.

Because it is the natural state for children to cycle between strong moods, it can be difficult to know when patterns become extreme or dysfunctional, such as when the child seems too expressive or moody or almost histrionic. This is not to say that some children do not indeed have an extreme and dysfunctional cycle of moods, but again it is rare that these children will meet the duration criteria of Bipolar Disorder.

Another aspect of Bipolar Disorder being rare is the criteria that the extreme moods are uncharacteristic for this particular individual. For a child to experience true mania or hypomania, the child must have a significant elevation in moods from the child's typical levels. To say someone is depressed means that they are feeling lower than their typical state. Some children are high strung, and when this is the case, the mood is not elevated; it is the typical state for this particular child. Or if a child cycles between extreme highs and lows and he does this often, this is not uncharacteristic. We must take into account individual differences, and not expect a child to feel like all other children. Bipolar Disorder requires that the child not only have mood cycles, but the moods must be extreme, an impairing condition, and be uncharacteristic of the child's typical mood state.

Now, I will turn the focus from discussing the disorder to discussing the expressed intent by some to have more children diagnosed and treated for one of the Bipolar Disorders. Initially I said I was going to briefly treat this constellation of disorders. There are several reasons for this brief treatment. First, regardless of the wishes of a growing number of parents and childhood Bipolar specialists, the diagnosis of Bipolar Disorder among children is rare. There is a large body of research on Bipolar Disorder in children, and nearly all of it indicates the diagnosis is rare among preadolescent children.

The primary reason for this is a definitional reality (advocates would say a definitional problem).

The present definition of Bipolar Disorder in children presents clinical criteria that are seldom met. The definition of a word in the English language can be found in a commonly accepted dictionary. Over time some words change their meaning and take on new or broader definitions. In the world of psychiatric diagnoses, there is essentially one dictionary, the Diagnostic and Statistical Manual of the American Psychiatric Association, the DSM. (The ICD-10 is another medical "dictionary" of physical disorders, and it takes its lead on psychiatric definitions from the DSM.) As with words in our language, over time diagnoses can also take on different meanings for both clinical and political reasons.

Advocates of broadening the net of Bipolar Disorder argue that there may be millions of undiagnosed Bipolar children in America. To which I reply: not as Bipolar is currently defined. Advocates of using this diagnosis would like to see the DSM change the criteria and even present a position that the current criteria are not only inappropriate but are causing tremendous harm to children and families everywhere. I am unconvinced by this argument.

Don't get me wrong; I support interested groups who want to influence the authors of the DSM to better define and identify problem areas in children. I personally would like to see specific adjustments in the next revision of the DSM clinical criteria for ADHD, Reactive Attachment Disorder, and Intermittent Explosive Disorder to name three. If advocates of a broader definition of Bipolar Disorder can successfully convince the larger clinical community (specifically the authors of the DSM-V), then more power to them, and I will consider more frequent use of the diagnosis because more children would then meet the clinical criteria.

The second reason I am treating this disorder briefly is that it is a descriptive diagnosis (describes a constellation of symptoms) and not a causative diagnosis (provides the cause of symptoms). The distinction between descriptive and causative diagnoses is my own. I prefer to use a diagnosis that helps explain a problem and not just describes the problem.

Some would say that Bipolar does explain the causes of the child's serious symptoms, a cycle of mood disturbances with probable causes in brain chemistry. However, to me Bipolar does not explain the causes of symptoms of mood disturbances any better than a variety of other descriptive diagnoses such as ADHD, Anxiety Disorder, Optional Defiant Disorder (ODD), and other diagnoses with similar symptoms. I see Bipolar as another way to look at symptoms in children, similar to looking at a crowd and defining the crowd by your characteristic of choice such as: gender, age, political party, race, religion, astrological sign or any other defining characteristic.

If the crowd is our nation's population of children whom I describe as refusing to participate in their own improvement or success, then we will see a great deal of whatever we are looking for, and some see millions of Bipolar children. If we are to change the definitional categories of the DSM, I would vote for Self-Regulatory Disorder rather than Bipolar. I believe this better states the problem rather than the symptom or what it looks like.

The final reason I am briefly discussing this problem is that Bipolar Disorder is nonspecific, and in my opinion fails to delineate in a clear way how symptoms of this disorder differ in quantity or quality from symptoms of other disorders common in children. Do many difficult children have mood problems? Yes. Do many of the children I am writing about act unpredictably, changeably, violently, and irrationally? Yes. But it is not particularly helpful to give something a name if the name does not rule in some characteristics and rule out others. To be of practical use, a given name or definition must delineate between other names and definitions, so that one can say this fits but this does not.

Some of the broad definitions for Bipolar Disorder in children include such sweeping criteria, that many other diagnostic categories can almost be called sub groupings. To represent the Bipolar lobby, I will cite a recent publication on Bipolar Disorder in children (Papolos & Papolos, 1999). I was interested in the proposed broader definition of Bipolar and the ability of this new definition to distinguish Bipolar Disorder from other disorders. Here are the results of my taking the first twenty symptoms of Bipolar Disorder mentioned in this publication, and comparing them with three other diagnoses receiving greater emphasis in this book:

Symptom	Bipolar	ADHD	ODD	PTSD
Inflexible	Yes	Yes	Yes	Often
Oppositional	Yes	Usually	Yes	Often
Irritable	Yes	Yes	Always	Yes
Explosive Tantrums	Yes	Usually	Yes	Often
Destructive	Yes	Yes	Yes	Yes
Assaultive	Yes	Often	Usually	Common
Sneaky and covert	Yes	Common	Often	Often
Rapid mood shifts	Yes	Yes	Yes	Yes
Anxious	Yes	Usually	Usually	Yes
Erratic sleep patterns	Yes	Often	Common	Yes
Excessive activity	Yes	Always	Usually	Common
Precocious	Yes	Often	Common	Often
Death preoccupation	Yes	Yes	Common	Yes

Symptom	Bipolar	ADHD	ODD	PTSD
Poor at transitions	Yet	Yes	Yes	Yes
Rigid	Yes	Yes	Yes	Often
Controlling	Yes	Yes	Yes	Yes
Over-timulated	Yes	Yes	Often	Often
Peer problems	Yes	Yes	Yes	Yes
Manipulative	Yes	Yes	Yes	Yes
Intrusive	Yes	Yes	Yes	Common

In the above cited book, there are many more mentioned characteristics of Bipolar Disorder in children than the above. These were mentioned first. Looking at the above, if Bipolar can be said to include all twenty symptoms, there are no symptoms in this list that provide any distinguishing element of the four diagnoses. Using empirical criterion keying (a statistical method of making distinctions), all twenty would be eliminated as unable to differentiate between disorders. If these are the top of the list of defining characteristics for Bipolar Disorder in children, then this label fails to distinguish itself from other frequently used childhood diagnoses. I would also say that this list of symptoms would not be helpful in distinguishing the other three diagnoses as well, since all are found in all four. Therefore, unless the symptoms can rule in or rule out children, how is the label useful?

Bipolar addresses extreme poles of a person's moods. The old name was manic depression, which identifies two poles. What should distinguish and set apart this disorder is the cycling of extreme mood swings from mania or hypomania to depression or a less elevated mood and back again. The above twenty traits may be associated with Bipolar Disorder, but as seen above they are also associated with many serious childhood disorders.

What many two-year-olds do all day can be unusual and very problematic from a co-worker at the office. Mental health disorders define the unusual, the extreme and by definition, the debilitating. The cycling of moods in children is neither unusual nor necessarily debilitating.

One of the joys of watching a child (as well as one of the challenges of parenting) is the excitement and joy she expresses when happy, and the sadness and anger she shows when she doesn't get her way. How many times does a normal child cycle from sad to happy in a day, or in an hour? The little guy becomes the man of steel in his superman PJs, and then cries like there will be no tomorrow when rain ruins a trip to the park.

Bipolar Disorder must identify extreme moods that last for unusual periods of time, and these moods must be debilitating for the child. Does this occur in children? In my experience yes, but more often than not, extreme debilitating mood swings are the result of other problems such as trauma, fetal alcohol or pervasive developmental disorder.

In my diagnostic work with children (who have included some of the most psychiatrically disturbed populations in our mental health system), I have never felt constrained by the tight criteria for Bipolar Disorder in children. I have been lobbied on occasion by a parent or professional to diagnose the child with a Bipolar Disorder, but I have seldom complied because the symptoms did not meet DSM-IV clinical criteria. As I mentioned earlier, if the criteria of Bipolar Disorder in children was broadened, then I would legitimately use it more, but I personally do not see the present criteria as problematic to get a child the help he or she needs to address the symptoms, regardless of the label we give it.

Part III

Advanced Parenting Skills

and Challenges

Chapter

7

Sexual Problems with Children

There is a great deal that could be said about the place sex plays in our culture. Few societies in the world promote and exhibit sexuality as much as the American culture, yet so little of this sexual emphasis fosters a healthy sexuality. We market sex as a "come on" and a taboo subject rather than honoring and respecting this aspect of human nature. The result of this is to create a sexual tension that is not and cannot be satisfied. This tension is found in adults who believe the press and the world of advertising that everyone else is sexually fulfilled. This tension is found in our high rates of sex crimes, sexual dysfunctions of all kinds, and our culture leading the world as consumers of pornography of all types.

Sexual tension can also be found with our children, and teen parents. We have a culture of adults and children who know more about the mechanics of sex, but less about healthy sexuality, than ever before. It is very clear that we do not know how to teach our children about healthy sexuality because we as a society do not understand healthy sexuality.

We market sex in our culture to help portray what we hold in greatest esteem -- youth and vitality. Where else but in America is sex used to sell cars, clothes, food, cigarettes, jewelry, whiskey, mufflers and entertainment? In our culture sex is used to gain attention, to heighten tension, and to hold out the forbidden fruit that is not available. We have an unhealthy fascination with body parts that is not found in cultures that see body parts and bodily functions as normal and natural. Where else but in America would one of the top ten news stories of the year be a medication to help men achieve a better erection? We restrict children from seeing breasts in movies, but violence is acceptable for them to watch. If there were a prime example of an entire culture with sexual "hang-ups," we are it.

With this societal backdrop, parents have the difficult task of raising children with a healthy attitude toward sexuality in a culture where sex is often anything but natural and healthy. This job is made much more difficult when the child has been initiated into a sexual world through abuse. Among sexually abused children, it often seems that the sexual light switch has been turned on much too early. Research has found what most foster parents already knew -- children sexually mature more rapidly when they have been sexually abused. However, this maturity is not a cognitive or emotional maturity, it simply means the plumbing is active before it is needed.

It is not unusual for abused children to define much of their interaction with others in sexual terms. They see sex as "bad" yet they can't think or get enough of this forbidden fruit. Often what parents must do for everyone's sanity is to change the subject, or try to have sex just go away until the child is older. This often does not work, but if it does, this creates other issues of concern. Again, the job of the parent is to initiate the child into a world that is natural and healthy, which includes sexuality. If the soup has already been spoiled, what does the parent do then?

When we look around at our culture, we see sex and power closely linked. The proof of being "sexy" is the ability to influence others. Can a woman turn heads by the way she dresses or acts? Can a man cause a woman to surrender and act against her better judgment? In America, sex is about power. It seems fitting that when a Hollywood male actor was recently voted "sexiest man alive," his response was, "I don't know what they are talking about. I don't even know what sexy means." I think he was just a bit more honest than our culture, because other than power, we do not know what sexy means either.

Our children learn from all the influences around them. Is it any wonder we have children wanting power and experimenting with sex to get it? Is it surprising that even young children have learned that any behavior involving sexuality is powerful and immediately gets the attention of everyone around? As our confused children grow up to be confused adults, we have a disproportionate number of individuals who are outside the boundaries of acceptable sexual behavior (boundaries which are already rather broad). We have European and Asian countries producing child pornography primarily for the American market. Producers of this material will say they do not know exactly why, but a strong American market can not get enough of this "sick stuff."

We have pedophiles, adults who seek sexual gratification from children, working to maintain the power position. We have a thriving sex industry where we teach young females that they have greater earning potential (power) in using their body than their mind. We have thus far the only truly profitable aspect of the Internet -- adult sex stores. And we have a greater problem with rape in our culture than in the rest of the developed world. Rape has long ago been correctly understood as more of a power crime than a sex crime.

As if parenting were not difficult enough, part of the job is to produce a healthy functioning sexual adult. In the larger context of a sexually confused culture, the issue of sex often becomes a whole list of inappropriate thoughts, feelings and behaviors. We seldom put healthy and sexual or erotic in the same sentence. I remember as a child wondering how big St.

Peter's book must be if (as I was told) all our impure thoughts were written in it. Remember President Carter's confession that he had sinned before by having lustful thoughts? The response he received was to be demeaned as being unhip, even silly, that anyone would be concerned about sexual thoughts. Even religious groups, the guardians of moral behavior, are viewed as out of touch with a contemporary world. A Mennonite woman recently told me a joke. She said "Do you know why the Mennonites discourage sexual intercourse? Because it leads to dancing." We truly have lost our "moral compass."

So what are you supposed to teach your children about sex? The "just say no" approach of collective denial appears to have mutated into the "don't ask, don't tell" thinking. For example, if you want to confound a group of adults, go to the blackboard and write down all the healthy and appropriate sexual expressions available to children in our culture. While most parents prefer the position that children are just too young for sexuality, it just so happens that children are sexual beings as well as adults. Particularly in our culture of sexual "come ons" and sexual tension, Pandora's box has already been opened, and parents are going to have to face the consequences, ready or not.

When looking at our culture it is easier to see why sex has the mystique it does in parenting. But your best bet is to downgrade this forbidden fruit to just another fruit in the garden. If you do not, you will signal to the child (as most of the other adults he/she has interacted with) that there is power in sexual behavior. It is almost always useful to consider problematic sexual behavior similar to all other problematic behavior. Stripped of its juicy, taboo, exciting, and gross qualities, sexual issues can be handled in a more natural and healthy way, just the opposite of all the societal modeling we get. If Johnny decides to enthusiastically scratch his special purpose (the name for a penis in Steve Martin's movie "The Jerk") in church, do your best not to blow a gasket, and handle the behavior just as you would the child chewing on his fingernails. If you don't, the behavior will be written in red ink in the great book of things that drive mom crazy. Remember the inscription chiseled in stone over the tomb of the unknown parent: "Overreact to any problem behavior and you will see it again before sundown." Do your best to respond to any sexual issue as you would any other issue; take the mystique out of it.

Another way to view putting sexual issues in a more natural and less frantic atmosphere is to understand that much of what we view as sexual from children is not motivated by sexual interests. Children use sexual terms and make sexual references that they see in the media but often do not understand their meaning. They draw breasts on girls and penises on boys (sometimes reversed) because they know that doing this is against the rules. They expose themselves or touch others in private areas because they know they can get an immediate response. When confronted with these and many other examples of sexual themes in children with a history of emotional disturbances, parents often see the sexual aspect of the behavior and catastrophize the situation by thinking, "Now what are we going to do? We have a sex offender on our hands."

Sexual behavior is enticing to many children not from a sexual orientation but from a power and control orientation. I recently confronted a child who was accused by a peer of sexually touching another child's anus. Her response was, "Gross, why would I want to do that?" I gave this some thought and I could not come up with a good answer to this question. This child let me know by this response and her energy that the allegation was probably untrue, which was soon admitted by the other child. Much of what is interesting to children is not sexual intimacy, it is the attention they receive. Ask yourself this question: if the child received no attention or reaction to the behavior, would the behavior continue as it is? Perhaps the answer is yes, but many times the answer will point to the main source of the behavior -- control over the environment.

How does a child gain control by sexual behavior? Let's consider a couple examples. Rachel comes from a foster home and is new to her third grade classroom. A week after she arrives, the recess monitor notices the boys suddenly playing with the girls as they whisper to each other. On checking this out, she finds that Rachel has taught other children how to play 'prostitute' like her mother taught her, and the little boys found this even more interesting than soccer (this actually happened in our program and as Dave Barry would say, "I am not making this up"). The recess monitor not only stops the game, but informs both the teacher and the principal. Parents are called, conferences are held, and Rachel is the source of a good deal of scrutiny and supervision wherever she goes. Is she aware of this? Do bees like honey? Is there any positive example you can come up with that would give Rachel the same amount of attention and influence on her environment? I can't.

Years ago I was working with an impulsive and highly sexualized boy. He had been showing improvement in reduced sexualized behavior when things took a serious turn for the worse. After I caught him trying to be sexual with another child, I told him I was disappointed that he was going back to his old behavior. The boy became enraged and yelled at me that he received much more attention from being bad than from being good. I have often thought of this statement ever since.

So if sexual behavior is used as power and control, what does the child attempt to control? The answer is you -- your behavior, your emotions and the mood in the environment. Be honest. Would it change your mood to walk into the living room and find your foster son doing sexual things with Muffy the family dog? Would the child have some influence over your feelings and behavior? Would this change the mood in the house? Can you think of any other ways a small child could get so much power? Neither can they.

In the face of the challenges of dealing with sexualized behavior, one answer is to become very comfortable with sexual issues. If, like most adults in our culture, you are not someone who can easily talk about sexual things, you need to work on this. If you get sweaty palms every time a child shows sexual curiosity or asks a sexual question, then you need to desensitize yourself or you will be an easy target.

If Travis, instead of being sexual with Muffy, was squirting ketchup on her, you would likely take the ketchup, tell him this behavior is not OK because ketchup is for a different type of dog. You would not be happy about the incident, but your blood pressure would probably not hit the roof, nor send you to the phone to ask the therapist, "What does this say about the safety of everyone in our family?" Learn to view problematic sexual behavior as you do any other type of problematic behavior, because that is what it is.

If you are getting more sexual themes than you care to have in your home, look around at any environmental stimulation. Look at what is being watched on TV, what music is being played through the headphones (just because you don't have to hear it, doesn't mean they should), what magazines are on the coffee table (a scantily clothed model on the cover with one of those looks offering "10 ways to put sexual excitement back in your relationship," and "8 dinners that will turn him on").

If you are saying to yourself, "Come on doc, lighten up, this kind of stuff is everywhere," I agree it is, and that is precisely the problem. We have so much sexual stimulation around us, intentionally placed there for marketing reasons, that we become desensitized to it. But many children are not.

Check out your world. Are you and your environment unknowingly overstimulating the natural, and not so natural, sexual curiosity and interest of a young child? Or are you understimulating them by not giving them developmentally appropriate information so they are always looking for more? When parents ask, "How do you know how much sexual information to give a child when they ask?" I usually reply, "When the child listens to you for awhile and then says 'Can I go out and play now?' he has received enough."

Remember that your job is not to turn a child into a non-sexual being. We often have to work to de-escalate the amount of sexual interest and sexual behavior with children. But make sure you are not the kind of parent who tells a child "Stop touching yourself down there, it's dirty, bad and gross; save it for someone you love." A seldom considered fact by both parents and therapists is that we all have a job beyond treating the effects of sexual abuse, and that is to replace negative sexual attitudes with positive sexual attitudes. We need to help the child have a healthy sexual outlook, not an asexual outlook.

Even with the many problematic issues surrounding sexuality with challenging children, they still need to learn and be exposed to positive aspects of this important part of their body and their world. Sex is not like voting. We can't say "just wait until you are eighteen to worry about that." Although most of us would prefer to find the sexual light switch and turn it off for a few more years (just when we would want to turn it back on is another matter), this approach is generally unsuccessful. So the best suggestion is to be ready, be comfortable, don't overreact, don't avoid, and realize that none of us is completely comfortable with all this, much less experts at it.

Sexual Issues

All sexual behavior is not the same. As mentioned above, some behavior we consider sexual is not motivated by sexual interests at all. If you want to effectively respond, step one is to determine just what you are facing. In the Appendices are two scales that may be helpful in determining the nature of sexual activity in children. The first is the Inappropriate Sexual Behavior Scale. Sexual behavior among children is a very complex and difficult topic for parents. In the past, all sexual behavior was wrong, and the suggested response was to punish the child with the hope of forestalling sexual behavior for as long as possible. The more "enlightened" response has been to see sexual behavior as normal, and to relieve children of the shame and guilt the parents went through as kids. However, neither of these approaches helps a parent to understand if and when sexual behavior is not only a problem, but perhaps pathological.

The Inappropriate Sexual Behavior Scale (ISBS) can help. The Scale is based on the premise that children should not be put into categories (which is popular). Each of the child's behaviors should be considered to see if there is a concerning pattern. In order to do this, there must be some measuring stick to consider a normal sexual behavior from an abnormal one. Once individual behaviors are reviewed, then the next scale can be useful, the Juvenile Sex Offender Risk Assessment Matrix (JSO-RAM). This scale uses the ISB Scale to determine concerning patterns of sexual behavior and to assess the likelihood of future acting out behavior.

When considering sexual behavior there are three more issues that deserve attention:

Sexual Reactivity

One of the biggest errors that is made in assessing sexual behavior is to mistakenly assume it is sexually offending behavior. There is a difference between a child who has been sexually abused and who does something sexual with or to another child, and perhaps a very similar behavior that is done by a child who has the intention of harming the other person. The first is what is called sexual reactivity (reacting to the fact that someone has involved them in sexual activity) and the second, sexual offending. It is not always easy to tell one from the other.

Sexual reactivity always comes from a child who has previously been sexually abused in one form or the other, and the behavior is in response to this abuse. Sometimes the child is not even aware of the behavior, such as with frequent masturbation. Sometimes there is a driven or fixated tone to the behavior, as if the behavior was in charge of them rather than the reverse. Sexually reactive children do not always know either what they are doing nor why they are doing it. There is generally a tone to the behavior that it is coming from somewhere other than this young child. It is important to spot sexual reactivity because it is to be expected in abused children, and is not a predictor of serious future behavior, as some people believe.

Sexual Offending

Offending behavior is much more serious and is a very real indicator of present and future concern. Offending behavior is almost always intentional, usually thought out, and is designed to place the offender in a dominant position over the victim. As with many adult offenders, the motivation is often as much power and control as it is sexual gratification. There is generally extra gratification for sex offenders when the victim is enjoying the experience much less than the offender is (remember the abuse is typically about power).

Like sexually reactive children, people who sexually offend may have a history of sexual abuse, but some research is suggesting not as frequent as we have believed in the past. As we learn more about the secret world of the offender, we are finding offenders are often experts at transferring responsibility and changing the focus away from themselves. One effective way of transferring blame when he is caught doing something sexual is to claim that he was a victim when he was younger. This is designed to take him off the hook and to create sympathy and leniency from either family or from the court system. The fact is that many offenders who say they were sexually abused, were not. Since truthfulness is not one of the characteristics of sex offenders, it is difficult to know the truth about their sexual past.

Offending behavior is very serious and should signal the need for professional attention. It is nearly always combined with a pattern of cognitive distortions known as thinking errors. Offenders generally have predictable cycles that include cognitions, feelings, and behaviors. With the right professional help, the behavior can be controlled first by the environment and then by the offending individual.

Identity Disorder

Some sexual themes are an indication of the confusion of the child's internal sexual identity. It is not unusual for very young children to have some period of identification with the opposite gender. However, some males may gravitate to female themes for a variety of reasons such as avoiding aggressive energy, liking the support females have provided, and in Freudian terms, over identification with the Oedipal drive. Females may either prefer the power role they have experienced from dominate males, or they may prefer to align with a male identity to pretend that they are not sexual females, as a way to protect themselves from further violation. Some identity disorders are complex and others less so. This issue may also be a reason to obtain some professional help if your efforts are not effective at helping the child discover who he is.

203

It is entirely possible that the little darling you have at home or at your office is providing you with a challenge that has not been discussed. If you need further help, go rent Woody Allen's movie *Everything You Ever Wanted to Know About Sex*. On second thought, that might not provide all the assistance you need. Do your best to remove the mystery and special status of all things sexual, or you will have more, not fewer, sexual challenges. Good luck. Do your best, and get help when you need it.

Chapter

8

Other Challenges

with Difficult Children

It is somewhat difficult to address all of the potential problems and challenges a parent may have to face, and cover the myriad of possible combinations. However, it is important to cover the most frequent conditions that are on the list of the most difficult to parent children. No list would be complete without a look at Fetal Alcohol Syndrome (FAS).

Fetal Alcohol Syndrome

Any treatment center that routinely serves young clients who have been abused or neglected will be very familiar with FAS. Clinics that treat populations from more stable and supportive families will undoubtedly see less of this condition. Information and reaction to fetal alcohol syndrome has sent many parents and therapists on a roller coaster ride for years. At times we have been told to believe that this condition is a life sentence with irreversible symptoms, and to some degree this is true. We have been warned to look out for the army of children who were to come our way due to the increase in adult drug use in the last three decades. However, this has never quite occurred in the numbers predicted. We have read that alcohol and pregnancy was a sure formula for

FAS, although it has always been the case that some pregnant mothers who were predicted to have babies with FAS, have not. Certainly there is some truth to the image of a pregnant woman drinking alcohol or taking drugs playing Russian roulette with the child, since we do not know how much or how often to be able to make accurate predictions. Over the last two decades we know more about FAS, and we know more about what we do not yet know.

There is no question that fetal alcohol syndrome is a preventable, senseless, and tragic burden to place on a newborn. In pronounced cases, FAS will follow the individual throughout his/her life and may indeed be a life sentence. It remains one of the primary causes of mental retardation, and among the many causes of birth defects. FAS is also the most preventable of serious disorders among children. This condition strikes thousands of newborns each year, and some of these children will be robbed of a normal life that could have been theirs without the assault on their development in utero.

The affects of toxins on the developing child can cause physical, emotional, and mental deficiencies. Physical problems can include arrested development producing low birth weight, small craniums, and at times abnormal development of internal organs such as the heart. Physical signs can include the lack of a filtrum under the nose, small and wide spaced eyes, an abnormal nose, and flat cheeks. Most affected children have some if not serious cognitive deficiencies.

But the picture does not stop with physical or mental disabilities; most of these children have moderate to severe emotional and behavioral problems. These problems can be the result of the child's initiation into a world that was uncomfortable and difficult before the first breath. Personal deficits and deficiencies can rob these easily frustrated individuals of the ability to understand the situation or know how to face the many inherent problems. Unfortunately, many of these children with organic impairments will grow up in a family environment that not only caused FAS to begin with, but continues to be unresponsive to the significant needs of these children. Because of this, and the fact that many of these children can behave in severe ways, a high percentage of children with FAS end up in some form of substitute care: foster care, adoption, or treatment programs.

FAS is one of the common ingredients in the mental health "stew" of multiple challenging conditions in children coming into intensive mental health programs such as residential treatment. FAS essentially always comes in combination with multiple other issues such as behavioral disturbance, trauma, ADHD, attachment difficulties, conduct disorder, mood disorders, and the list goes on. At times it has seemed to me when working with some of the more severe cases of FAS that this condition is the fire that heats all the other problem areas into a boil.

I referred earlier to the roller coaster of understanding this condition. Although medical science always prefers to be black and white with diagnostic categories, it is not always possible with disorders such as FAS. There is no litmus test for FAS, no blood test to indicate that you are not a carrier. This has caused over-diagnosis at times and under-diagnosis at other times. For years the common practice in assessing children with behavior symptoms of FAS was to consider the criteria of the medical diagnosis. If the child did not have dismorphology directly associated with FAS, as well as proof of a significant history of alcohol or drug intake during pregnancy, often the child would either get the diagnosis anyway or was coded as FAE, fetal alcohol effect or FADE, fetal alcohol or drug effect. In some areas of medicine, this diagnosis became so common that it nearly lost its diagnostic importance. Children with abusive past histories or children with unknown prenatal development who had symptoms were likely to receive the label of FAS or FADE. Many of these children may have been appropriately labeled and many were not.

Over the last decade, more care has been taken to distinguish a diagnosis of FAS from children that act like FAS children but do not meet the clinical criteria. While this is a more accurate and precise diagnostic position, it has also tended to have the pendulum swing to the other extreme. In recent years some medical practitioners have avoided the difficult and diagnostically messy business of FAS by preferring not to use the diagnosis. This has been done by requiring the diagnosis be assessed only by a very limited number of experts, and only when there is irrefutable proof of "hard" physical symptoms and a history of drug and/or alcohol abuse during pregnancy. In our state, there were only one or two medical facilities that would affix a diagnosis of FAS and only after extensive review. The lesser code FAE or FADE began to be looked down upon by experts since it was technically a constellation of symptoms and not a specific medical diagnosis itself. This may be more precise, but the question must be asked: at what cost?

Soon fetal alcohol effects were "soft" signs and often ignored, although there is no question that many children were negatively affected by drugs and alcohol with all the hard signs necessary for the formal diagnosis. In the last few years a common sense middle of the road position is more apparent. FAS as a diagnosis should only be made if the case meets the criteria. But if there is information of drug or alcohol exposure, in combination with the many behavioral and emotional symptoms in children, there has been more willingness to indicate the probable influence toxic exposure in utero has had.

Working with Children with Fetal Alcohol Syndrome

Understanding FAS is crucial in knowing what to reasonably expect of the child. Fetal alcohol syndrome affects the developing brain exactly at the most vulnerable time. Specifically, alcohol directly affects cell viability and migration, both essential for brain development. The effects of alcohol on the cellular level set into motion abnormalities that cannot be undone. There is no way to go back and provide the child what was needed during critical periods of development.

Although there is much we do not know about FAS, we do know that the resulting effect on children can run the continuum from slight to severe. We also know that the effects of FAS are irreversible and permanent. However, we also know that this is not another way of saying the situation is hopeless.

A dozen years ago, fetal alcohol syndrome received national attention due to a best-selling book by author and parent Michael Dorris. His book was called *The Broken Cord* (Dorris, 1989), and in a compelling and startlingly vivid fashion he presented the story of his adopted son Adam. It was difficult to read this book and not feel a long list of emotions effectively portrayed by the author. However, most of these emotions were on the pain and suffering side of the continuum. It would turn out that Adam's life would end as tragically as it began. As haunting and helpful as *The Broken Cord* was, some parents viewed the book's message as the FAS cup half empty. If this was the case, then the FAS cup half full is found in the later book *Fantastic Antone Succeeds!* (Kleinfeld & Wescott, 1993). From the title of the book to the last chapter, a hopeful message is directed to parents and teachers of children with FAS. Both books are well done and worth reading, and both acknowledge the same points but with a very different emphasis. I must say that because of the populations I work with, Michael Dorris' FAS cup, half empty or not, is the one I most often see confronting children with serious FAS. However, everyone needs to focus on the positive in life and no one more than a parent of a child with FAS.

Parents with children who have FAS are particularly appreciative of knowing this diagnosis because of the effect this knowledge has on expectations of the child. A multitude of "misbehaviors" of other children are to be expected of children with FAS. Without knowing the common results of this diagnosis on the behavior of children, the frustration of parents would reach critical mass very quickly. It would be like expecting a child with retardation to take honors courses in school.

Since FAS frequently affects the cognitive ability of children, this analogy is pretty close to reality. For many of these children, life is like facing an honors curriculum without the gray matter to figure out what is being asked, much less to come up with the right answers. It is unreasonable to have the same expectations of children with FAS as other children. Parents appreciate knowing why these children respond as they do. Just as they would do for children with low cognitive ability, which is the case with many children with FAS, the parents must adjust their expectations of children with FAS. Perhaps the best way to work with a child with FAS is to identify frequently used parenting or learning strategies that are often found successful.

Using external cues, props, and reminders -- do not take anything for granted with children who have FAS. Make your instructions and your expectations demonstrably clear by red spray paint on the wall (well, almost).

For getting dressed, give the child pictures showing the socks being put on, left shoe, right shoe, and tie the left then tie the right. Put masking tape on the floor indicating where the shoes go at the end of the day, color code clothes for play and for school. Put red tape on the toothpaste, white on the toothbrush and blue on the cup, so they can remember the order: red, white and blue always go in that order, don't they?

Set an alarm for the shower if you want some hot water left; telling the child to turn off the water in ten minutes will get lost in the experience of the moment. Put pictures on the dresser drawers: socks, underwear, shirts, etc. Post the family rules on the wall (a good idea for all children). Put up calendars with special events marked -- Halloween, Dad's birthday, and a trip to Grandma's. Have the child carry 3 x 5 cards with a list of things to do when he gets home from school, but remember to put a reminder on the wall to take the card out of his pocket to look at it. Give the child three poker chips when there are 15 minutes left before bedtime, then take one chip each 5 minutes. You get the idea.

Using external structure to compensate for the lack of internal structure -- To some extent all children need to begin self control with someone providing external control. We are taught how to think, how to act, and to a large extent how to feel. The experience of a child with FAS is like an experience with the little gray writing board that when you lift the plastic sheet, what you wrote disappears. For these children, past experience makes little lasting impression. For this reason, structure needs to come from the outside. Even learning routines is a form of the structure coming from outside the child. These children need reminders, they need road signs through life as the rest of us need signs on highways: when to start, when to stop, to merge, to use caution, to speed up and to slow down. Over time the external structure seeps in, but often at a surprisingly slow rate.

Using routines and repetition -- There is nothing quite like repetition for learning. But these children must repeat many more times than other children to learn even a fraction as much. Encourage the child to do the same tasks in the same way. Make as much of the child's day as predictable routine. We eat at the same time, I use the same green plate, I eat my salad first and dessert last.

211

Reducing stimulation -- I compare FAS to being unlucky enough to be in the grocery store on pay day. Too many people with too many overflowing carts having wheels that don't go straight. Anywhere I stand, there is a woman over 87 who is trying to get past me. I just want to get out and find a quiet place. A child with FAS has a brain that often sees the world as the grocery store or rush hour traffic. Normal stimulation becomes the accident during rush hour; no more thoughts are going down this freeway any time soon.

Calm the child or better yet, calm the environment. Limit the distractions, turn off the TV or stereo in the background. Cut down on the number of stimuli that yell at the child, "Hey, look at me!" Limit noise, activity, chaos. If Bowser barks a lot, don't have him around when it is homework time. Develop quiet spaces in your house, and teach your child to voluntarily use those spaces often (you might do this as well).

Teaching internal calming -- I do not think humans are born with an instinct to relax. In fact, we know that our primary drives are avoid pain, pursue pleasure, fight, or flight -- none of which is relaxing. One definition of being alive is detectable stress in the body, at least in brain activity. We must learn to relax. If muscles stay tense they cramp and hurt, and if people stay tense they do the same. You will need to spend extra time teaching relaxation and calming techniques to children with FAS. They hate over stimulation and they go toward it every time. I teach these children meditation and concentration, starting with being still. We have quiet contests. I tell a group of the children that "T Rex" from Jurassic Park is in the room and the next one who moves is lunch (now there's a calming thought).

Reducing changes and surprises -- This is another way of saying routines and structure are important. Don't vary dinner and bedtime by one or two hours. Have a predictable schedule; it may seem boring to you but there is still plenty of excitement for the child. Surprises are everyone's favorite, right? Trust me, surprises will often backfire with children who have FAS. Anticipation is part of the excitement at Christmas or waiting to leave for vacation. But these children do not experience anticipation; looking forward to a positive experience, they experience anxiety and stress. In our program we routinely do not let these children know if we are going on a field trip until minutes before. Otherwise the anxiety often puts them into a tailspin and they can't handle going on the trip. Of course, this approach must be balanced with limiting surprises.

Using physical touch -- I believe the first and most important language of children is touch. Touch freely but touch firmly and supportively. Make sure your touch is not causing anxiety or over-stimulating the child. Take both of the child's hands in yours and then deliver your message. Tell the children you love them with frequent hugs and embraces as you walk by. When the child gets overanxious, a firm touch on the shoulder or taking the child's hand firmly in yours may calm the situation. Particularly for younger children, if you can send the message with touch and without words, give it a try.

Modifying verbal interactions -- Who says the best instructions are verbal? We have a deaf child in our program, and he has taught me the limited value of words. We use hand signals, a very good idea with children struggling with FAS. Have a signal for "calm down," "listen to me," "what do you need to do next," etc. When using words use familiar words; ask the child to give you eye contact. Use short sentences and brief instructions. If you can say something in a simpler way, do so.

Using pneumonic aides -- Specialists in memory will tell you that our mind remembers information better if it is associated with another piece of information. In this case the other information is a song or saying. How do you remember how many days there are in the month of October? I must

213

admit that I learned several sayings and songs so well, they remain the only way I can remember the information. If I was on Jeopardy and Alex said, "This month begins with a 'J' and is one of four months with 30 days." I would never get to the buzzer first, because I would be saying to myself "30 days hath September..." I can still spell encyclopedia only if I see Jiminy Cricket in my mind singing the letters.

Remembering in this way is part repetition (how many times have I repeated "30 days hath...") and part association (how we remember the words to a song on the radio we have not heard since junior high). Children with FAS need every advantage possible. Create a song about bath time "soap, soap, soap your bod, gently rinse it off, dry, dry, dry, dry, until it is enough" or something similar that gives the child a way to remember the steps to a daily routine. I mentioned earlier a child I presently work with who has fetal alcohol and ADHD (a frequent and challenging combination), and how he dresses each morning in a different way. He is amazing in his inefficiency because he sees the task as something he is doing for the first time. A saying or song could be helpful to a child like him.

When the whole is the sum of its parts -- Tasks might seem logical and simple to you, but not to a child with FAS. "Bill, please set the table for dinner" may seem straightforward to you, but a child with FAS might think, "Set it where, what table, sit on the table, sit what on the table, dinner is on the table, set the dinner on the table and sit on it, now where was I..." You must break down even simple tasks into parts, step 1, step 2 and only then, step 3. Even something as simple as washing hands. Turn on the water, rinse hands, put soap on hands, rub hands, rinse soap off hands and dry hands. You do it many times a day without thinking, but if these steps are in any other order it doesn't work. In the same way, to tell a child with FAS "Go pour yourself some cereal" is not going to work unless you say, "Get a bowl from the cupboard and bring it to me...good, now get the milk in the fridge...well done, now..." Think about needing to do something complex on the computer (this usually means anything you haven't done before), or when you are in a strange town looking for a phantom street and are getting directions from Bubba, don't you want the steps explained clearly and given slowly? Children with FAS are not only visiting a strange town, they are living permanently in a strange world.

Three behaviors that have not yet been previously addressed can prove to be very challenging: enuresis (bedwetting), destructive behavior, and eating disorders.

Enuresis

Bedwetting is a fact of life for all children and parents at some point in time. Most parents can understand and stay patient with the child who is learning sphincter control, or who occasionally has an accident. It can be another matter entirely when bedwetting is an everyday occurrence, and the child is entering the teen years. Sometimes even more challenging are children who have wetting incidents during waking hours. And the top of the challenging ladder in this area are the children who intentionally choose to urinate at times and in places that are not appropriate. Few parenting programs talk about what to do when you find your favorite potted plant in your living room suddenly dying, and you notice an unexpected but familiar odor around its roots. This may be when you could use a "quiet room" in your home, not for the child, but for yourself, in order to calm down before you address the problem.

Let's start with common bedwetting. Essentially, all males do this and a large percentage of females. I do not know this for a fact, but my experience tells me that nearly 100% of traumatized children, males and females, wet the bed beyond when it is developmentally expected. When it comes to children with serious problems other than trauma, the percentages go up as well, and the problem can last much longer.

The first question to ask when a child is bedwetting is whether this is the time to come up with a plan to reduce night time enuresis. Most children grow out of it with little intervention. Many children with one or more serious problem areas need a program to address this problem because it just may not go away on its own. Bedwetting programs can take several forms. The most standard are strategies like cutting off fluids after six in the evening (reduce the source), awakening the child an hour or two after going to sleep (teaching the child to get up and use the bathroom), having a star chart with rewards for dry nights (increasing motivation to learn self regulation), and sometimes increasing fluid intake in connection with getting the child up (increasing attention to the sensation of a full bladder).

Regardless of the plan, some children, particularly those who have been traumatized, can become amazingly accustomed to bedwetting to the point that they express little or no discomfort with it, or interest to work on it. For this and other reasons, I would always suggest that the child who is five, six or older remove soiled sheets and put on a new set without you providing maid service. Isn't this a bit young, you ask? Above the age of four, I have worked with no young child who could not do this task more or less proficiently.

When waking up a child, you will need to take most of the responsibility to get the child up at first. One of the common aspects of enuresis is deep sleep when the child is not aware of bodily sensations. After awhile it may work to have the child take the responsibility of getting up by setting a personal alarm. This encourages self sufficiency and can also train him to be more aware of his bodily sensations by sleeping less deeply.

There are also mechanical devices that can help. These are often moisture sensitive electrodes that are placed on a pad on the bed or attached to the child's sleepwear. When moisture hits the sensor, an alarm goes off, waking the child, who can then go to the toilet. For the most part, my experience with these gadgets has been good. They are particularly helpful for children who are motivated to fix this problem. The child who doesn't care about wetting the bed continually will either turn off the alarm or sleep through the alarm.

Some parents consider electrodes in the underwear to be invasive. I have always viewed urine soaked clothing as even more invasive. I have been surprised how rapidly this approach has shown success in some cases. I have had children turn this problem around in a couple weeks with this device. I even had one child who had the alarm go off only once, and he never had the problem again. For children who are ready to work on this problem, this device can be an important aid.

Perhaps the most controversial method of treating enuresis is with medication. The two most frequent methods are prescriptions for a nose spray or the medication Imipramine. The nose spray has fewer potential side effects but is not as effective as Imipramine. However, Imipramine can be toxic at a large dose and must be monitored carefully.

Destructive Behavior

The second problem behavior in this triad is destructive behavior. There are few behaviors that will keep parents and the entire family on edge quite like a child who frequently loses control or seeks negative attention by destroying property.

Step one is to find out "What's Eating Gilbert Grape?" The source of the destructive behavior may be a number of factors, some of which you can address directly, but others may be much more difficult. When possible go after the problem, not

217

the symptom. If Billy is upset because he received his annual letter from his biological mother promising him a new bike at Christmas and letting him know that she has married for the fifth time and moved to the other side of the county, be ready for Billy to blow. Knowing that the conditions are ripe for a destructive episode, you may be able to address the problem. Rather than find yourself in a power struggle and subsequent destructive tantrum, when the whole time the issue was really about mom.

For example, depending on the child, you might be available to listen to how Billy feels about the letter or mom is moving again. If he is not a talker, you could let him know that you know it is tough for him. You could plan a swimming trip to get out some of his angry energy on the water slide rather than on the family. If you know what the problem is, you are way ahead of the game.

Unless destructive behavior is intentional and solely attention getting, this behavior is an outward manifestation that the child has lost the sense of internal safety. Many destructive children will be remorseful after breaking the radio they received on their birthday, but others show little sense of remorse. Either way their actions are communicating that they are not able at times to ensure their own safety. In these cases it is essential for the environment to provide that safety. Safety comes from limit setting.

Being destructive of property must be added to the list of dangerous behaviors because in the process of his outbursts, he can be damaged just as the objects on which he is venting. Providing external safety can mean setting a verbal limit, it can mean being close to the child to support her (and to stop her from being destructive). Or providing external safety can mean to physically protect the child and property from his destructive rage. Although these children will often tell you that you are hurting or abusing them when you physically step in, you are providing a sense of limits, support, and safety that the child desperately needs. In the midst of a physical altercation with a raging child, it is generally a good idea not to engage in verbal debate, arguments, or even try to reason with him. Tell the child in a calm voice to calm down, and the matter can be discussed later.

If the destructive behavior is attention seeking, as with all other manipulations, do not reinforce the behavior by giving the child 24 karat gold attention, which is your emotional energy. Obviously it is difficult to ignore a child being destructive in your home or at the shopping mall. Step in and handle the situation but with as little emotional energy as possible. The manipulative child is always gauging whether he has gotten to you by reading your frustration, anger, or annoyance. Most manipulative children feel like they won if they got you upset, no matter what else happens. Since these children love to be in control (particularly of you), they will try the same successful behavior again, and this is not what you want. Review the section on manipulation and tantrums.

For children who are hard to read or who are unpredictable, it may help to adjust your home to at least temporarily make it more destruction proof. Look around the house for easy projectiles. Put that favorite photograph of your mother in the antique frame in your room for now, etc. Ask yourself if you will be able to handle the destruction of readily available items in your home because you may not always be able to get there in time.

In cases where there is a known cause of the potential outburst, predicting an angry episode can sometimes be effective. You might mention that Billy's feelings about the letter from his mom are understandable, but being destructive like in the past will not help the situation. In this case, come up with "Plan B" if he is available before the anger builds. You could say that in the past mom's letters have been upsetting, so let's take those feelings and hit some balls in the park, or some other favorite activity.

As with other problem behaviors, if you are not able to determine the cause of the problem, or if your continued efforts do not seem to be helping, don't be afraid to ask for professional assistance. A good step with explosive children is to make sure that the behavior does not have a physical cause. There are some medical conditions that could produce explosive or unpredictable behavior.

Eating Disorders

Raising a child with an eating disorder can be an invitation to lose your mind as a parent. Of all the issues that someone becoming a parent would anticipate as a challenge, this would not be one of them. Eating disorders such as anorexia and bulimia are insidious problems, first of all because of the secrecy often involved. Secondly, they represent one of the most difficult realities for a parent -- you cannot control what goes into or comes out of a child. Without being abusive, you cannot make a child eat, and you cannot make the child digest what she has eaten. So in a very practical way, eating disorders require the cooperation of the child, which just happens to be the problem in the first place -- that the child is not cooperating with her own body's physical needs and is not cooperating with you.

I will not be addressing the most serious forms of eating disorders such as anorexia nervosa or bulimia; I will leave this to experts in this area. I will focus on children who have eating problems well short of these serious issues.

Because food is a requirement of living, it is also very symbolic for children (as well as adults). Food can represent how we treat ourselves and reflects what we think of ourselves. If a child is having serious emotional and/or behavioral problems, it is not unusual for this to be represented in some way in eating habits and patterns. Because of their symbolic value, eating behaviors are ideal for the principle discussed in several areas of this book --

translating the child's behavior to determine its meaning. There are a wide variety of meanings that could be involved with eating problems. Because the child is not exercising personal care, both not eating and overeating can have similar meanings. To intentionally not nourish one's body can be a sign of anger against oneself or others; it can also show a self hatred or an attempt at distancing the self from the body.

For sexually abused children, cutting off one's nourishment may be an attempt to eliminate the source of desire of an adult who has been sexual with the child. Food may reflect a fixation with body image and an over-concern for how others view the child. Eating disorders can be a way some children act out harming themselves or even attempting suicide, either quickly or slowly. Eating can be a way to keep others away or to have others notice. In short, all eating disorders do not have the same message, but I think it is safe to say that all eating disorders carry a message that is critical to understand.

More so than most disorders, eating problems are best addressed at an early stage of onset. The long term issues of starving the body (not to mention the symbolism of starving the soul), go much deeper than what can be externally observed. Weight gain and loss can often be detected, but their effects on the body's internal organs and functions may not be apparent until advanced stages of breakdown. But the eating issues of primary concern here are not life threatening, and thus the most concerning aspects of habitual eating problems are psychological. Early detection is not always as easy as one would think. Some children disguise and hide the problem, compensating in ways that would not always be obvious to parents or other adults. Clothing can sometimes hide the results of eating problems. Some teens combine eating issues with acceptable activities such as sports or other excuses for gaining, or more often, losing weight. Early detection is always best, but it will take a parent who is close to the child and is observant to changes that may seem subtle.

The majority of eating problems that I have encountered with young children have been attention-getting in nature. This is not necessarily better or worse than other motivations, but at least you know what the source of the behavior is. I recommend translating all problematic behaviors of children. If the source of the behavior appears to be attention-getting, like all other manipulations, and you give the child what she wants because of this behavior, you will get more of the problem behavior in the future. Since by definition we want to reduce problematic behavior, avoid giving attention to behavior that is designed to demand it overtly or covertly.

In most cases the best solution to attention-getting behavior is to ignore the behavior, while giving the child increased attention connected to issues other rather than the behavior. In this way the child gets what he wants but not connected to the eating problems. In our residential treatment program we have frequently had children, usually girls but not exclusively, who say, "I just won't eat and then I'll starve." We literally might ask the other children "who wants a larger portion of dinner" and divide it among them. Does this sound insensitive? There are only a few children who have passed on two meals in a row, and when the child compares the results of the behavior -- hunger with no increase in attention or control over others -- she often goes in search of another way to be noticed.

But what do you do if a child appears to be serious about self harm, or if she is developing a serious habit with eating behavior? My suggestion is to get help from an expert in eating disorders. The best advice I can offer is that if you are closely aware of the child and have serious concern, you will at least be catching the issue at an early stage. To find an expert in eating disorders, call your local mental health authority or contact programs that work with adolescent females. Both should have a number of referrals for you.

Low Intellectual Functioning

The first place to start with comments on intelligence is to talk a little about what intelligence is, or perhaps more precisely what it is not. The truth about intelligence is that there is no one definition that is generally accepted in psychology. Yes, this means that we don't really know what we mean by intelligence. The term is commonly used to describe how smart children are, but this is not a precise definition. It is also used to identify what the capacity of a child is to understand the world around them, but again this is not the full picture. Many believe that intelligence is a capacity that we are born with and will follow us through life basically stable and unchanging by definition, but this does not quite fit either. It turns out that intelligence is not as stable as we have believed.

When very young children are tested for their "intelligence" it turns out that there is no reliability to this score when compared to testing the same child ten years later. It does appear to be true that an elementary-aged child who scores in the well above average range is very likely to be in this range as a young adult. But if we talk about well above average intelligence, let's get back to the question of what intelligence is.

The main point to remember in measuring intelligence is that it is more of a comparison with a cohort (peer) group, than it is about some factor of inherent ability. Common sense would tell us that some people are obviously smarter than others. But what does it mean to be smarter? There are many answers to this question in the world of psychology, and there will likely be more diverse opinions in the future than there are today. I am going to stay within the discipline of psychology, because if we go to engineering or the arts, the meaning of intelligence gets even more complex.

From a statistical perspective, intelligence testing is basically coming up with a sample of questions, asking a broad representative sample of individuals to answer the questions, and then comparing scores through statistically meaningful scores, such as standard scores or percentiles where one child is compared with 99 other children. For example on an intelligence test a child may be at the 43rd percentile. This would mean that if you lined up 100 children, she would be number 43; 42 children would be behind her in line and 57 ahead of her. That sounds pretty good, but what does it mean?

The answer becomes more troublesome the deeper you look at this question. Of course there is always a problem in comparing human beings. A low score might mean that a bright child has not had the exposure to information, or a child is "smart" in math but has no common sense. When we compare people or talk about intelligence, we need to approach with caution and humility.

There have been many examples of the bias that is built into every currently available IQ measure, even those that claim to be "culturally fair" tests (attempting to take out the influences of culture or socioeconomic factors). We know that different cultures, races, and socioeconomic levels tend to score differently from others. With the magic of statistics, all this variation can be factored into what appears meaningful on paper, but is it?

There are so many factors that go into scores on a test, that the most psychologists should ever definitively say is to provide an estimate of cognitive ability based on the scores of a test that has a good track record (psychometric strength). These estimates can and do change over time. These estimates do not measure "intelligence" as a global concept. And perhaps most importantly, these estimates do not tell us how smart a child is. This is because being smart is the ability to figure out what needs to happen to accomplish something in a particular situation, and there are as many types of being smart as there are problems to solve.

One child can be smart in math, while another is smart at fooling adults. Another child is a whiz on the computer, while another is a natural at music, or sports, or animals, or spirituality. Are all these kids smart in the same way? No. Would their level of being smart show on an IQ test? Probably not except for school smarts. Are school smarts important? Yes. But we all know that being bright in academic subjects does not make you a success in life, which is yet another definition of being smart -- to figure out the answer to the problem of being successful in a challenging world. This is why most of us run across people who have been identified as having limited cognitive function and notice that they seem so much smarter than their scores.

Many children score in the below average or well below average range and seem at times to be quite bright. This is a basic misunderstanding of cognitive measurement. Low intellectual functioning does not necessarily mean that the individual is not quite smart in some areas or even gifted in other areas. It simply means that on the fund of knowledge tested the child did not score well compared to peers. There is much more that could be said about measuring intelligence, but suffice it to say that IQ tests can be reliable, valid and useful, but it depends on how they are being used.

I have not started with these comments to take a hard line, as many others have, to do away with estimates of cognitive ability. You can find those in psychology who believe the above problems with testing intelligence and others not mentioned, indicate that we should stop the practice altogether. I am not one of those people. I use testing instruments for intelligence and other reasons and find them valuable. But again, be sure you know what a test is measuring and what the score means before you jump to a very unfortunate conclusion for the child. Studies have found that when adults believe a child is slow, sure enough he or she is often challenged less and the expectations are lowered, and over time the child becomes even slower. Conversely children thought to be bright and challenged more with higher expectations generally respond and become even brighter. IQ tests are not about putting people in boxes, categories, or clubs (unless it's Mensa). Measurement tools can help to identify trouble areas in learning and assist in teaching to strengths. But an IQ test cannot measure motivation, endurance, or nontraditional thinking, all of which are keys to being "smart" and being successful in our complex modern world.

Within this context of what IQ tests can and can not tell us, what about children who are diagnosed as low intellectual functioning? It is first of all important to say what conclusions should not be made. The diagnosis of mental retardation does not mean that the child cannot learn. It does not mean that these children do not have specific areas of strength. And this diagnosis is not necessarily a good indicator of success or happiness in life. It probably does mean that school learning for this individual will be more difficult than for his/her peers. It may be helpful in estimating the level of academic success and the likelihood of higher education, but not always (don't forget that motivation and determination are not effectively measured on tests).

Understanding everything that has been said about low intellectual functioning, there are some important factors to consider with many children who have this challenge. These children are often compared to their peers in school and do not match up well. For most of us, we gravitate to what we do well. If learning in school is more difficult for you than for your peers, there will be a strong pull to dislike and even avoid school learning.

Because school is essentially the main career of young children, poor performance in school starts these children off as less than successful; and this is precisely the population that needs extra support and encouragement to take on the challenge of school learning. So what often happens with slow learners is that they switch from school learning to other types of learning such as learning how to get more attention than the "smart" kids (by acting out). Many struggling children mask their learning struggles by putting the focus on problematic or extreme behaviors. Some are even "smart" enough to figure out the answer to school; while getting the undivided attention of their teacher, school counselor and perhaps their principal, they escalate until they are suspended.

Our schools are one of the few places I can think of where if the child does not want to go badly enough he simply acts out and is rewarded by being suspended. Fortunately we don't take this approach with people who don't want to obey the law. Any time a child is having serious behavior challenges in school, the question that needs to be asked is "What is this learning environment like for this child?"

Of course, some children are slower cognitively than others, but again, few children do not have some areas of strengths that can be encouraged and can be the basis of confidence in learning to be functionally smart in life. Acting out is not the only common defense of the child who finds academic learning slow going. Some children develop selective hearing problems, others develop somatic ailments, and still others daydream to extreme. All of these adaptations are designed more or less to lower the expectations of the adults in the child's life.

As you have already guessed, I think lowering the expectations that children sense from adults is not the way to go. It is true that for many children, a higher education may not be the key to their success. But there are many learning challenges in life that take a great deal of work that do not involve universities. Do not handicap a child by communicating verbally or non-verbally that he is unlikely to be good at learning. The key is to find what he learns best, realizing it is unlikely to be an academic subject.

For many of these children, success in learning is not only a challenge in school. Although this can sometimes be selective, learning can also be a problem at home, in social skills, understanding rules and expectations, and struggling with functional skills and abilities to get along in the world. When this happens, it is important to look closely to see what the real problem is. If it is understanding and comprehending that is being expected of them, then adults must compensate by being clearer, developing better ways of communicating with these children, and providing the extra support and encouragement for them to continue to do something that they sense they are not good at.

Take a second and ask yourself what activity you do very poorly that you enjoy and do as often as you can. Can't come up with anything? Neither could I. This is what we are asking children to do at times -- continue to come back and bang your head against the wall without any signs that you will be any more successful this time than the last time. This is why the child needs our extra encouragement. I am not just talking necessarily about math and science in school. It may be getting along with other kids on the playground, being appropriate in church on Sunday morning, or even keeping track of his shoes. We all tend to avoid what we do poorly or have little past success in doing. When these children are resisting something, consider that this may be a statement that he or she just does not like failing, and acting out is one thing at which any child can quite easily learn to accomplish.

All special needs children require parental endurance and enormous amounts of patience. Children who are cognitively challenged are no different. You can often teach them how to do something that they want to learn, only to find that they don't remember moments later. For some children who have auditory learning difficulties, you may find yourself explaining something relatively simple only to look into the bland face of the child as if you were speaking Latin to them.

It can be difficult to tell at times when the lack of learning is genuine or simply an excuse not to listen, or to avoid something undesirable. One way to tell the difference is to consider whether the child is motivated to learn. If she is and she still has difficulty, it is probably a function of a learning problem and not a self-inflicted problem.

Repetition is an important element of learning for children with low intellectual functioning. In groups of these children that I have run, I always plan to go over every concept at least three times in the session (actually not a bad habit for all children, for adults repeat more often). Repetition can be combined with encouragement from the adult so that the child believes they can and are grasping the content. Encouragement can be something like, "This can be difficult to learn but you are understanding several parts of it really well -- good for you." This type of encouragement works with all of us, and it is essential for a child who is climbing a difficult intellectual mountain with less than perfect equipment.

I made the case earlier but it bears repeating: motivation can take a child a long way, so focus on motivating the child. Everyone has an opinion of the modern educational system. I will weigh in on this topic and say that most of the failure of education is caused by the inability to motivate the learner. In classrooms that I have run, most of my focus is on the excitement of the subject rather than on the facts. Once a child is motivated, you can't stop him from learning. Can you imagine telling a child that for homework they will need to practice manual dexterity for several hours per day manipulating a keyboard in response to visual cues? But if it is Super Nintendo or Play Station, they willingly do this for hours above any other activity, including eating. I have always felt that learning is all about presentation. When I consider some of my education in school, I wonder why I bothered. One thing I have learned -- special needs children can't be bothered unless they can be motivated.

As with other issues, it is important to consider how other challenges in the child's life are affecting cognitive performance. Some environmental issues are obvious factors in making the child appear slow academically. Anxiety can hinder intellectual success, hyperactivity can seriously block sustained concentration, and traumatic child abuse in the past, or even present, can look much like a cognitive problem rather than a family problem.

Although I evaluate children for cognitive functioning, I am quick to say that one sample or exposure to a child is not nearly as useful as individuals who have observed the child in numerous settings. Test anxiety, fear of being evaluated, and fear of strangers or strange situations are only a few factors that can play a role in low test scores. A good evaluator is supposed to be able to sense the level of effort and anxiety the child is experiencing in the testing situation. But if the child is new to the evaluator, it may not be clear if something is adversely affecting the results for this child. One point that comes up time and again with special needs children is that the norm is not relevant or helpful. These children need to be compared with their own pasts and the progress being made.

So in closing on this brief treatment of children who struggle with cognitive skills: understand the child's struggles, support the child in the challenge of school, help her find what she excels at, and do not communicate to her that you have lowered your expectations of what she can do in life.

Autism and Pervasive Developmental Disorder

This range of problems is important to mention in the context of challenges with children, but will not be covered here. Briefly stated, autism is a disturbance of communication and behavior, which can be on a continuum from severe to mild. Disorders on the autism spectrum are under the larger category of pervasive developmental disorders of childhood. Children with autism most often have difficulty with speech, language, and communication of all types. The child shows poor capacity to relate to others. These children often have unusual responses to sensory stimulation, and have delayed development in multiple areas. This category of disorders can be chronic and continue throughout life. This challenging and difficult disorder is complex and deserves more focus than can reasonably be provided here. For more information, further reading has been provided in the Reference section.

Chapter

9

Parenting Children
with Multiple Impairments

Like most aspects of parenting, there are few right and wrong ways to approach children with multiple problems; there are simply effective and ineffective approaches. Just to make sure you stay challenged in your role as parent (or therapist), what worked yesterday may not work today, and this should no longer surprise you. Some children, like adults, are very consistent in their thinking and behavior. And then some children seem to lack any sign or pattern of thinking and behaving that provides the important clues to what the parent can do to prepare the child for the world with the challenges he or she will face. Many of the children found in these pages have one commonality -- inconsistent attitudes and behavior. So instead of saying to yourself, "I need to find the approach that will work with Dustin," you may want to change that to, "I need to learn how Dustin thinks and acts, and then be prepared to alter my parenting based on what I learn from him."

If you are a parent of a child with multiple challenges, do not approach professionals such as therapists, psychologists, and psychiatrists hoping to find sympathy for your plight in life (ministers and perhaps bartenders may be a better source of this). The fact is that these children scare professionals, or better said, the difficult challenge these children present is scary. To fully hear your frustration, and at times your hopelessness, can be a dark alley that professionals do not want to walk down for fear that they may end up in the same place as you.

Most professionals have an optimistic outlook; you want them to, don't you? Few parents want to hear from a professional, "I have to tell you, this is the worst case I have ever faced in my career!" The dilemma is that as parents, sometimes we do want to hear this, in order to feel like someone understands our lying awake at nights wondering, "What did I do to deserve this child?" But as much as we want to be understood, we also want hope, not sympathy. If the therapist told you "I know just how you feel," you wouldn't believe her anyway. So rather than sympathy from professionals, look for ideas and practical suggestions that might help improve your resilience and/or the atmosphere in your family.

The challenge for professionals as well as parents is that understanding and working with children with multiple issues is like understanding the dynamics and interactions of giving a child multiple medications. It appears that no one can accurately predict what is going to happen as a result. There are simply too many factors, complications, and unknown possibilities. However, knowing what to look for, what to avoid, and keeping a keen eye on the desired result are all important aspects of the road map to take with you on this journey.

Although this can be very complex, it is important to try to identify just what the issues are that are affecting your child. Sometimes a child's problems are like a stew -- there is a little of this, a little of that, mixed with a lot of something else, and all simmering to a boil. Just like a stew, it can be difficult to distinguish each individual ingredient when they all come together. However, it is critical to begin to break down the challenge into individual pieces, while realizing that the whole problem becomes more than the sum of its parts. This reverse synergy will likely lead you to get the best help you can find to figure out your child, much less to try to help your child.

There will likely be factors that are internal to the child as well as external in the environment. While complex, consider when the stew comes to a boil and what factors are involved. At times, it is very clear what compounds the problem, as long as someone is taking a step back far enough to see the forest for the trees. Here is where a professional can be of help. Sometimes asking the right questions can make all the difference in the answers.

Once the main ingredients of the problem have been identified, work first to isolate each and address the symptoms. It is often true that one factor compounds negatively with another, such as fetal alcohol or drug involvement with hyperactivity, or childhood trauma and attachment problems. However, the opposite can also be true. If the symptoms of one problem can be effectively addressed, at times more than that one problem can show considerable improvement.

It is important that you and your child experience some improvement on some level, and the sooner the better. Although some adults do not realize this, before many parents begin to feel helpless and hopeless with a child, the child often beats them to this desperate place. There is nothing that gives hope quite like some limited but specific success. Before you can improve his behavior and his success in school, you may be able to help him improve his bedwetting. Before you can help her with her raging anger, perhaps she can improve her reading and improve her view of herself.

One question that comes to a parent's mind immediately in medical matters is "Whose help do I need?" If it is your child and there is a medical problem, there must be a specialist to go to. However, parents don't often ask this same question when it comes to a child's mental rather than physical health. But there are specialists who can be found for most problems in children. Get the help that you need or at least the help that is available. Do not forget to go to the Internet and look around. I have people contact me from around the country and around the world, so I know you can find resources and ideas if you put in the effort.

In developing a plan to address problem areas in search of some success and improvement, it is important to have an idea of what to address first, second and third. It does make a difference at times. Generally, don't go after the biggest issue or issues first. Do not focus on something that has been an active problem for seven years, if there is a specific issue that has shown up in the last seven weeks. Remember that one of the most important initial positive steps is to see some improvement for both you and your child. Think small, think specific, and think positive.

In order to see improvement, you will have to be looking. As obvious as this seems, at times parents of children with multiple problems may in fact have some success and quickly realize all the problems that are not better. This is the "Yes, but" game that everyone loses. I understand that over the summer Johnny has significantly decreased his lying; "Yes, but he still isn't getting along with his sister." I notice that Sara has a much better report card than last term; "Yes, but she still talks too much in the classroom and frustrates her teacher."

At times parents don't hear themselves throw away some hard fought gains. No success is too small to overlook. It may be several small steps that become a springboard to large steps. Like a child growing taller, if you live with him each day you don't always see the change. To avoid this, set goals that can be measured or get outside help where it is much easier to see growth, or the lack of growth, because of the external objectivity.

In this difficult and confusing journey, commit yourself to the destination, not the route. Although you may at one point in the journey have full confidence in one path to your goal, it may turn out that you were reaching a dead end or worse, a circular path back to the beginning. Keep your eye on where you want to go, and if your path does not show signs of heading in that direction, then it may be time for a new road map or highway. This may include a medication, a treatment method, a particular therapist or teacher, or a combined approach.

Be aware of the principle in social psychology that the more we invest in something, the more we put our faith in it whether it works or not. There are some very expensive therapies, schools, and training being offered. More than once has a family spent a great deal of money with little to show for it, but they continue to believe in the route to the goal. Remember, whenever there is a desperate consumer, there will always be someone to sell you a quick and easy solution, for a price. Almost universally, the solution is not good enough and the price is too high. Get your priorities straight; it is the destination you are after, not any particularly path to get there.

In addition to the things that you may want to do to address children with multiple problems, there are also some things that you may want to avoid. The first thought to avoid is the irresistible desire to think that there is a cure for the problem(s) your child has. Cures are usually a part of the quick and easy solution culture we live in, where the most serious problems are resolved by the end of the movie or television show. It may be that there are some things that can be done to make the situation much more workable through a medication or different way to work with the child. But leave the quick cures to Hollywood, and if by chance your effort does come up with one, you can be doubly grateful, but you will not be disappointed if the answers are neither easy to come by nor quick.

The more I learn about people and particularly about children with multiple problems, the more I distrust systems or "one-size-fits-all approaches." Wise trainers and therapists know that their way, as effective as they may have found it, is only one way. It seems more true to me all the time that it is the unwise expert who wants to sell you a packaged deal; you just need to suspend your questions and your own thoughts and do it according to the "X" method. If it does not seem to work then you must not be doing it right -- try harder or suspend your judgment even more.

"But wait a minute, Dr. Z, aren't you cautioning parents against using approaches in this book?" If you think so, I have not effectively presented what I have learned from difficult children. I will be the first to tell you to try any of the suggestions I offer, and if they don't work, try something else. Don't buy snake oil from me or anyone else that is packaged in the latest psychological wrapper. This is not to say that all the approaches out there might not teach you something very useful, but nothing works with all children all of the time. Long term problems are not fixed quickly and easily, and spending a great deal of money is not the same as getting the help you need. If someone or some system promises any of this to you, realize that you want to believe it, and then use your own wisdom and move on. Then go and find the approach that levels with you that you may well have a very difficult situation, that the answers may take more work than you may want to put into it, and you will figure out solutions that fit your unique situation together.

Another situation high on the avoidance list is working with professionals or any experts who keep you in the dark. Over time there are rare individuals, such as a Milton Erickson, who are able to provide you what you need without the necessity of your understanding. But most of the time, when someone is keeping you in the dark, that is either exactly where they want you, or that is where they find themselves with your situation.

The last item on the list of things to avoid is being only a full time parent. This is not to say that you can lapse into irresponsibility at convenient times. There is no way to avoid being a full time parent, but if that is all you are, you will not be of much value to the people around you. This is one of the best times for the saying, "All work and no play, makes Jill a dull mom." I know it is difficult to even imagine taking up skydiving, much less to do it, but you must develop aspects of your life that return more to you and your energy level than parenting does. The list of possibilities can be long. If you are stuck, ask yourself what you used to do before you became a full time parent and go from there. Get a beeper, get a cell phone for when you are out of the house, but get out and do something other than being a mom and dad.

There are a few other thoughts to offer concerning children with multiple complex problems. As the saying goes, "If you don't know where you are going, any road will get you there." It is important to have a good idea of your desired destination or where you want to be headed with your child. Once you know where you want to go, do your best to steer in that direction. You may not find the going any easier, but at least you are making headway toward your goal.

There is nothing worse than the feeling that the journey is not only brutal, but you don't even know where you are likely to end up. This is a prescription for hopelessness and giving up. But if your goal is the top of the mountain, it may be very difficult but each step in an upward direction brings you that much closer to your goal. It can make a great deal of difference. This is why for your own mental health, get the help you need to know within yourself that you are headed in the direction you want to go.

Part of knowing where you want to go with your child is a relatively simple list of what you want to see more of, and what you want to see less of. It may be complicated to know how to do it, but preparing the list should not be complicated.

Part of this journey is learning how to reduce the impact on you and your family. A marathon runner will not finish the race, and the mountaineer will not reach the summit, if each mile takes a greater toll than the stamina they have within them. It is the same with parenting. There are many aspects of wear and tear that are self-inflicted such as worry, guilt, anxiousness, anger, resentment, impatience, frustration, intolerance, judgmentalness, and obsessing on factors over which you have little or no control. Admit it: you have an old friend or two on this list; most parents do. But each of these impediments is like friction -- they slow down your progress and build up a lot of heat.

Avoiding frustration is the ability to keep your hopes and your goals in mind, while accepting the reality of where you are at any particular point in time. To want to be other than where you are is what frustration is all about. Frustration can perhaps increase your effort to achieve your goals, but more often it decreases your enthusiasm and your energy. Generally frustration is a trap, and when you realize you are in it, get out as soon as possible. The best mantra or affirmation for frustration is "I wish I was further ahead, but here is where I am right now, and that's OK."

Success has been called a combination of a journey and a dream. The dream is the destination, and the journey is the path that leads there. If you get too focused on either and neglect the other, you will not succeed. Any parent who gets in a hurry to produce a successful human being, what we earlier called the most difficult task there is, needs to slow down, develop a pace that can be sustained, and keep moving forward.

Mental health can at times be very similar to physical health. Some problems need more drastic solutions than others. It is important to know when you need a Band-Aid and when you need surgery. When it comes to children with multiple disturbances, there are no magic Band-Aids, and in fact, you may need more help than can be provided in your home. Part of the solution to your child's problems might be to remove him or her from your home for a drastic step like residential treatment.

Speaking of which, I need to briefly clear the air on this subject. But first, I must declare my lack of objectivity in that I have run several residential treatment centers for over eighteen years. This may mean either that I lack objectivity or, on the other hand, it could mean I know firsthand what I am talking about -- you decide. In the last few years there have been many people who talk about residential treatment programs like they are part of the problem rather than part of the solution. Many of these people are journalists who know that everyone has an opinion on how children should be treated, and that a sensational exposé sells stories. Others are professionals and researchers who are quick to recount abuses that have been uncovered.

Being someone who is very concerned about children's rights, particularly the right that is seldom mentioned, to get the help they need to succeed in life, I notice that outspoken critics of residential treatment usually have no direct or personal experience on the subject. They do not run residential programs nor work in them, they have not consulted with one, received help from one, or had a child in one; but they look in from the outside and find fault with the messy, unpleasant, and rough aspects of this work. Without direct experience many professionals know that residential treatment programs are bad for children. They know this because they have read this.

The reality is that the orphan asylums of the past are not the residential treatment centers of today. The care and sophistication of treatment centers overall has never been better than it is today, nor have the industry standards and the number of programs that meet and exceed these standards ever been as high. I read the investigative newspaper articles of some program described as using "dark ages methods" and "hog tying" children. The simple fact is that for every child who is mistreated, injured, or worst case -- even dies -- in a treatment center, there are thousands of children who face these fates in their own homes and communities. Residential treatment centers are critical elements of the solution to difficult children. They are places of support, healing, and doing the difficult work of addressing the messy, unpleasant, and rough aspects of treating very disturbed children.

Whatever someone says to you, and whatever you read in a newspaper, do not be afraid to get your child the help he or she needs from a residential treatment center. How do you make sure it is a good program? Ask around, check with accrediting bodies, look at the program's track record, and ask several knowledgeable people and see what programs are positively mentioned most often. When you find a program that comes highly recommended, call and ask your hard questions. There are no perfect hospitals, and there are no perfect residential treatment centers, but if you need physical or mental health surgery, do not go to the corner outfit for Band-Aids and aspirin, get to the causes and start the healing.

Medical Conditions

There are a multitude of physical impairments and medical conditions that can make the job of parenting considerably more challenging, particularly if the medical condition is combined with one or more psychological conditions. The following treatment of this topic is a quick overview of some of the more pronounced and frequently encountered medical conditions. Each problem deserves significantly more detail than will be offered here. The important point is to know when a medical condition is complicating the parenting picture, and how medical issues combine with psychological problems. The reader is encouraged to find out more about these and other medical problems that are all too common.

Exact numbers of children with debilitating medical conditions are difficult to obtain because of standardized criteria and the presence at times of more than one condition in the same child. However, a general number that is often cited is that .5% of the childhood population has some medical condition that has a direct impact on the child's life and the child's ability to take full advantage of opportunities. This percentage may sound small, but this adds up to a great many children, and the level of impact on many children goes far beyond the child being just another statistic. Many of these children have the added complication of repeated trips not only to the doctor's office, but often to the hospital for short, and at times long, stays.

Some children endure invasive medical procedures as an everyday part of life. This can have a secondary impact on the child's emotional health. For example, early prolonged hospitalization is the primary factor other than the trauma of child abuse that can affect the child's ability to form a bond with his/her parents or primary care providers. Hospitalizations can have an impact on family life and on attendance in school. This can in turn disrupt opportunities for social interactions with peers, reduce opportunities to learn, and give the child the message that either she is somehow different than other children, or even worse that something is wrong with her that can not always be fixed. This message can at times become internalized, and the child can develop personality traits that can include helplessness, isolation, social withdrawal, lack of tenacity, or the use of a medical condition as an excuse for a variety of negative attitudes and behaviors.

I must say at this point that the parents of many of the children I have worked with who have medical and physical problems never cease to teach me about mental strength. They show me that love can mean not being overly influenced by disability to the detriment of improving ability. I have often observed with deep respect the parents of these children as they overlook the emotional pain they experience themselves at watching their child struggle to do things that come easily for other children. These parents have helped teach me the true meaning of support, which is less about holding someone up, than it is about giving them the strength to hold themselves up. I am talking about parents of blind children who will not accept self-pity, the parents of children in wheelchairs who encourage the child to explore his world on his own power, and parents of children with Spina Bifida who expect their child to look upon self catheterization as other children view combing one's own hair.

But of course, the world is not an easy place for children with physical disabilities. Many parents who give their child confidence, at the same time wonder if they could handle it if they were in the child's shoes. What these parents can teach the rest of us is that what we see has a lot to say about where we look. It is not difficult to find sadness or reasons to think life has dealt these children a hand that they did not deserve. But how will this help the child? Perhaps the real challenge for these parents is to see beyond the disability and focus instead on the ability; and in this way teach the child to do the same in life.

Everyone has one form of disability or another. If you spend your life making a list of your disabilities and finding out just how significant they are, it may be that you have just wasted precious time that could have gone into enhancing one or more abilities that everyone has as well. Can parents look beyond the symbolic emotional power of a child's medical or physical struggle? If not, how will the child be able to do so?

The implication in the above comments is that when everything is considered, children with physical challenges are more like other children than they are different from other children -- unless, that is, adults are successful in having the child believe the opposite.

A physical disability can at times be a powerful motivator. I have climbed a number of mountains in my life but never Everest, but a man with only one foot made the summit of Everest. Yes, one foot. I have run a couple of marathons in my years, but a man with cancer and only one leg ran the width of the North American continent. Yes, one leg -- covering 4,000 miles. I did a 25-mile bike ride once, but a man with testicular cancer won the 2,400 mile Tour de France, twice! Obviously these are rare accomplishments by rare individuals, but they symbolize the choice all people have with their limitations: either dwell on them or go beyond them.

There are many medical conditions that can be a serious challenge for children and for families. Three will be mentioned here primarily because of how frequently they are encountered in our population. Three of the medical conditions that account for a large percentage of disabling physical problems in children are Cerebral Palsy, Spina Bifida, and Epilepsy.

Cerebral Palsy

Cerebral Palsy (CP) is just what the name implies -- the person has difficulties in motor development with movement and posture due to damage in the brain. This condition most often affects children at birth or very early in life. The causes are many including oxygen deficiency at birth, illness, premature birth, blood type incompatibility of parents, and illness in the mother while pregnant such as German measles. Less common in children is acquired CP due to illness, accidental head injury, lead poisoning, or even child abuse. This medical condition is not progressive throughout life, and new cases affect several thousand children each year. The degree of impairment can be variable from mild to severe. The use of advanced technology has had a significant impact on people with Cerebral Palsy through assistance in communications, living needs, educational and career alternatives. Like other medical conditions, living with Cerebral Palsy can be extremely challenging, but a child and an adult can learn to thrive as a person even with this condition.

Spina Bifida

If you don't have a child with this medical problem and you know what it is, give yourself credit for being more informed than most adults. In brief, this medical problem is an abnormality where the spinal column does not completely close around the spinal cord. This physical abnormality can run the gamut from severe all the way to very mild. However, when all cases are considered, this may be the most common of all physical abnormalities in children, perhaps affecting up to 100 million people in the US. Yes, you heard right; Spina Bifida Occulta (usually mild) Meningocele, and Myelomeningocele (severe) are all forms of this abnormality and may exist in up to 4 out of every 10 individuals in this country, including the author. And yet you and many of the people who have mild forms probably have never heard of it, and will not even hear it on "Jeopardy." Most of us who have the Occulta type aren't even aware of a problem unless a specialist looks closely at a spinal Xray. This mild form is often accompanied by few or even no symptoms. However, the other two types are anything but mild.

In the more serious cases of Spina Bifida the spinal cord is not protected by the spinal column and is exposed on the child's back at birth. Some cases can be repaired with minimal damage to nerve pathways, but many more cases result in a lifetime of required accommodations to this serious condition. The serious cases are often accompanied by paralysis below the area of the spine affected. Muscle weakness is common as is loss of sensation in the lower regions of the spine, often affecting bowel and bladder control. At the other end of the spine, the brain often has an accumulation of ventricle fluid that requires surgery to implant a shunt to relieve the fluid buildup and prevent other problems such as blindness and seizures. If this illness sounds unpleasant so far, there is more.

In the not too distant past, essentially all children with exposed spinal cords at birth died (approximately 1 in every 1000 births). Now medical science can save the majority of these children. However, they must start life with serious surgeries, and later on learn not to be toilet trained but learn the catheterization process. This is placing a tube into the bladder to urinate. At first others do this for the child; the maturing child learns to do this for himself or herself. Many of these children have multiple cranial surgeries to have the shunt put in place and keep it functioning properly. If the shunt unexpectedly does not work or decreases its effectiveness, a variety of symptoms are possible that can change the child's cognitive functioning. Children with serious cases are wheelchair bound. It is not unusual for these children to know a large number of medical professionals by first names since they have frequently been in and out of surgery and hospitals. These children often need support from clinics for ongoing evaluations and addressing complications.

All of these medical factors can have significant psychological ramifications. These children are not like others; the child's freedom of movement can have significant limitations, and the medical focus of the child's world can affect social, educational and occupational development. As with many other medical conditions, the parent's task is to address the medical needs while working to normalize the child's situation when possible and encouraging the child with Spina Bifida, like all other children, to learn skills for independence within reason.

Epilepsy

A third medical condition that affects many children and adults worldwide is epilepsy. In this country an estimated 2,000,000 individuals live with epilepsy, with most new cases being diagnosed among children and teens. Epilepsy may be the most well known of the medical conditions mentioned here. It is characterized as a disruption in the normal functioning of the brain, and can affect, on a short term basis, speech, movement, and at times consciousness, otherwise known as seizures or convulsions. Epileptic seizures can affect parts of the brain or have more generalized impact. Due to a seizure, a child may repeat movements and later not remember the episode.

The impact on the lives of children with epilepsy can be significant. Like many other misunderstood medical conditions, the impact on children can be made worse by the misunderstanding and fear of other people. This condition makes others uncomfortable. They fear seizures and may stay away from the child. Epilepsy is one of the many medical conditions that essentially invites parents to overemphasize the impact of the condition. The child and the family can have the world fit around this medical problem rather than the other way around. All children at one time or another use illness to gain attention or get something they want. Children who have epilepsy and other psychological problems can use the symptoms to control others, or as an excuse for ignoring adults and doing what they want. It takes a very special parent to effectively address the serious aspects of a medical condition like epilepsy, while not giving the illness undue influence over the child's life.

Although this has been a very brief overview of several prominent medical and physical conditions that complicate parenting, the presence of other mental health issues along with these physical issues can make parenting an extreme challenge. Remember, the best you can do is your best. Work to have your best be enabling the child with the confidence to focus on his/her abilities not disabilities, and not letting the child allow physical limitations to dictate emotional health as well. Once again, a tall order, but do your best. With these principles in mind, review the sections in this book on the emotional issues and put the two together. Also, remember that the first thing that every child needs from a parent is reassurance that he or she will be safe, and that the situation will work out. The child may attempt to sound tough or unaffected by what is going on around him, but even more so than adults, a child's insides keep score.

Chapter

10

Strategies for Successful Parenting or How to Maintain Your Sanity

The following is an adaptation of Chapter 20 in the Handbook for Treatment of Attachment-Trauma in Children *(B. James, Ed., 1994) written for adoptive parents. Some of the points that pertain to adoptive parents can be generalized to all parents of special needs children.*

Families that contain children with serious problems can be much like the state of modern marriages: too many dissolve with pain for everyone; others stay together but everyone is miserable; some get by with everyone lowering their expectations; and too few are a wonderful experience of loving, learning, and growing for all concerned. To be successful, a family needs as much care, thought, and skill as a good marriage. As with a marriage, the goal is not merely to survive and get by, but to thrive and grow stronger from the challenges involved.

Maintaining More Than Your Sanity

Maintaining a healthy family despite the odds can be compared to maintaining an automobile. There are issues that

251

need attention, and as the ad goes, "You can pay me now or pay me later." Here are some comparisons:

Check the radiator	Keep it cool, don't overheat
Check the steering/brakes	Stay in control at all times
Keep the battery charged	Keep your energy up
Tune up for performance	Maintain your power
Check the plugs	Keep your spark
Clean the windshield	Watch where you are headed
Don't run out of gas	Don't run out of gas
Check wear on tires	Realize when you are wearing down before you burst

Contained in each of these suggestions is all you really need to know about maintaining health as a parent. The best truths are simple ones. A best-selling book once surprised readers by proclaiming that we learned in kindergarten everything we need for a happy, fulfilled life. Well, some of us may have gotten it all the first time, but most of us could use a refresher course (and some people go through life as if they are repeating kindergarten for the twenty-eighth time). If you got it all the first time, then stop here. But if you need to hear a bit more, read on.

Many parents feel like failures with special needs children for a variety of reasons. Some feel like it is their fault that a child has such difficulties in life. Others feel out-of-control and watch as everyone in the family is hurting, and then they feel powerless to change the situation. Other parents desperately try to balance their limited energy, dividing it up between a difficult to raise child and one or more other children, a spouse, perhaps a career, and a self who often comes in last place. Even if a parent sees some gains in the challenging child, the parent may feel the guilt that it is at least partially at the expense of one or more of the other family members. It can seem like a no-win situation. Faced with this challenge, there are constant invitations to get depressed, get frustrated, or to give up entirely; all of which can add further to the guilt and stress of parenting.

Many parents are all too familiar with the elements that feel like failure in parenting. This primarily comes from a belief that the child's behavior is the report card for the parent. For many parents the failures are much easier to see than the successes. Some parents also have the curse that if the child is doing well, it must be because of a multitude of factors (the child may even get some of the credit), but if the child is failing in life everyone knows it must be at least partially the fault of mom and dad. We do not need to focus on failure, we all know what that looks like. But what does success look like in a parent?

Successful Parenting

Successful parents of a special needs child tend to have a lot of TLC. Tender loving care, you say? Absolutely not. Tender loving care is almost always in abundant supply with parents who struggle with difficult children, as least while their energy holds up. This type of TLC is wonderfully effective with most children, but if love was enough, your child would be president of his class and currently being recruited by Harvard out of elementary school. Sadly, the first lesson many of us learn is that love is not enough with special needs children. But few parenting manuals tell you what to do when regular TLC fails. The type of TLC needed with challenging children means something very different:

T = Translating correctly what is really going on with the child in order to understand where the child really is. It is important not to attach too much importance to words. It is commonly known that manipulative teenagers (aren't these two words redundant?) talk in opposites. It is often a safe bet to retranslate what teens are saying into the opposite to get closer to the truth. Practice by retranslating the following: "I

253

don't want rules," " I'm not worried about my future," "I am all caught up on my school work," and "I'll be home early tonight." This same principle of opposites often works with special-needs children. Translating is much more than considering a child's words. It is understanding the child's energy, the motivation, and moving from the child's "world view" to the specific situation, and what the child may be saying, not with words but with actions.

L = Learning from the challenges of parenting a difficult child becomes one of the indicators of success, not how smooth it is going for everyone. But parenting is not smooth -- it is either constant trouble or a series of challenges, depending on your point-of-view. The one factor that has helped me to determine if a parent will be able to hang in there with a challenging child is if they view the situation as a challenge and not merely as yet another problem. The parent who comes to family counseling with one goal -- to change the child -- is unlikely to climb this mountain. However, the parent who explains the problems in the family, and then asks for help to understand and impact these problems, has a better chance for long term success. The more you see a problem as a challenge to learn from, the better candidate you are to be a successful parent of a difficult to raise child.

C = Stay in Control at all times in all situations involving the child. This child did not get to be so difficult on his own; he had lots of help often times from chaotic, abusive, and neglectful experiences in his past when safety and security were in short supply. Do not confuse being in control of your behavior and your feelings with being in control of the child. When you are in control of your inner world and the family environment, the child who is interested in driving you to drink doesn't have much of a chance. Constant control may sound pretty heavy, but if you parent one of these children, he or she will constantly test to see just how in control you are. If the child is able to gain control of you and the situation, everyone loses; if the child can't gain control of you and the family, everyone wins. It is that simple.

TLC -- Translating, Learning, and being in Control -- is easier said than done. But here is part of the point -- What does parenting a difficult child offer you? It offers an opportunity to grow yourself, as you attempt to give the child what she will need to succeed in life. Only parents who want to grow need apply for this job.

Seven Strategies For Success

1. Understand the real needs of the child. It is not often helpful to listen to the child's words, or even to accept the child's behavior at face value because of the "rule of opposites" mentioned above. If the child has had an abusive or neglectful past, then his needs are pretty straightforward despite the way he acts. These children need the following:

♦ Safety -- Will I be safe in a nonviolent environment where my basic needs will be met?

♦ Security -- I need a structured situation where a parent is in charge and I can just be a kid.

♦ Acceptance -- I need people who can accept me as a person even if they don't like or accept my behavior.

♦ Belonging -- I need to belong to someone. I need to be connected to others and learn to give and receive affection.

♦ Trust -- I need to learn to trust and be trusted, be treated fairly with honesty, respect and firmness.

♦ Relationship -- I need to be in relation to others in a way that no one is victimized and both sides are enhanced.

♦ Self-Awareness -- I need to learn how to make changes in my personality and behavior through self-understanding.

♦ Personal Worth -- The final indicator of my being a success as a person is, "Do I believe in myself and my own worth?"

2. Positive discipline is the quickest route to your maintaining control and building the child's personal worth at the same time. Techniques include: separate the child from the behavior, don't punish -- discipline (which means to teach), and don't let "time outs" become a disguised punishment. Use logical consequences. Don't ask the child to lie by asking questions you know the answer to, and avoid power struggles. Have the child fight with herself, not with you. Keep your sense of humor and don't let the child decide what you will feel (don't let her anger you when she is trying to). Allow the child to change, and to be more responsible by not locking her into past behaviors.

3. Learn to win the manipulation game. Don't let the child use your rules against you. Don't be completely predictable to a manipulative child; you become an easy target. Keep him off balance when he is trying to beat you. In general, if the child is manipulating to get something, do your best to prevent her from getting her way, or you will get more manipulation (because it works). Stay a couple steps ahead of the child by predicting in your mind what he might do and what you will do in return. Don't respond emotionally; you don't think very creatively when rattled. Parenting is best done by a team, so talk over your next move and get advice and ideas. If the child has you on the run, she wins the manipulation battle and you both come closer to losing the war.

4. Get the help you need from the right source. Frankly, some counselors who don't understand these children can make the situation considerably worse. It is not much of a

challenge for a manipulative child to be perfectly behaved and even charming one hour a week in someone's office. It is often not difficult for these children to handle being the center of attention. If the counselor starts looking at you the parent like you must be the problem, get someone else. Ask a prospective counselor about their experience with children like yours. An expert mechanic with Fords may not be much of an expert with a Toyota. Better yet, go to a counselor who comes highly recommended for skills with a child like yours.

5. The only given is that parenting a demanding child will be a challenge, but it does not have to be terrible. The difference is something you have complete control over -- your perspective of the situation, your emotions, and your sense of humor. A wise man once said, "If you lose your sense of humor, the world just isn't funny anymore," and parenting is like that.

6. Make sure you are more than a parent. If you are a parent 24 hours a day, you have become pretty dull. Be a wife, a student, a hiker, a volunteer, a square dancer, an artist, a husband, or whatever, but don't get stuck in the parent role where there is a whole lot more giving than receiving. Batteries don't last long if they get drained but never recharged.

7. Don't get in a hurry. In a culture where we expect Captain Kirk to save the solar system in one to two hours, some parents want problems solved in a couple counseling sessions, or at least a couple of months. Pace yourself; there has been no proven way to parent a successful human being using short cuts. If anyone promises you a quick solution, save your time and your money and look elsewhere.

Chapter

11

Physical Touch and Parenting

Providing a young child with significant amounts of physical contact does not sound like it would be questioned or need to be mentioned in a discussion of special needs children. But in some forms, physical touch has been seriously questioned in some surprising circles. In the following pages the role of touch will be covered for all children, particularly those children who react in negative ways to touch.

Next to food, water, and shelter, the most important survival need of human beings is physical touch. It may seem odd to say it is a survival need, but this has been graphically and disturbingly proven. Before the development of human subjects review committees more than fifty years ago, some psychological research took on ghastly qualities. We are hearing more about subjecting adults, particularly soldiers and prisoners, to research in medical and psychological domains. But perhaps even more difficult to imagine now are the studies done on orphan children in England and other countries during the great world wars.

In some research into human touch, infants received all physical needs but were purposely deprived of human touch, while control groups had the same basic needs met along with being held by care providers. The results were a clear indication that indeed man does not live by bread alone. How

259

did they learn this? Children deprived of touch had severe adverse effects and many died. Did researchers actually let the study get to that point? Yes, apparently this was the same thinking that went into justifications of exposing people to radiation and chemical gas which was "for the good of humanity." We do not extend the same justification to Nazi human research, but they lost the war. I would dare to say that these are studies that will never be replicated, at least hopefully.

We have learned that as a species, we do not do well without being held, cuddled, tickled, stroked, fondled, patted, rubbed and generally petted from our first days of life. Adults can learn to manage without this basic need, but only after years of denying themselves the closeness of human contact. I think it is fair to say that the healthiest humans are those who have a life-long experience of ample human touch from cradle to grave.

While writing this book, I was surprised at the amount of energy generated throughout the country on the topic of touch with children who have serious problems. This is not the way the issue was framed, however. The controversy revolved around the use of coercive touch in therapy or physical restraint, and holding children who become enraged and violent to themselves and others. These topics were not originally planned to be included here, but found their way in at the last moment. The reason for this late inclusion is to help bring some much needed balance to the debate on intervening with violent children for both parents and professionals. Once again, I believe I may have something to offer here, since I have found myself unintentionally at the center of two different debates on this same topic.

In the first debate I found myself in the middle of while in front of national network television cameras concerned "holding therapy" used by some in treating children with bonding and attachment problems. While it was not my intention to take on this contentious issue, I was informed by the national media that they could not find knowledgeable professionals who were willing to speak out. My position on the subject has already been briefly covered in Chapter 3. I will only briefly repeat this position here.

Although I do not question the importance of physical touch with children with attachment problems, the who, when, how and why are critically important with these children. My principal complaint with "holding therapies" is the risk of reactivating traumatic experiences and symptoms for children who have been seriously abused when they were very young. Despite the assurances of some of these therapies that re-traumatization or reminders of trauma is avoided in the process, I believe this cannot be guaranteed, and the unproven rewards are far too great to justify the substantial risks involved. Remember the first rule of medicine and psychology, the Hippocratic oath, "Above all else, do no harm." But as I mentioned above, my complaint did not center on the actual touch involved in the process. So if "holding therapy" was modified to include touch by the right people in the right way at the right time, I'm on board.

The second controversy involving touch that has recently spread across the country like a grass fire in California, is the use of physical methods of intervening when children become violent to themselves and others. Before addressing this issue in more depth than "holding therapies," let's briefly look at interventions with children that can greatly assist the protector and the teaching roles of parents.

Few places on the planet have had as much opportunity on a daily basis to work with difficult children as a residential treatment program. I am often asked to explain how our program intervenes, when and why. I have included our Agency policy here to provide some insight to our approach, which views touch in a very different manner than many other programs.

261

Interventions at SCAR/Jasper Mountain

Over the years, new staff and parents have repeatedly asked for an explanation of how and when interventions take place at Jasper Mountain. Most of the time what these people are really asking for is an easy to understand formula as to what the adult should do in a certain situation. However, a formula or cookbook approach to interventions has been resisted since the Agency began. Instead, staff and parents have been trained and encouraged to become skilled clinicians with a growing understanding of the artistic qualities of treating children. The following position statement is both a policy and procedure and is meant to outline the philosophy of the Agency regarding therapeutic interventions.

The word interventions is a generic term to indicate the manner in which steps are taken to accomplish a prescribed goal. Treatment programs are fundamentally about accomplishing prescribed goals, and are, therefore, fundamentally about interventions. Over time therapeutic interventions, be they verbal, nonverbal, physical, environmental, or chemical, have maintained a positive and important place in the functioning of a treatment center. Although this is still the case, the modern world of regulations and liability has placed a spotlight on physical interventions. In some ways this is good if a heightened awareness brings more effective physical interventions. However, this focus can also put a very effective form of treatment into a category of a crises, and this line of thinking maintains that all crises are best prevented.

Understanding treatment and the purpose of an intensive treatment setting includes the recognition that in this unique setting problems cannot be ignored, behaviors cannot be allowed to go underground, and explosive issues cannot simply be avoided with skilled crisis prevention. Using a medical analogy, hospital treatments are not simply focused on comforting patients and maintaining the status quo. Hospitals are places people go to heal, and sometimes, as in surgery, you have to get worse before you can begin to really heal. It is similar in our psychological hospital. The goal of residential treatment is to achieve the treatment goals in the most expeditious way possible given the unique situation of the child. It is therefore important that treatment centers and their staff have the latitude to use all interventions that are clinically appropriate. Clinically appropriate interventions are not good and bad, they are effective or ineffective. Saying that one form of intervention in all cases is better than other forms is to not understand the purpose of a treatment program.

The role of therapy and the therapist is an extremely delicate one. The power held by the treating clinician has been and will continue to be controversial. This is even more so when it comes to treating children. There are many reasons why the clinical staff in a treatment center must be knowledgeable of their role, and how best to accomplish their goals. The better the clinician, the better the program and the better the results for children in residence. The following issues are presented to assist staff and parents in reviewing the complexity and the development of "best practices" at SCAR/Jasper Mountain.

Of the interventions covered here, physical interventions will receive the most attention. This is not because they are the preferred intervention. Most educational settings, parent trainings, college courses, and other training programs cover verbal and nonverbal interventions effectively. For this reason, staff members coming into a treatment program are generally much more knowledgeable about verbal interventions than physical ones. The first issue addressed will be verbal interventions.

Verbal Interventions

Clinicians usually rely heavily on verbal communication because they are most comfortable interacting on a verbal level. This is why many therapists prefer working with adults or teens rather than young children. It is important to understand that verbal interventions can be relied on too heavily with children. Most children in treatment settings have learned how to have the words of adults "go in one ear and out the other."

Although clinicians are more highly trained in verbal interventions than any other type, the belief that most communication occurs with words is not often true. Training programs stress what is said to a client more so than any other form of communication. The basic verbal skills of communication such as active listening, attending behavior, tracking, reflection, summarization and many others are important for all agency staff to be familiar with. They are helpful to parents as well, but will not be covered here.

One of the most important principles to understand concerning verbal communication with children is actually its limitations. Verbal therapies and interventions with preadolescent children are often not as effective as other forms. Actions do speak louder than words in treatment settings, as well as in homes and schools. Children will primarily learn by watching the modeling you demonstrate. How you handle your feelings, conflicts, and frustrations is far more important than what you tell a child about these things.

Verbal interventions are a critical aspect of an effective treatment program. However, be cautious not to rely overly on verbal interventions to teach, to counsel, to calm down, to provide reassurance, nor to facilitate various aspects of socialization. Words can be powerful in some treatment situations, but they are only one way to intervene.

Nonverbal Interventions

Words are less than 25% of any verbal interchange between people. Facial expression, posture, tone, cadence, volume, gestures and other components of communication add to the full meaning of words. Children are particularly sensitive to nonverbal messages. In part this is due to the years when communication took place between parent and child without the benefit of both speaking the same language. An effective parent or clinician will know how to use nonverbal communication to achieve therapeutic goals. Children learn to read nonverbal messages from caretakers long before they understand verbal messages. Most educational programs in the field of social sciences and parenting programs will cover nonverbal communication. It is primarily through experience and awareness that nonverbal communication skills will be developed in a family or residential treatment setting.

Chemical Interventions

Physical interventions are not the only controversial topic in treatment approaches. Some programs have a philosophical leaning toward the use of chemical interventions, and some lean away from their use. SCAR/Jasper Mountain takes no position promoting nor discouraging the use of chemical interventions. It does take the position that if a chemical intervention can safely facilitate treatment progress for a child, it will be considered. External progress must always be weighted with empowering the child to make internal gains as well. If a chemical intervention is chosen, the best approach is to effectively take advantage of the intervention by using a therapeutic dosage, and not to over nor under medicate. Chemical restraint, using drugs to calm down a child in a crisis, is never used in the Agency.

Specific decisions concerning the use of therapeutic medications are not the concern of treatment staff, but are made by the psychiatrist. However, a basic knowledge of chemical interventions will enhance the effectiveness of parents and staff members. Psychopharmacology is an extremely complex area of medicine and physiology. Basic understanding of how medications work on the brain and how specific medications affect behavior are areas all parents and staff should expose themselves to.

The Purpose of Physical Interventions

The first language of the child is touch. Research has shown the critical importance of basic human touch in physical growth, cognitive development, and personal and social attachment. Touch is the primary language of children for years following the beginning of language development. An effective family setting and treatment program will use touch as a potent means of communication.

As stated earlier, the role of a treatment center is to accomplish the treatment goals of each child. To borrow from an investment commercial, at SCAR/Jasper Mountain we measure success one child at a time. Understanding physical interventions also entails understanding crisis prevention. However, it is also important to understand that in the controlled setting of a treatment center, not all emotionally laden issues and situations that might bring out intense reactions and behaviors (which some would call a crisis) are to be prevented. It is a failure for a treatment center to graduate a child who, with the assistance of trained staff, has avoided situations that precipitate antisocial or violent reactions, only to surface after leaving a tightly controlled setting. It is important to know how to prevent such a crisis; it is not important that all treatment enhancing situations of this type be avoided nor prevented.

There are a variety of reasons to physically intervene with a child in a family or treatment center. All these reasons can be consolidated to say that a physical intervention is designed to let a child know that you are there, you are prepared to handle any problem, and the child is in good hands. There are some who say that a child has a basic right not to be physically restrained in any circumstance. However, there is an even more basic right -- to be safe. The adult's presence in the above ways constitutes safety and predictability for the child. It is important from the outset to state that physical interventions are not negative, punitive, nor a symbol of failure on the part of either the child, parent, or the staff person. A child needs physical touch, and he needs tangible reminders that a competent and caring adult is working with them. It is common for a child to push limits until she finds that the adult will step in and take charge. Emotionally disturbed children need these reminders more than other children. When done in the right way and at the right time, physical interventions can be some of the most potent aspects of a clinical regimen, particularly in the early stages of a child's residential stay.

The Types of Physical Interventions

A discussion of physical interventions will begin with saying what interventions are not appropriate for use in the Agency. Mechanical restraints are never used, the Agency does not believe in the concept of seclusion rooms for isolating traumatized children, and no type of punishment, or harmful, painful or punitive interventions is appropriate in this treatment program. A child may need to be removed from being around other children if he is being physically or verbally abusive to others. Children removed from other children due to serious behavior are to receive particularly close supervision. In addition, the agency prohibits degrading punishment, corporal or physical punishment, painful aversive stimuli, forced physical exercise, punitive work assignments, group punishment for one person's behavior, medication for punishment, mechanical restraints, extended isolation without contact with peers or staff, depriving children of food or other basic needs, and preventing contact with family members when contact is not prohibited nor contraindicated by the treatment plan. All interventions used are within the guidelines of the state-approved crisis management system -- Crisis Prevention Institute or CPI.

Physical interventions are not restricted to taking charge of an out-of-control child. Physical interventions include any situation where there is a therapeutic gain possible through physical touch. Depending upon the situation, this might include a hug, a back rub, a hand on a shoulder, sitting close to a child, giving him a piggy-back ride, having her sit on your lap, or holding her hand. Too often people think of physical interventions as negative interactions when there are problems. It is often the case that the types of interventions mentioned earlier can help desensitize a child to physical touch when difficult situations do arrive where more firm action may be necessary.

Before going into more involved physical interventions, it is important to mention the concept of being firm and friendly. According to our program philosophy, providing a balance of firmness and caring is important to avoid manipulation by the child (accomplished through firmness), and to avoid the perception of punishment (by being friendly). This does not mean that a parent or staff person can be both firm and friendly in every situation. Many situations do not allow this. It does mean that overall you must be able to establish a relationship with a child that is characterized by firmness or you will not be taken seriously, and using a friendly style or you will be viewed as another punitive adult in his or her life. For most physical interventions, if you are able to be both firm and friendly, you will come out ahead and so will the child.

In addition to the interventions mentioned thus far, there are interventions of a more firm physical nature:

Escorts or Moving the Child -- Physically moving the child from one place to another may be needed in situations such as a child refusing to get out of bed to go to school. To a child who has learned to test adults and be powerful by oppositional behavior, this intervention can be critically important. The child should be given the opportunity to respond to adult instruction in an appropriate way, but if she will not, then there is a good likelihood that this is a situation in which she is testing the resolve of the adult and the structure of the environment. Few children in residential treatment have tested the resolve of adults in a former environment and found that the adults were physically and emotionally in charge of the situation. Because of this, the child needs to test not only you as a staff person, but every other staff person (see the Building Blocks of Treating Emotional Disturbances). If the child is testing the adult and the child wins, the adult has failed the test and more testing will be necessary. It is important to consider all factors in situations that may require escorting or moving a child.

Brief Redirection -- this can include holding a child's arm or shoulders. These interventions are brief and require a minimal amount of containment of the child. When this is done in the right way and at the right time, it can answer the questions behind a child's testing behavior, and can at the same time be very reassuring to the child.

Seldom is a child's response to a hold immediately positive. He will generally struggle physically or verbally to see who is in control of the situation. Many times only later (if ever) can the child admit that it was good to know that the adult set limits and then enforced those limits. In translating the meaning of a child's behavior, do not overlook the obvious. If a child knows that a certain behavior will end up in a hold and she proceeds anyway, there is a good chance she needs to be reassured by being supportingly touched by the adult.

Children are not always testing when needing a hold. At times children may have reached internal limits to be able to handle the emotional demands of a situation. At such times, children may begin to act in violent or other hurtful ways either to themselves, to others, or to property. When a child becomes violent, immediate steps must be taken to contain the potentially dangerous results. This is one of the most critical times for a traumatized child to hear, see, and feel the reassuring protection of an adult who is acting in the child's best interests.

Containment Holds -- The term restraint is not the best of words. It means something mechanical to many people. In our setting a restraint is actually a therapeutic hold used to contain the child from causing potentially serious harm to self, to others, or to property. These holds are used to contain the child's body, arms, and legs, all of which are most frequently used by young children to be violent. The child usually responds to being restrained by resisting or seeing if you have control of the situation.

Once the child finds that you do have the situation under control, he often sees if he can emotionally be more powerful than you, as he has over other adults in his past. This often takes the form of screaming, head-banging, verbal insults, or yelling that you are hurting him and you are therefore a child abuser. For many of the children coming into our programs with violent pasts, they will often need to go through many or all forms of this testing before they see that in this situation the adult can manage violent behavior, and is in control of the situation by preventing anyone from being hurt.

For many emotionally disturbed children, only after all this testing has occurred can he or she begin the steps of moving beyond the violent and controlling behavior that hides internal fear, sadness, and pain. If a staff person and a treatment program cannot get to the place of reassuring protection, the therapeutic work will often not occur.

There Are a Wide Variety of Ways to Handle A Situation

Parenting challenging children requires skill and considerable brain power. Many of the children we work with have developed problem behaviors to an art form, and are often much better at the game than most adults are. Here is where brain power plays an important role. There are programs that have prescriptive interventions that essentially give the staff several types of interventions and when to use them. This is comforting to many staff because it is clear and easy to know what to do. However, we must realize that most of our children have run into adults in the past who were experienced and worked hard to help the child achieve but with little success.

Successful work with the children we intentionally accept into Agency programs requires more than a cookbook of therapeutic interventions. Success with the level of disturbance and sophistication of many of our children requires staff to become skilled therapeutic artists. A staff member must take the situation into account, understand the interplay of the situation and the imprint of the personalities (including his own) on the situation, and must lead with his mind and his intuition. This is the clinical staff person as a therapeutic artist, creating one-of-a-kind interventions that precisely fit this child and this situation. Not all interventions work the first time, and this is where experience as well as evaluating the intervention becomes very important.

Standard Intervention Steps

There is no therapeutic cookbook in our Agency to working with all children in all situations. An individual child will have her own unique background, ability to understand, and motivation system. Because of this, individualized treatment plans are the fundamental road map for a particular child. However there are standard intervention steps that can guide the staff member in situations where a child needs to learn social conventions. Effective socialization is the key to being a success. Most children in a residential treatment program have failed in multiple social settings. Learning to respond appropriately in a social context is essential, and this is why it is the purpose of a treatment program at times to allow conflict to surface and not to simply prevent conflict.

The following five steps should be involved in most physical interventions:

1. Respectfully request the child to do what you need him or her to do. A good habit is to end the request with a please. Polite words such as please and thank you are excellent modeling as well.

2. If the child does not appropriately respond, make the direction very clear, including when and how you expect him to respond.

3. If the child continues to be oppositional, consider the individual child and the specific situation; there may be an appropriate reason why the child cannot or will not respond. If follow-through is therapeutically indicated, ask the child if she needs your physical assistance to proceed with the instruction.

4. At this point, do a self-check of your own energy and motivation. If you are upset or angry, or if you are feeling a need to prove you are stronger or more physically powerful, stop! A power struggle with a child is not therapeutic. Regain your own internal control before attempting to handle the situation.

5. If the child does not respond and the situation calls for it, physically intervene using the least physical and emotional energy possible to resolve the situation.

The above steps give the child the opportunity to take care of the situation by a personal decision. If you have to physically intervene, keep in mind that the eventual goal is to have the child make his own choice to fit within the social bounds of a situation. This is the fundamental nature of socializing a child. At first she fits into the social norms because she is required to, then because she prefers the positive reinforcement pro-social behavior brings, gradually she does so because she chooses to, and because it is the right thing to do (showing progressive steps toward social and moral reasoning).

Repeatedly going through all steps with the same child may indicate that another intervention is required. As mentioned earlier, these steps are not always possible; there is no one process of intervening that fits every situation. But more often than not, these five steps can be a helpful guideline. There are several special cases that require more detail than this brief overview of interventions. These are: manipulation by a child, understanding and working with power struggles when consistency is critically important, and when creative inconsistency is the better therapeutic choice.

The Mental Components of Planning an Intervention

As mentioned earlier, working with challenging children takes brain power. The following are steps that point out just how important it is to think and act smart in clinical situations.

- ◆ Always come from a philosophical base. If you do not, then you are intervening without solid footing.

- ◆ Plug your philosophical premises into this specific situation.

- ◆ Translate the meaning of the child's behavior and affect.

- ◆ Rely on your experience to help you. If you have little experience, rely on the experience of your team members.

- ◆ Trust your intuitive sense of what is going on and what might work in the specific situation. Be willing to try an intervention that is creative as long as it is appropriate and safe.

- Work as a team, and use the creative brain power of your team members.

- Put these steps together and choose an intervention.

- Evaluate the immediate and the subsequent effects of your intervention. Usually this requires you to modify what you do based upon your evaluation, at which time you may need to return to step one.

All these steps might need to take place very rapidly. The more you work with emotionally disturbed children, the better you will become. However, the above steps are much like playing the piano; if you do not work at it, you will not improve.

Environmental Intervention

It is a fundamental belief of SCAR/Jasper Mountain that the most potent influence on children is the synergy of all aspects of the child's environment. This environment is composed of the atmosphere, the architecture, the people, the lighting, the sounds, the activities, the relationships, and all other components that interact and interplay to form the treatment environment. Considerable energy has gone into the physical qualities of Agency programs. To develop the optimum impact of environment as an intervention, it is important to understand the effect of all the aspects of a child's life, and how they create a positive or negative influence. In the final analysis, our programs will succeed or fail not on the basis of individual therapy, medications, skilled verbal or physical interventions or any other single aspect of the program. It will be the overall environment that will promote or delay the child's progress toward an integration of the child's overall health and personal and social development.

Questions and Answers

Should physical interventions be the last resort? Not necessarily. There are many situations where some form of physical intervention might be the most effective step. If your intuition tells you that this child will push until you firmly step in, do so sooner rather than later. However, if the child is manipulating you to enter a power contest by controlling you to instigate a therapeutic hold, avoid doing so, because it will not be therapeutic. Additionally, a therapeutic hold should only be used when the child is a threat to self, to others, or to property.

Should it bother me as much as it does to restrain a child? Probably. None of us works with the Agency to be involved in unpleasant interactions or wrestle with young abused children. None of us wants to be potentially viewed as an abuser or to be called an abuser by a child. However, all of this comes with our work. It gets a little easier with experience, but the tension inside never completely goes away.

Should physical interventions only be used when a child is out of control? No. There are a broad range of physical interventions discussed in this position statement. Most of them can be used with potentially effective clinical results in a variety of situations, not just when the child is out of control. Containment holds, however, should be used to ensure the safety of all involved.

Should a physical intervention be used to gain the appropriate response from a child? In some cases, yes, others no; it depends. Remember there is no one-size-fits-all in this business; however, oppositional behavior is more often the result of testing than other reasons. Testing by a child is done with the conscious or subconscious hope that the adult will pass the test. A variety of physical interventions short of therapeutic holds may be very helpful with oppositional children.

Should I be slow to use physical interventions with a child new to the program? In general, probably not. Orienting the child to what is expected early on can be very helpful to the child and to the program. Most children will push until they find the limits, so let them find the limits sooner rather than later. Some children will respond to a firm and friendly approach. Other children will push to find the limits of being violent. Again, handling these situations depends on the age, previous trauma, and the individual personality and resilience of the child.

Should children be fully contained if they are not following directions? The only reason to exert full control over a child is to prevent the child from harming self or someone else, or from damaging property. A variety of physical and nonphysical interventions can be used for less serious situations.

Should I bargain with a child, lay out potential consequences, or even ignore as much as possible rather than physically intervene? Again, there is no cookbook answer. Go through the principles listed previously; if ignoring might possibly work, then ignore and evaluate. However, if a physical intervention appears inevitable to insure safety, then intervene calmly and firmly, sooner rather than later.

Is a child's fear of a physical intervention an effective deterrent? It may seem like it is, but actually it generally isn't. Most children continue to act in ways that get what they want. Fear will play less of a role in the child's behavior than if the behavior has been reinforced by the desired result. Often what may seem like fear from the child is the child's frustration at not getting his or her way. If he can get his way by being violent physically or verbally, he may just do so. If she looks at you and knows that you are prepared to fully handle the situation and anything she does, she will often not push to extreme limits.

Can I get to the point that I don't need to use containment holds very often? Yes, with most children. Once they have the experience with you that climbs the steps of the Building Blocks (see Figure 1 in Chapter 1), the only time you may need to restrain that child again is if he gets to a position where he needs reassurance. Staff who can give children reassurance by personal energy will do far less restraining.

Should I restrain a child in a forceful or gentle manner? A containment hold is often not a gentle intervention. The goal is to prevent the child's dangerous or destructive behavior. The key to achieving this is to be firm and to demonstrate in a physical manner that the child and the situation are safe and in control.

Should I restrain a child who has made me angry? Avoid physical interventions when angry. At such times, you are less aware of the physical power you have. When we are angry, our brain power is less available to us. At such times, have another staff person take over while you ask yourself what is going on inside of you.

What does it mean when multiple children act out seriously and often? It may mean that the children don't respect the staff or they don't believe the staff will be able to handle testing behavior. It may also be a cry for more structure which may include effective use of physical interventions. Chaos in a program for any period of time must be handled decisively so that children know that everyone is safe. This requires that the adults are in charge of the environment. In chaotic situations in programs where multiple children are acting out, and there could be potential danger, stabilize the situation first and address the emotional issues of children and staff after the situation has been calmed.

Should I talk to a child in a restraint? Use your judgment. When a child is being loud and verbally venting, it is often best not to talk to him. At such times, your presence is what speaks the loudest. As the child begins to calm down, you may find that he or she is more personally and emotionally available. This may be an excellent time to verbally intervene.

Should the child's diagnosis and past be considered in how to intervene? Yes. Treatment of a child follows the prescription outlined in the treatment plan. The plan combines important issues such as the child's past and her diagnosis to outline a course of treatment. This is one of the main reasons why treatment must be individualized and cannot follow a cookbook approach.

This is all so complex! Will I ever be good at it? Hang in there; some of our best clinical staff took months, if not years, to learn the subtleties of being a therapeutic artist and an effective clinician.

Working with Violent Children

Violent children have been in our treatment programs, foster homes, schools and community streets and playgrounds for many years. Over the last half century (roughly the period of time that treatment programs have "organically grown" from orphanages), a variety of methods have been used to deal with out-of-control children, and adults as well. It is not surprising that the most often used method to intervene with violent and abusive behavior has been to stop it from harming anyone. That makes reasonable sense. There has been a heightened awareness over the years of how to do this in less crude, painful, and restrictive methods (outside of many criminal justice facilities, that is).

The use of inflicting pain, "snowing" children with tranquilizers, depriving children of food, and mechanical methods such as straightjackets, four-point restraints, and handcuffs have all but disappeared, and fortunately so (however, some of these can still be found in some psychiatric hospitals and detention centers). With the coming of national standards of care, the primary methods of dealing with violent behavior have evolved to using crisis prevention methods to de-escalate the violence, and when necessary the use of physical restraint and/or seclusion implemented by trained staff. This seems reasonable enough, but not to everyone.

Due to some of the abuses of the past, and the current practices of some poorly run programs that do not strive to meet industry standards, there has been an outcry for more restrictions on handling violent behavior. This has come in the form of restrictions in foster homes, state standards for the use of seclusion, and even proposed federal government regulations on the use of physical interventions of all kinds. Where has this recent energy come from? Much like celebrated cases of child abuse by parents can focus the attention of the government and private sector to take steps to further protect children, the same appears to have happened in regards to treatment programs.

The following section is an adaptation of an article accepted for publication in the *Journal of Residential Treatment for Children and Youth* called "To Hold or Not To Hold...Is This the Right Question?" Initially, the primary audience for this discussion was treatment programs, but the topic of intervening when children get violent and destructive is also a very important issue for parents with difficult-to-manage children.

Many states regulate the use of physical holds in foster care. Often these regulations focus more on what parents can not do than what they can do to keep violent children and those around them safe. This chapter contains a review of the professional literature in the area of therapeutic holding as well as an attempt to place the issue in a practical and reasonable context. At a time when more violent children are in substitute care in both programs and families, there has been increasing pressure to handle extreme behavior with non-intrusive methods. Advocates of this position frame the issue by asking if the use of physical holding or seclusion should be allowed. This issue will be reframed here in terms of what is both professionally appropriate and what actually works. Traditional methods of handling extreme behavior are discussed and compared. The discussion ends with suggestions for building a response to violent behavior in children.

Introductory Background -- The Present Climate in Substitute Care

Substitute care providers, including treatment programs like the one I run, and foster and group care, are facing growing scrutiny concerning methods used to ensure the safety of children and reduce aggressive and violent behavior. At a time when there has never been more focus in treatment programs on professionalism, clinical best practices, and meeting national standards of excellence (including national accreditations such as: COA, JCAHO, CARF, and NCQI), some voices are saying we have not done enough.

These voices of concern seem to come from at least two camps. First are those who speak out under the banner of human rights for children, and second are those who express the more legalistic concerns over liability exposure. The author's primary interest is in intensive treatment programs for children under the age of twelve, but the issues raised are applicable to other settings as well.

While human rights advocates are apparently well meaning, the question can be asked as to whether their concerns represent a balanced perspective. Supported by examples of sensational journalism as well as some professionals with a theory or packaged approach to sell their system of care, advocates speak out for "rights" that appear to be neither human rights nor, at times, common sense for children in substitute care.

A recent newspaper series from Hartford, Connecticut, has found its way across the nation (Altimari, Weiss, Blint, Poitras, & Megan, 1998). One of the headlines, apparently designed to shock readers into being concerned, reads "Deadly Restraint: Killed by a System Intended for Care." However, close inspection of the facts in the series of exposé articles indicates that nationally an average of one child under the age of ten died in substitute care every five years during the period of the paper's investigation. Most of the deaths discussed involved adults or older teens. All reported deaths involving physical holding occurred from methods unsanctioned by accrediting bodies or crisis intervention systems.

While it is true that even one accidental death in substitute care is one too many, the article does not consider how many children every year under the age of ten die from intentional abuse at the hands of parents, from accidents in their own homes, or even from suicide. Therefore, the question can be asked, how many deaths were likely prevented by placement in various forms of substitute care?

Some advocates have spoken out for children in substitute care and the child's "rights" to unrestricted access to tele-phones, not being placed alone even in their own rooms, freedom to do anything the child wants to do as long as it is not dangerous, and the child's "constitutional right" to be obnoxious and oppositional (Smith, 1993). As a society, do we grant these "human rights" to our own children at home or in our schools? For children in substitute care who need additional structure and supervision, and who have pathological behavior or oppositionality, common sense would seem to question such "rights."

The legal liability arguments are somewhat easier to understand. State agencies and departments that place aggressive and violent children in substitute care must listen to the advice of lawyers and risk managers who know the financial exposure of liability related to these difficult chil-dren. At the same time, there must also be a balance between liability concerns and the treatment needs of the children. If a balanced perspective is not reached, most substitute care providers may follow the lead of the programs that currently screen out aggressive and violent children. This could leave few, if any, community resources for the most difficult to manage children in our system of care.

While writing this, I spoke to a treatment program that turned down a child I was referring because she was too difficult to manage. I was told "our treatment program only accepts children who are likely to be success stories." But isn't that the point? Aren't treatment programs there to work with children who without such help are *not* likely to be success stories?

In addition, parents who are willing to take difficult children into foster or adoptive homes may end up frustrated by a system of care that makes their job more difficult to the point of no longer being willing to help these children.

The scrutiny on care providers must be considered along with the current reality that more aggressive and violent children are being referred and placed in substitute care than ever before (Bath, 1992; Crespi, 1990). Despite a common misconception that teens are most often aggressive and violent, it is settings that work with young children that most often face violent behavior (Miller, Walker & Friedman, 1989). Violence is most common among young males (Measham, 1995). At a time when more resources for the management and treatment of aggressive and violent children are needed, legitimate and effective methods of working with violent behavior are now coming into question by outside critics, who themselves infrequently understand or treat violent populations.

A recent focus has been on the question of whether children and adolescents should ever be the recipients of physical interventions, even when the child is a risk to self or others, or seriously destructive of property. The question frequently being asked of substitute care providers has become, "Is it appropriate to use physical interventions such as holding or restraint?" This overly simplistic view appears to be the wrong way to frame the issue.

The job of substitute care, particularly treatment programs, is to manage violence and to provide treatment not only for the behavior but the underlying issues that cause the behavior. The primary job of treatment programs working with violent children is to return a less violent child to the community as soon as possible. In families, the goal is to significantly reduce violence and unsafe behavior for everyone's benefit. Because of this, the better question to frame the issue is, "What ethical and clinically appropriate physical interventions can be used to manage and treat aggressive and violent behavior?"

An Historical Perspective

The methods used to handle aggressive and violent behavior have changed radically over the last century, as have the standards of what is ethically and clinically appropriate in working with children. Current methods of managing extremely violent behavior range from chemical restraint, mechanical restraint, seclusion, and physical intervention (Troutman, Myers, Borchardt, Kowalski & Burbrick, 1998). Over the last twenty years, the question has justifiably been raised, "Do these methods effectively resolve an immediate crisis and reduce future outbursts?"

Chemical and mechanical restraints have been viewed as the most intrusive of these approaches, and are generally limited to acute care hospital settings. The limited research on these interventions does not present a strong case for being effective in preventing serious episodes (Measham, 1995).

Most violent children remain in homes in part due to a shortage of residential treatment resources throughout the country. The only method in the above list that is available in families to handle violence is to step in and physically stop the behavior, as well as physically ensuring that the child and others in the environment are safe. However, in some states foster families are prevented from physically holding children who become out of control. This restriction only adds to the challenge families face taking difficult children into their homes. These same states do not have the same restriction for dealing with biological children. It appears to be common sense to ask, why would any adult not do his best to stop a child from being violent to others? It is more perplexing to consider why foster homes have this restriction when biological families do not.

Seclusion and Physical Interventions

The less restrictive of generally used interventions for extreme behavior in treatment programs are various forms of seclusion and direct physical interventions to resolve the crisis. The equivalent in a family setting is to have the child "cool off" alone in the child's room or other suitable location in the home. There are at least two theories on the preference of these two approaches.

Some believe that an episode is best handled by providing the violent child with a less stimulating environment where he or she is able to regain control without the stresses of the situation that caused the problem. There are many variations of this concept from locked seclusion, quiet rooms, time out rooms, soft rooms, or freedom rooms (Dougherty, 1982), or when foster parents have the child spend some time alone somewhere in the house to calm down without an audience. Part of the thinking with seclusion is that there is less likelihood of injury if staff or parents are not directly involved with the violent child.

Critics of seclusion point out that what is intended and how it is received by the child may be very different; similar criticisms are leveled toward physical interventions as well. Children may experience seclusion as rejection and marginalization which could continue a pattern of past physical separation (Benjamin, Mazzarin & Kupfersmid, 1983; Miller, 1986; Wadeson & Carpenter, 1976). Other questions have also been raised such as: "How can we best get a non-cooperative violent child into the quiet area, and what about self harm if the child is left alone?" and "In the long run does seclusion return the child to the regular social environment quicker than other approaches?"

Others argue for person-to-person interventions using safe methods of staying with the child throughout the crisis in order to maximize the therapeutic openings often provided by stressful and emotional events. Advocates of physical intervention point out that violent young children need support and structure that is best provided by a person, not a padded room. The argument is made that violent children will as often target themselves for harm as others, precisely because the child feels unwanted, "bad," or not worthy of the love and attention of others. To those trained in physical interventions, close supportive and caring touch is literally "just what the doctor ordered."

The most important question when working with volatile children is, "What will reduce the amount of violence in the short and long term?" To address the effectiveness of seclusion and physical interventions, the professional literature was reviewed to address four factors: 1) Are risk factors addressed with this approach? 2) Is there flexibility of the intervention to fit an individualized case? 3) How long is the crisis period with this approach? and 4) Is it effective in preventing future episodes?

As I mentioned in the first section, research is always suspect in my mind unless it is objective. I run a treatment program that holds a bias on this issue. If a child is in a crisis, we want a supportive adult with that child. Because of this bias, I wanted to ensure that I was not somehow selective in considering professional literature that agreed with our program's opinion and ignoring what did not. The way I resolved this was to have the literature search done by people with no bias. The literature review was done by a medical doctor, a psychologist, and two graduate students. All literature found was included in this discussion.

Most of the information reviewed was on therapeutic holding, perhaps because it is the most commonly used response to violence. Before discussing the literature, it is clear that many more studies need to be conducted with experimental designs and without the researcher using the study to further the professional's own preferred approach or agenda. In the professional literature, there are many more strong opinions than strong research findings.

Comparing Seclusion to Therapeutic Holding

Clear preferences for one approach over the other often appear in the professional literature, but most commentators acknowledge a place for both seclusion (usually preferring some form of time-out) and therapeutic holding (Bath, 1994).

Seclusion has been found by some to be preferred to physical interventions for several reasons. Some are concerned that physical touch is essentially reinforcing to the child, perhaps increasing aggressive behavior (Wong, 1990). Another argument against physical interventions is that physical holding may be perceived by children as aversive (Wong, 1990). Some are concerned that a child will experience reduced personal dignity when physically restrained. There is the concern that parents or staff have a greater likelihood of an injury due to the physical proximity to a violent child. There is always the concern that physical interventions can become punitive "counter aggression" by an angry adult.

When seclusion is evaluated on the four criteria previously mentioned, the results are mixed. The first criterion is managing risks. Risks can be mitigated to some degree, but it may be difficult to closely supervise a child if he or she is alone in a room, unless the room is designed for this purpose (much easier in a treatment program than in a family). Even if a child is required to be alone for some period of time due to violent behavior, physical intervention may still be required if the child is attempting self-harm or if the child refuses to comply with being alone. The most complex aspect of addressing risks is how to address the inherent message of seclusion which is separation, which can be interpreted by the child as another rejection.

The second criterion is whether seclusion is flexible enough to be individualized. This is problematic. It is possible to individualize the time a child is to spend alone, but seclusion presupposes the availability of a specific space. This approach would not be usable on a field trip, during a soccer game or whenever the child was not in a situation where there was a space to have the child spend some time alone.

The third criterion is whether seclusion reduces the period of time the child is in crisis. The research reviewed indicated seclusion prompted longer episodes than other interventions (Miller et al., 1989). The fourth criterion is whether seclusion reduces future episodes of violence. No research supporting a reduction in subsequent episodes could be found.

There is an obvious difference between a child sitting on his bed to cool down and the same child in a padded room with concrete floors. Either way, some prefer the therapeutic advantages of seclusion or some form of time-out. At the same time, seclusion is frequently a target of concern. Long periods of seclusion in locked rooms have received the most criticism (Garrison, 1984; Irwin, 1987). Seclusion may reinforce deep issues of rejection and exclusion (Robin, 1982). Others not only criticize the many forms of seclusion but call it anti-therapeutic (Curtis, 1991; Fahlberg, 1991; Smith, 1991).

In treatment programs, concerns have been raised that by their nature seclusion and time out rooms are barren settings where children are left alone rather than being taught to work with an adult, and children can still act in severe and dangerous ways in seclusion (Rolider, Williams, Cummings & Van Houton, 1991). Concerns surrounding the use of seclusion have resulted in Massachusetts and Pennsylvania outlawing seclusion for minors in treatment centers. Due to concern about the punitive potential of seclusion, the Boys Town Family Home Program explicitly prohibits seclusion or time-out rooms (Daly & Dowd, 1992).

More than one study has found therapeutic holding superior to seclusion in reducing the length of the violent outburst (Bath, 1994). In one study the average length of a therapeutic hold was 21 minutes compared to four times longer for seclusion (Miller et al., 1989). In the reviewed literature, physical restraint was viewed as preferable to seclusion in a broad range of situations when there is a choice between the two (Bath, 1994). Physical holding has been found effective in increasing receptiveness to social contact with autism (Rohmann & Hartmann, 1985; Von Stosch, 1986). Physical containment has also been recognized as avoiding giving the child a sense of control over adults or reinforcing admiration from their troubled peers (Bath, 1994).

A general problem with therapeutic holding has been acknowledged in that it is universally distasteful to adults who must use it, or who observe it. In some ways the act of exercising control over the child and the situation can seem somehow violent and antithetical to a calm therapeutic environment. However, Drisko points out, the overwhelming majority of writers in psychiatric and child care literature acknowledge that physical intervention may be necessary to protect aggressive and violent children and others around them. In fact, some call a failure to intervene physically "a serious mistake" when the failure comes from a reaction of distaste for the process, because physical interventions are the most legally and ethically sound methods to protect dangerous children (Drisko, 1981; Sugar, 1994).

Physical interventions appear to measure up to the four evaluative criteria reasonably well. Criterion one addresses risk. Unquestionably there are risks associated with physical interventions: injury to the child or parent/staff, misuse, punitive intent, and the possibility that the child may experience the intervention in a similar way as past trauma. These risks are addressed in all nationally approved crisis prevention and violence response systems. Correctly trained parents and programs with well-trained staff that monitor all physical interventions can address the potential risks.

Criterion two asks if physical holding is flexible and conducive to individualization. Because there is no requirement of a physical room, physical interventions can be used in any setting (public places can be challenging), and can be adapted to the level of intensity needed by the child and required in the situation.

Criterion three addresses a reduction in the length of the crisis. As was mentioned earlier, more than one research study has identified physical holding as superior to both mechanical restraint and seclusion in reducing the length of the crisis (Bath, 1994; Miller et al., 1989).

The fourth criterion is whether physical holding prevents future episodes of violence. Studies have found physical restraint effective in reducing severely aggressive behavior, self-injurious behaviors and self-stimulatory behaviors (Lamberti & Cummings, 1992; Measham, 1996; Miller et al. 1989; Rolider, Williams, Cummings & Van Houten, 1991).

Physical Holding and Traumatized Children

A frequent concern expressed regarding physical containment of traumatized children is the possibility of the child re-experiencing previous trauma or viewing the intervention as traumatic. All crisis systems address this issue and most recommend individualized interventions that take into consideration the situation, the needs of the child, and special factors such as previous trauma (Crisis Prevention Institute, 1987).

Physical interventions to address violence have been found effective for traumatized children. In contrast to secluding aggressive and violent children, many find that forms of physical interventions best address the problem. Having a trained parent or staff person stay with the child throughout the violent episode has been described as engendering security and comfort in the child (Robin, 1982). Some find that the essential element of an intervention's therapeutic quality rests on its ability to teach pro-social skills. Therapeutic holding has been found to prevent a previously traumatized child from continuing to see adults as hostile, rejecting and punitive.

When physical holds are done correctly, the adult maintains a safe control of the situation and conveys a caring, nurturing, and reassuring message to the child (Barlow, 1989). Hands-on physical interventions were found helpful in treating aggression with dissociative children (Lamberti & Cummings, 1992). The close proximity of the staff or parent in physical interventions rather than seclusion gives them better information on the child's state of mind in order to respond more appropriately (Miller, Walker & Friedman, 1989), which is particularly important with traumatized children.

The role of physical interventions as an aspect of re-parenting has also been recognized. Traumatized children, in particular, need to learn essential aspects of limit-setting that have frequently been absent in the parenting styles that behaviorally disturbed children have experienced (Fahlberg, 1991). The most important element in ensuring that an intervention is effective with a traumatized child is to know the individual child, use an individualized intervention, and be in close enough proximity both physically and emotionally to understand how the child is experiencing the intervention.

The Purpose of Physical Interventions

From this discussion, physical interventions, when done properly, appear to receive the strongest support of all methods to effectively handle violence and to treat violent behavior in children. I have found this to be the case which is why our program holds this bias. To be effective and therapeutic, physical interventions must be done for the right reasons and in appropriate ways.

The purposes of physical interventions appear to be broken down into three areas. The first addresses managing the behavior and the last two address treating the child. First, physical interventions can contain the violence and reduce the length of the crisis (Bath, 1994), while providing protection from harm to the child and others, preventing serious destruction of property (Stirling & McHugh, 1998). Second, they can help the child experience limit-setting from a supportive parent figure, therefore having a re-parenting quality (Fahlberg, 1991). Third, they can provide cognitive restructuring of the meaning of physical touch and closeness in emotionally charged events, particularly for children who have experienced abuse in previous crisis situations.

Building a Response to Violent Behavior

Of the most common interventions to severe aggression and violent behavior, chemical restraint and mechanical restraint are most appropriately left to acute care settings. There is some consensus in the literature that both time-out spaces and physical interventions have their place in treatment settings. In families, using time-outs and using physical holds are the two available choices. Decisions concerning the least restrictive of these two interventions should be made on an individualized basis (Myers, Borchardt, Kowalski & Bubrick, 1998). Of these two approaches, physical interventions are more flexible and thus adaptable to the individual child and specific setting. Several factors are essential to the appropriate legal, ethical, and therapeutic use of physical interventions:

Safety must be ensured -- The intervention must be safe for all concerned, requiring nationally recognized interventions that are approved by a crisis prevention system. Staff and parents must be adequately trained with periodic refresher courses, and crisis episodes must be handled without emotional investment from the adult, who must guard against counteraggression or punitive energy. In treatment programs the episode should be discussed with peer staff, reviewed by a supervisor, and fully documented, and in a family the incident should be discussed with the family therapist/coach.

Internalization -- The teaching opportunity of any crisis is helping the child learn internal skills for self-control, anger management, verbal expression of frustration, internal impulse control and self-management. Any crisis intervention that leaves the child with the message that an adult must do the limit-setting and provide the controls further moves the child into a cycle of an external locus of control. The improper use of physical holding can make the situation worse. But in two studies, proper physical holding produced rapid gains in internal behavioral control (Miller, Walker & Friedman, 1989; Sourander, Aurela & Piha, 1997).

Individualized -- The intervention must fit the child and fit the situation. Prescriptive and one-size-fits-all interventions may be taught by some theoretical approaches, but unless the intervention is individualized, an important opportunity for the child to learn may be lost. It is also important that physical interventions make up only one small part of an overall therapeutic environment that supports, encourages, and teaches the child a repertoire of skills and behaviors leading to social success.

Therapeutically driven -- In families and particularly in treatment centers, all events in the child's life, particularly intensely emotional events, are opportunities for therapeutic gain. In many settings the purpose of crisis intervention techniques is to prevent emotionally-laden episodes; however, in treatment centers the goal is not to prevent opportunities to help teach the child, but to make maximum therapeutic use of all events in the child's life. The issue of liability exposure must be recognized but cannot take precedence over meeting the child's treatment needs. The purpose of treatment programs is not the limitation of liability; if so, difficult children would not be the target population. The purpose of treatment programs is to work with children who have not been successful in less restrictive settings. Returning a safer child to the community must be a top priority.

Effectiveness -- Individual interventions as well as general types of interventions must be evaluated to ensure that they work and produce the desired results.

Conclusion

Despite the many voices attempting to say that parents and treatment programs should not use physical means of controlling violent acting-out by children, these interventions remain the best methods according to the vast majority of intensive treatment providers (Barlow, 1989; Bath, 1994; Drisko, 1981; Rolider, et al., 1991; Sterling & McHugh, 1998; Sugar, 1994). Accrediting bodies, state regulatory agen- cies, and the American Academy of Pediatrics (Committee on Pediatric Emergency Medicine, 1997) maintain that physical interventions used to address extreme aggressive and violent behavior are not only sanctioned but essential in many situations. Dr. Howard Bath in his excellent 1994 article on this subject summed up the issue in a manner that is difficult to improve upon:

> Quite apart from the collateral benefit of
> containing a dangerous behavior (most often the
> protection of other children and adults and the

293

prevention of "contagion" effect), sensitive employ-
ment of physical restraint can effectively demonstrate limits for a child, provide a timely response
to a child's need for protection from his or her own
impulses, and prevent a child from receiving
reinforcing rewards for aggression. In contrast to
the use of seclusion, it achieves these ends in an
interactive and inclusive manner. Additional therapeutic benefits may be found in attachment-related
possibilities. A care worker with an understanding
of a child's temporal responses to confrontation
and the typical phases of temper tantrums will
allow and channel the expressions of anger and
rage and be alert to the opportunities that the
resolution affords for mutual bonding. Physical
restraint is not a management tool that should be
employed when less intrusive approaches will
suffice, but when used appropriately it can have
significant therapeutic benefits (Bath, 1994).

Chapter

12

Parenting As Spiritual Growth

If the title of this chapter does not make immediate sense to you then what is written here will probably not be of interest to you, and it may be a good idea for you to skip over this last chapter. However, if the title of this chapter drew your immediate attention, or if you read the contents and went first to this chapter, then the following is included here particularly for you.

Some of us are strongly motivated by a spiritual need that drives most of what we do, at least the things we can tell others. We look for meaning in all aspects of our lives. We ask the why question a lot. Why me? Why now? Why is this happening? I use the pronoun "we" because I am one of these types. Those who do not consider themselves driven by a spiritual need call it something else -- science, gratification, success, living in the now, living a good life, etc. However, these form spiritual needs in a generic sense. What we are driven by is at a core level our spiritual makeup, for wherever you store your treasure, there shall your heart be also.

How We Think

Even if you are interested in this topic, don't expect this chapter to make a great deal of sense to your linear mind. If you get to the end and you are exasperated with the circular logic and ambiguity, then it has probably been good for you. Of the famous quotes about the mind (this does not include Dan Quayle's "the mind is a terrible thing to lose"), I like Chang Tsu's observation that "the mind is a wonderful servant but a terrible master." Many spiritual teachers such as Lao Tsu, Swedenborg, and Krishnamurti have known this. Many eastern spiritual traditions are suspicious of the linear mind. For this reason, there are Zen koans and the Hindus have Yana Yoga, or using the mind to overcome the mind.

Our linear mind can help in many ways in our everyday lives, but it may, in fact, be a terrible master because it does not think "outside the box." In our culture the only place that thinking outside the box is really encouraged is in business, where this expression has come to really mean thinking of new ways to make money. We don't want students to think outside the box in our schools, which are often a political landscape where the "smart" students figure out what the instructor wants and are rewarded for giving it back on tests.

We don't reward thinking outside the boxes in mental health, or you may find yourself rewarded with an involuntary chat with a psychiatrist. We don't even encourage free thinking in our spiritual traditions in the western world, where free thinkers historically have received condemnation because of scandal or heresy. In fact, religion somehow became the epitome of developing the box we are to think within. And this despite the fact that the founder of Christianity tried for a full three years to challenge and confuse the linear minds of the lawyers and teachers of the dominant spiritual tradition of his time ("unless you become like little children...unless you eat my body...unless you are born again...the first shall be last and the last first").

To understand the deeper way that parenting a challenging child can build your spirit you must use more intuition than logic. You must go beyond what may make sense to your mind. You must look up at the mountain and see it from a completely different perspective. If you are able to do this, the whole game just may change and in a very positive direction for you, your child, and your family.

I am happy to tell all of my comrades who are reading this and who belong to the unofficial "Why Me Club" that by far the number one task that can bring meaning and purpose to your life is to be a parent. If you want to go farther, you can parent a special needs child. If this is not "taking up your cross," then what is? Parenting just happens to have absolutely all the ingredients of the perfect spiritual path. The following is not necessarily in any priority order.

Losing Yourself in Your Work of Service

Parenting is not about you, it is about the child. Parenting is about loving, giving, consuming yourself in the service of another. Parenting is about the ultimate "I Thou" journey. Parenting is about oneness, the goal of every spiritual tradition. Parenting is about working with your preferences or your selfish attachment (the Burger King approach to life -- wanting it your way). Parenting brings you face-to-face with your greatest joys and your biggest fears. Parenting demands that you learn more about yourself than you ever wanted to know, to look at parts of you that you would rather not see. Parenting can make you feel more, cry more, laugh more than any other aspect of your life ever will. In short, parenting is the best spiritual teacher you can ever find.

As with any spiritual journey, the teaching may be available but if the student isn't interested, all the effort, the pain and opportunities are missed. For those of you who resonate so far with these words, step number one is not to figure out how to be a better parent, it is to figure out how to be a better student of the teachings that are available through parenting. If you can become the student, you will not be able to avoid the teaching.

Other than death, there is nothing as grounding and as real as being a parent. Even love relationships we have all had are situations we can, and do, walk away from. Not that parents don't ever walk away from their children, but the heart and soul of a parent will trouble them from then on. Is there more I could have done? What was I lacking to make it work? What do I do with my love and commitment now? The fact is that once a loving, committed parent -- always a committed parent. The only other aspect of life that you just cannot run away from is death.

An Act of Love

We can almost universally say that parenting is solely an act of love. There is little to be gained in being a parent other than the spiritual gains of participating in the act of creation, bringing a new life into the world, passing on your family traditions, and giving back the life that you received. There are a couple complications, however, to calling all parenting an act of love. To some the unfortunate focus is on the act of sex, not the act of love or procreation. I find the method God chose to encourage and ensure procreation the ultimate irony. For a moment of bliss in intercourse and conception, there is a lifetime of challenge, struggle, and worry. There are other parents who have an image of what bringing a child into the world is going to be. I would wager that image does not include the 3 a.m. feeding. But with all things considered, parenting is an act of giving and an act of love.

Children often do not go easy on parents; you knew that already, didn't you! Children don't tone it down or lighten up on you. In fact, children often go right to where it counts, where you are most tender. The child often seems to have an uncanny ability to get you where it hurts, where other adults don't sense your vulnerability. Children can be more intuitive than adults, particularly if they want something from you. Intuitively being able to point out the deficiencies of the pupil is one sign of a good spiritual teacher.

As parents we feel compelled to take our roles seriously. We are the bottom line for our child. This is not like high school where we carried an egg around all day to feel some of the responsibility for a child, only to have the egg break in second period. In one moment our child's life can change horribly if we blow it. This is the real thing; this isn't practice for the big game. Parenting grabs our deepest desires and fears more than any other part of our lives. This is a great help for spiritual growth. Parenting immediately gets our undivided attention, which is essential to being a good student. So the teachings are there, our attention is there, and we realize that this is perhaps the most important responsibility of our lives. So now what is it we need to learn?

We can start with learning unconditional love. I know this is like jumping into the deep end of the pool to learn to swim, but parenting is a big step. I remember a cool rainy morning on November 3rd, 1982, the first day I became a foster parent. I had been a counselor for over ten years already, but nothing prepared me for that day. It wasn't anything like I expected it to be, which was my first lesson. Parenting is hardly ever what we think it will be. My life has never been the same following that day, as I have played a parent role for several hundred foster children in our home. I got up this morning to get my kids up and off to school, and this morning was not what I expected. When this happens as a parent, what do I do? Get anxious, angry, become controlling, get depressed?

Learning About Ourselves

Parenting tells us about who we are and how we handle the most challenging aspects of our lives -- important things that do not go the way we want them to go. The good spiritual student studies himself or herself. You have to be oblivious not to learn about yourself as a parent. You are not an idiot, you would never invite a friend or partner into your life who would turn everything upside down like a child will. Most of us (I hope) do not look for a partner who thinks only of himself/herself and is mostly interested in taking and not giving, like a child does for years. So here are the opportunities that you would never wish on anyone, much less yourself, and now it is time to watch how you manage them.

Parenting is a little like evaluating candidates for the presidency. I have trouble voting for anyone who would want to be president of the United States. Being a candidate tells me right away that the person must be a little crazy. All parents are a little crazy for taking on the challenge of their life. Part of my job at times is to give my support to parents who ask to foster or adopt a special needs child. There are many reasons not to do this -- fill holes in your life, turn the child around, become important to someone, feel needed, or strengthen your marriage. One of the best reasons to do this is to start a spiritual journey of discovery unlike any other journey of your life. But any good spiritual journey will result in the person who ends the journey not being the same person who started. Only adults who want to lose themselves need apply to be a parent.

Give Until It Hurts

There is a tricky aspect to any spiritual journey: you go because ultimately you want something, but spiritual development is about giving not getting. For example, the not so secret key to a happy life is to love and give of yourself to as many people as you can. Joy, happiness, fulfillment, peace, purpose, meaning and all the other things we all want only really come to us if we give, not receive. The same paradox can be true for parenting. Parenting has little to offer the self-absorbed. A child doesn't start out returning caring and some would say that most children take much longer than expected to return a fraction of what they receive.

Parenting has within it the seeds of the most fulfilling aspects of living. Most parents will say that their children are high on the list of their most important and significant contributions to the planet. What is it that gives back such a lofty reward? Selfless giving is the answer. There is no human activity to compare with selfless giving. There is no kind of receiving that even compares on the Richter Scale, other than receiving love which requires giving as well.

Have you noticed that stories of people blessed with receiving the most our materialistic society has to offer seldom have happy endings? Why do people take a chance with their money on the lottery when they find out what it does to the lives of the few who ever win? Why are there always aspiring actors and actresses who want to be stars and be famous and then spend the majority of their stardom trying to escape the attention they once craved? Why do we have so many presidential candidates ready to face the grueling gauntlet of a national campaign when the prize is the end of a private life as they know it forever? No, we have a society that maintains its focus on receiving despite the overwhelming evidence that giving, not getting, is the key to life, liberty and the pursuit of happiness.

I am reminded of the ten-year-old boy who one holiday season said to me, "Dave, I know you want me to understand that giving is better than receiving. But you also have taught me to be truthful, so I need to tell the truth and let you know that this Christmas I am mostly interested in receiving." This is the motto of our society, although seldomly stated with as much honesty as with this young boy.

In the face of a culture that maintains that you have inalienable rights that are mostly about receiving, there is one very popular activity that does not seem to be losing any of its appeal, and that is being a parent. However, the appeal of being a parent is all about giving and going against the cultural myth of getting yours, and going for the gusto. The only reasonable answer to why parenting is still popular is that deep within us, unrecognized by many, is the need to give. To those who consciously understand this can go the greatest rewards. Which brings us back full circle to the spiritual paradox of parenting: we receive most when we give most.

Now we must turn this discussion into parenting children who "could give a rip." If you find yourself in this role unexpectedly or even if you (gasp) chose to parent a difficult child, you have two fundamental choices. First, you can try your best, give until it hurts, continue to care no matter what, and let the results of your efforts drive you raving mad. Or second, you can try your best, give until it hurts, continue to care no matter what, and let the results feed your spiritual heart. Doesn't sound much different, doesn't look much different, doesn't always feel much different, but your state of mind makes all the difference.

Have It Your Way

Siddhartha Gautama (also known as the Buddha) said 2,600 years ago that the cause of all suffering is that we are attached to things going the way we wish them to in life. At least in our culture it appears that we have not been listening because we have made an art out of Frank Sinatra's anthem "I Did It My Way." From the evidence, it does appear that Frank did much of it "his way," but the problem is that few would place him on the list of America's most fulfilled role models of finding meaning and purpose, despite receiving everything this materialistic society had to give.

Parenting is perhaps the greatest challenge in life to do your best, and then you have to live with the results (your child) usually for the rest of your life. We all want a great deal for our children and from our children. However, children seldom want the same things for themselves as we want for them. As parents we seldom get it our way, so we can be miserable or use the opportunity for our own spiritual growth.

Unconditional Love

It is easy to say "use your struggles in parenting as spiritual growth," but what specifically does that mean? Another spiritual teacher 2,000 years ago from Nazareth broke it down to one word: there is faith, hope and love, but the greatest of these is <u>love</u>. Unconditional love, to be specific. To love without conditions, can anyone do that? To love someone and not even expect to be loved in return? To give love and receive deceit and disrespect in return? Yes, this is the steep path of the spiritual journey that is difficult and few travel it. But for that which other spiritual seekers look their entire life (to learn the lessons of unconditional love), parents have their own private spiritual teacher down the hall and to the right. Yes, in the room that has that strange odor coming from within.

The shift in perspective from "what do I get out of this" to "what more can I give" is what has made simple humans bigger than life -- Albert Switzer, Tom Dooley, and Mother Theresa. It is just this shift in perspective that can change your parenting from a living hell to being on the path to heaven. But remember, the externals do not look much different. You cannot cheat and secretly just want to receive even if it is spiritual growth. This is just another form of materialism -- spiritual materialism. You must give and continue to give, but the joy comes not from what you accomplish (what you get), the joy comes from the giving. So you do not have to go to India, join an esoteric belief system or perform rigorous daily rituals; you just have to parent your child in as conscious a way as you can.

OK, I really don't want you to read this and just end up confused, so you can turn on your linear mind again and consider some examples of turning parenting into spiritual growth.

You have already figured out that unconditional love seems to be a concept first developed by a parent struggling with wayward children (perhaps this is a good analogy with God the father and all us difficult children which started in the Garden of Eden). It is not hard to make unconditional love specific and make sense, but it is entirely another thing to actually love unconditionally. Every time you write a personal letter (now, tell the truth) don't you want to hear back from that person? Every time we give a Christmas gift, doesn't it occur to you to prepare to get one back or at least get a thanks?

It seems that only in parenting is there the given expectation that you will always give a great deal more than you will receive back, at least in tangible terms. That is what parenting is all about. We make some sense of this by saying that our parents did it for us, so we can do it for our children. With more than a little satisfaction, we get a chance as grandparents to watch our children struggle with their own perpetrator of the "terrible twos," which just happens to be a phase many children are in until age 22.

The challenge with practicing unconditional love is not to understand the concept or whether you agree that it is something you believe in; the challenge is to remember at the time that here is a situation in which I can unconditionally love. So the key is to find ways to continually remember to practice loving as unconditionally as possible. This is one definition of spiritual practice or religious observances and activities.

Parenting and Faith

It turns out that basically all of the central aspects of spiritual development of the major belief systems of the world can be found in parenting. Along with loving which has been mentioned, there are also faith and hope. Some spiritual systems view faith as less of a virtue than a gift from God. In a sense, faith is a share in the divine understanding of how everything fits together, and therefore a realization that the difficulties of life are not random but play a part in an overall plan.

Faith fits quite nicely with parenting a challenging child. Parents spend days and nights wondering if the hard work, the frustrations and the disappointments are anything but punishment. Faith is not logical but it can fill your spirit with a deep sense of meaning. There is a very good reason to get up each morning and keep trying, giving and struggling with the world's most challenging job. Faith is often viewed as a gift because you cannot think your way into faith; you feel faith deep within yourself. In a sense, it is either in there or it isn't. Some people seem to have this inner feeling and some do not; it is hard to understand the difference, so it is often seen as a gift of God. For the parent of a difficult child, faith is a precious gift.

Hope Springs Eternal

Hope also fits very well with parenting. Somewhat different than faith, hope is more participatory. It requires ongoing effort by the person to nourish it. Hope can be described as an abiding sense of the possibilities in all situations. We "hope against hope" when our logical mind says that a positive outcome appears very unlikely. Hope helps us to not give up on either ourselves, others, or the daunting task before us. Hope can change our energy from static (why bother any more) to dynamic (there is always a chance). Hope is at its core a positive outlook, a refusal to succumb to a negative outcome that appears inevitable, and therefore a situation that appears to be hopeless. Hope is a virtue because it comes from within ourselves and allows us to do what we would otherwise not be able to motivate ourselves to continue to do. Sounds like a good amount of hope could be useful in parenting a challenging child, doesn't it?

There is a story told of the very old man who spent an entire day in the heat digging a hole, amending the soil, planting and watering a tree that would take ten to fifteen years to mature and bear edible fruit. When asked why he would labor so hard for an outcome that he would never see or benefit from, he said that some old man must have done the same for him many years ago and now it was his turn. This story, which is meant to impart a spiritual message, has a very direct application to parenting. I often tell parents to look at their difficult work as a process of planting seeds, some of which may sprout and some not. You may not be around for the fruit of the harvest but it is very important that the seeds are planted. As a parent you are the old man; someone did plant seeds in your spiritual garden, they labored to give of themselves to you without any assurance that they would see any return themselves. And now it is your turn.

Peace in the Midst of Conflict

Some spiritual principles need little comment in how they fit parenting -- patience, forbearance, forgiveness, tolerance, and self-sacrifice. It is not hard to plug these qualities into a day's work with a child who is angry at the world when he gets up in the morning, and whose mood gets worse throughout the day.

There is another spiritual principle that seems important to cover in this discussion. It has many names depending on various spiritual traditions. It has been called the Atman, Nirvana, Equanimity, the Tao and the Peace of Christ. More or less each of these concepts points to a state of mind that infuses a massive amount of wisdom and understanding into what is often a perplexing and perhaps overwhelming situation, and produces an inner calm and a sense of certitude that cannot always be explained in words. This state of mind is the goal of Buddhist meditation, of living in the Tao, of monastic contemplation; and it provides the missing link in life that hints at how it possibly all makes sense at a deeper level than we normally see or experience. But it is important to point out that unlike cartoon images of navel gazing or the bearded sage in the lotus position on the top of the mountain, this attainment can only come from a head-on collision with the world and all its most difficult aspects (lessons).

You cannot talk about Nirvana without talking about facing all the pleasures and pains of living, facing them directly and finding a place that goes beyond them while still surrounded by them. Remember the rich young man in the New Testament who said to Jesus, "I follow the command-ments, what more must I do to be perfect?" Jesus said, "Go sell all you have, give the money to the poor and come follow me." We are told that he went away sad because he was a man of much wealth. You cannot talk about the Peace of Christ without remembering that there was a cross prominent in the picture. I say this quite sincerely; can you imagine at the end of your demanding day with your child taking her insults, her misbehavior, her disrespect and saying, "Forgive her, Father, for she knows not what she is doing." If you can get to this place, you are on the spiritual path of parenting that can shift the experience from one of suffering and feeling hopeless to one of the most direct routes to spiritual growth and understanding.

As the Bible says, "The path is steep and narrow and few travel it," but it is there nonetheless. The spiritual path of parenting is the only guaranteed winning scenario despite the outcome or results of your efforts. If you travel this route, you are in an excellent position to expand your journey not only to parenting but to every aspect of your life. And all this because you have a challenging child at home. What a deal! Can you see how the whole game changes based on how you approach it?

Happy parenting, and I hope your journey is filled with much challenge and a deep sense of peace!

Appendices

The following three instruments are offered here for use with children and adolescents with sexual behavior problems and attachment difficulties.

The Inappropriate Sexual Behavior Scale was developed to be a practical, not theoretical, tool to assess the sexual behavior of children. It provides a basis to determine the severity of behavior both in pathology and in legal reportability to child protective services. You are free to copy and use this instrument. It has been used for thirteen years with hundreds of children. However it is not offered as a normed or psychometrically tested tool and as such, should be used with caution and not used as the primary reason to make decisions concerning a child.

The Juvenile Sex Offender Risk Assessment Matrix is similar to the ISBS above and the two instruments are complementary. The JSO-RAM is designed to be a practical tool to consider the likelihood of future sexual offending behavior. As with the ISBS, this instrument has been used for more than a decade. However, it is not normed or psychometrically tested and should not be the sole criteria for assessing the dangerousness of a child or used as the primary reason for making decisions. The instrument can be copied and used as it may be helpful.

The Attachment Disorder Assessment Scale is an instrument that was developed a decade ago and has been used to assess the severity of attachment problems in children under twelve. Research on the instrument is ongoing.

Inappropriate Sexual Behavior Scale

Dave Ziegler, Ph.D.

Abstract

In the early 1980s, there was a startling realization that children are often sexually victimized by other children. With this understanding has come a serious confusion as to what constitutes normative sexual expression and what is sexual exploitation. This article discusses the two stances that have been prevalent: 1) discourage or ignore sexual behavior in children and hope that it goes away, or 2) persistent sexual behavior, particularly with other children, is either pathological or a definitive sign of emerging pathology. The disparity and myopic nature of both positions makes them unacceptable. How do we then take a more balanced and accurate view of childhood sexual expression, given our new sensitivity to children exhibiting sexually offending behavior? The Inappropriate Sexual Behavior Scale is presented as a tool to take into consideration normative sexual themes and behavior in children and the possibility of developing sexual pathology.

The Discovery that Children are Sexual Beings

Historically, it is difficult to determine just when the realization occurred that children, as well as adults, are sexual creatures with all the resulting ramifications. From a sociological perspective, it is clear that what our culture still considers part of childhood (11 to 18 years of age) in many cultures would have already undergone the rite of passage to adulthood. With this passage comes the responsibilities and privileges associated with adulthood -- work, conscription into the army, leaving home, taking a partner, and freedom to be sexually active. Presently, in third-world nations, large percentages of their armed forces are younger than the legal age to view R-rated movies in the United States. It is ironic to the point of absurdity what children in our culture are exposed to, concerning sexuality and the restrictions we place on their response to this exposure. Television, movies, magazines, and even comic books frequently depict mild-to-strong sexual themes such as nudity, sexual suggestiveness, sexual behavior, and sexualized dominance and violence. Yet, about the only culturally agreed upon sexual behavior of children is to ask a biology question or two. When it comes to sexuality, the disparity between the physical or hormonal clock and the cultural clock exacerbates the difficulty.

But, even with younger children under eleven, the presence of sexual themes and issues was given credible scrutiny by Freud. In theory at least, all human beings have sexual feelings, drives and motivations including children.

Pushing Sex Underground

With an emerging complex society, the age of maturation has been driven higher and higher. For adults over fifty, it was not unusual that children of twelve contributed to the family income in the 1940s and 1950s. Child labor laws and other mechanistic changes have pushed children out of the work force and further from the rites of passage to adulthood. The puritan answer to young people ready to experience sexual expression, but considered by the culture as too young, was a rigid good-and-evil construct. Sexual behavior, and even sexual thoughts, were wrong and punishable by possible insanity here and eternal damnation in the hereafter; while abstinence was virtue with rewards one-hundred-fold -- later on. This state of affairs has produced a cultural protocol to punish sexual behavior and to ignore sexuality in children with the hope that it will somehow go away.

While the prevailing strategy is still to pretend that children are not sexual beings, the inescapable fact is that the average first-grader witnesses more sexual behavior in a year of viewing prime-time television than Sigmund Freud dealt with in his career. The most that can be said about our culture's position on sexuality is that we know it isn't working -- teenage pregnancies and adolescent sexual offenders are two of the many indicators of this.

Our Eyes are Opened to Sexual Abuse

Twenty years ago, few professionals questioned the presence of sexual abuse among children and as a 1975 psychiatric text stated, it could be found in one in every million homes [1]. In the last twenty years, we have come to realize that sexual abuse may be in one in every four-to-ten homes. A more recent realization is that sexual abuse is often perpetrated by another child. Children's sex games are no longer viewed with attitudes like "boys will be boys" or "they are only kids." In the state of Oregon during 1985, over 1,000 arrests of children under the age of 18 were made for sexual offenses. A surprise finding was that the majority of children arrested for sex crimes were under the age of 14 [2].

The national media have helped our society understand the prevalence of sexual abuse. Stories abound of the school teachers, police officers and ministers who have lived a secret life of harming children. It is now clear that, for incarcerated pedophiles, their disturbance began to manifest in their early teens. "Sex play" can no longer be ignored or merely punished and pushed underground. It must be exposed, understood, and responded to effectively.

But, in our new awareness of sexual pathology, the pendulum has swung to the dark side. In the last three years, sexual expression by children is being treated and referred to by many professionals as pathological or pre-pathological. Certainly our culture has learned that children are sexual beings and will present sexual themes and behaviors which are normative by definition and not signs of disturbance. Understanding sexual expression has now become extremely difficult.

The Inappropriate Sexual Behavior Scale

The challenge that faces us is to sift through the complex continuum of normative behavior to sexually exploitive abuse. The following Scale is a tool to help with the analysis of childhood sexual expression:

Sexualized Expression	Cooperative Sexualized Expression	Emotional Abuse of a Sexual Nature	Emotionally Coercive Sexual Abuse	Physically Coercive Sexual Abuse
Sex writing Sex drawing "Dirty" talk Masturbation Childish sex calls	Mutually consenting sex games Curious/ exploration	Exhibitionism Voyeurism Obscene calls Frottage	Premeditated genital contact with narcissism Manipulation Thinking errors	Forcible demeaning and/or brutal sexual contact

Not all behaviors in the first two categories are necessarily inappropriate in themselves. However, it is a given for the Scale that the mentioned behaviors have become problematic in a specific setting. The Scale allows any inappropriate sexual behavior to appear somewhere on the point scale. The higher the point scale, the more serious the behavior and the greater the potential or presence of pathology. Point scores of 3.5 and higher indicate issues best treated in the context of a specific sex offender program (3.5 would indicate behaviors in this category that are frequent or habitual). Scores above 3.0 are reportable to police agencies as delinquent sexual behavior. Scores above 4.0 are reportable to the proper authorities as sexual abuse.

Attitudes and Behaviors

As with all problematic behavior, inappropriate sexual behavior in children needs attention. The type of attention depends upon the facts of the incident. The who, what, when and why of the situation must be carefully considered. It is critical to identify the early signs of a developing sexual disorder, particularly potential sexually offending attitudes and behaviors. The population of sexually abused children is a significant group to watch.

Although the Inappropriate Sexual Behavior Scale can be a useful tool in understanding a specific sexual incident or pattern of incidents, it is not in itself a predictor of future sexual behavior. However, the earlier sexual pathology is identified, the better the chance of successful treatment. Of equal importance is not attempting to "desexualize" children. To respond in punitive or even corrective interventions to normative sexual themes and behaviors gives an unhealthy message to children about sex; particularly those with moderate-to-severe distortions to begin with (resulting from abuse). Treating sexual abuse victims requires identification and treatment of pathology, as well as an environment with sensitivity and understanding of normative sexual expression. Controlling behavior is not a sufficient long-term justification for further distortions of the healthy role of sexuality in growing up. In treating sexually abused children, great care must be taken to resocialize healthy viewpoints while avoiding new, however subtle, distorted messages concerning sexuality.

References

[1] Kohn, A. (1987). Shattered innocence. *Psychology Today*.

[2] Avalon Associates (1986). *The Oregon Report on Juvenile Sexual Offenders*. Salem, OR: Department of Human Resources.

O'Brien, M., & Bera, W. (1996). Adolescent sexual offenders: A descriptive typology. *Preventing Sexual Abuse, Fall*.

Wenet, G.A., & Clark, T.F. *Juvenile Sexual Offender Decision Criteria*. University of Washington.

Ziegler, D.L. (1987). *Childhood Sexual Behavior In Residential Care*. Jasper OR: SCAR/Jasper Mountain.

Juvenile Sex Offender Risk Assessment Matrix (JSO-RAM)

Dave Ziegler, Ph.D.

The following matrix is designed to take into consideration a variety of known dimensions of offending behavior and their antecedents. It is composed of four parts:

1. History
2. Environment
3. Personality
4. Clinical Assessment

This matrix has been developed to require minimum technical knowledge or training in offender treatment on the part of the evaluator. When fairly specific factors are considered a score is determined which, after following the formula, will result in a Matrix Score and can then be evaluated by the Matrix Scale to determine first the risk and second the suggested treatment response.

Part I

Sexual History/Environment/Personality

Of the many factors that go into predictability of future inappropriate sexual behavior, there are three major categories:

♦   History of sexual behavior

♦   Environmental characteristics

♦   Intra-psychic or personality traits

Each of these areas have a number of significant factors that assist in an overall evaluation.

Category Factors and Attached Weight

PAST SEXUAL BEHAVIOR -- Of the many factors that lead to the risk of future sexual offenses, the most important is past behavior. Even with a strong environmental predisposition and a personality that is similar to a sex offender, some individuals still do not become offenders. However, once this line is crossed the odds are very high it will be crossed again. For this reason, past behavior is the single best indication of future behavior and in this matrix, holds the highest weight. The significant past behaviors are those sexual in nature. To assist in the assessment of these behaviors this Matrix uses the Inappropriate Sexual Behavior Scale.

ENVIRONMENTAL CHARACTERISTICS -- The background, socialization, stress level of the family of origin and present living arrangement all influence risk of offense.

INTRA-PSYCHIC AND PERSONALITY TRAITS -- The predisposition to offend is the beginning of the molestation paradigm. Does the juvenile fit the traits often found in offenders?

To best understand the categories within the scale, it is important to understand that each has corresponding behaviors and attitudes. The same behavior can have a completely different quality depending upon the attitude behind it. In the following list, the behaviors and attitudes are neither all-inclusive nor will all attitudinal states necessarily be present:

Category	Attitudes	Behaviors
1 *Sexualized expression*	Unsophisticated Curious Naive Spontaneous Explorative Fascinated Scared/excited	Masturbation Sexual graffiti Sexual notes Sexual "dirty talk" Sexual phone calls Looking at underwear **ads** Staring at body parts
2 *Cooperative Sexualized expression*	Impulsive Inquisitive Opportunistic Curious Mutuality Secretive Consenting Experimentation	Sex games Mutual touching Visual exploration Observing eliminations Sexual mimicry of adults Generalized sex play
3 *Emotional abuse of a sexual nature*	Anxious Fixated Lacking self-control Obsessive Preoccupied Prurient interest Premeditation Isolation	Exhibitionism Frottage Voyeurism Sexual harassment Fetish theft Obscene phone calls
4 *Emotionally coercive sexual abuse*	Narcissism Premeditation Manipulation/trickery Lacks remorse Thinking errors	Genital contact that is: Chronic/progressive Progressively intrusive Threatening words or acts Exploitative Multiple victims
5 *Physically coercive sexual abuse*	Antisocial Domination Generalized anger Character disorder Poor impulse control Psycho-social dysfunction	Genital contact that is: Aggressive Demeaning/humiliating Violent Use of weapon Causing injury Non-sexual serious antisocial behavior

Use the following procedure to arrive at scores to be inserted into the JSO RAM Score Sheet:

Factors	Points	Score
#1 Behaviors	3 (x 2 for a repeated pattern)	
#2 Behaviors	5 (x 2 for a repeated pattern)	
#3 Behaviors (one or more)	20	
#4 Behaviors (one or more)	40	
#5 Behaviors (one or more)	60	

Environmental Factors		Score
Victimization	10	
Offender Modeling	8	
General Family Dysfunction	5	
Exterior Controls Lacking	5	
Inadequate Sexual Socialization	3	
Economic Environmental Stress	2	

Intra-Psychic or Personality Factors		Score
Narcissism	10	
Substance Abuse	5	
Manipulative	5	
High Sexual Arousal and/or Sexual Fixations	5	
Defensive	4	
Low Intellectual Functioning or Low Self-control	4	

Deterrence Points

There is an allowance for the interest and ability of the individual to overcome problematic behavior and for the positive influence of the environment (assisting in internal and external inhibitors to molestation - Finkelhor).

Successful Treatment	-10	
Willingness for Treatment	-5	
Strong Supportive Family	-10	
Intensive Supervision	-10	
Deterrence points are subtracted from the RAM score		
Total Sexual History/Environment/Personality Score **(for Part I on Matrix Score Sheet)**		

Part II

Clinical Assessment JSO-RAM

In the past, the closest assessment of risk has had to come from the best clinical judgment of the professional. While this had been found inadequate, given the new information and research on juvenile sex offenders, research has nonetheless shown that clinical judgment has in fact shown some predictive validity. Clinical judgment was shown to be a poor predictor of further sex offenses (Smith & Monastersky) but no juveniles, who were rated as low-risk, subsequently offended. This points to the fact that clinical judgment correctly identified the factors of high risk, but tended toward false positives (overstate potential of future incidents). Therefore, the following questions can be an important supplement to Part I and Part II. To be of maximum use, it is important that a therapist, caseworker or probation officer have previous experience with juvenile sex offenders and have sufficient contact with the juvenile to be able to answer the questions. Your best clinical judgment is the goal.

			Score
1. Is this juvenile's personality like or unlike that of other young sex offenders with whom you have worked? [ ] like [ ] unlike			
2. Is this juvenile's family environment like or unlike that of other young sex offenders with whom you have worked? [ ] like [ ] unlike			
3. Is this juvenile's sexual interest like or unlike that of other young sex offenders with whom you have worked? [ ] like [ ] unlike			
4. Check the character traits or attitudes in the following list that fit this juvenile:			
A	[ ] *Anxious* [ ] *Fixated* [ ] *Lacks Self Control* [ ] *Obsessive*	[ ] *Single-minded* [ ] *Preoccupied* [ ] *Prurient Interest* [ ] *Loner*	
B	[ ] *Narcissism* [ ] *Lacks Remorse* [ ] *Antisocial* [ ] *Character Disorder* [ ] *Psycho-Social Dysfunction*	[ ] *Manipulation/trickery* [ ] *Thinking Errors* [ ] *Poor Impulse Control* [ ] *Domination of Others*	
5. In your overall clinical judgment, does this juvenile pose a [ ] low [ ] moderate [ ] high risk of future sexual offenses?			
Total Clinical Assessment Score (for Part II on Matrix Score Sheet)			

Scoring: For questions 1, 2 and 3 : [X] like -- counts 5
For question 4: A checks count 1
and B checks count 2
For question 5: Low counts 5,
Moderate counts 10 and
High counts 15.

JSO/RAM Matrix Score Sheet

1	#1 Behaviors	3 points	___	
	#1 Behaviors (existing pattern, above x2)	6 points	___	
	#2 Behaviors	5 points	___	
Past Sexual Behavior	#2 Behaviors (existing pattern, above x2)	10 points	___	Total
(Inappropriate Sexual	#3 Behaviors	20 points	___	#1
Behavior Scale)	#4 Behaviors	40 points	___	
	#5 Behaviors	60 points	___	___
2	Victimization	10 points	___	
	Modeling	8 points	___	
	Family Dysfunction	5 points	___	
Environmental	Exterior Control	5 points	___	Total
Factors	Inadequate Socialization	3 points	___	#2
	Low Income (financial stress)	3 points	___	___
3	Narcissism	10 points	___	
	Substance Abuse	5 points	___	
	Manipulation	5 points	___	
Intra-Psychic/	Arousal/Fixation	5 points	___	Total
Personality	Defensive	4 points	___	#3
	Low Intelligence/Low Self-control	4 points	___	___
	Successful Treatment	-10 points	___	
Deterrence Points	Willingness for Treatment	-5 points	___	
(to be subtracted	Strong Supportive Family	-10 points	___	Total ___
from score)	Intensive Supervision	-10 points	___	

Total RAM Score (without optional Part II)	
Clinical Assessment (optional) **Total Clinical Assessment Score from Part II**	Total ___
Total RAM Score (with optional Part II)	

Score Analysis

Overall score analysis will depend upon whether Part II and/or Part III have been included:

Without Part II		
Under 30	Low Risk	
Under 50	Minimal Risk	Psychological Treatment Recommended
50 - 60	Moderate Risk	Psychological Treatment Required
61 - 70	High Risk	Specific Sex Offender Treatment Required
71 - 80	Very High Risk	Specific Sex Offender Treatment in Residential Setting
81 - 90 +	Extreme Risk	Residential Sex Offender Treatment with Maximum Supervision/Security
With Part II		
Under 40	Low Risk	
Under 70	Minimal Risk	Psychological Treatment Recommended
70 - 85	Moderate Risk	Psychological Treatment Required
86 - 100	High Risk	Specific Sex Offender Treatment in Residential Setting
101 - 130 +	Extreme Risk	Residential Sex Offender Treatment with Maximum Supervision/Security

[Note: The above treatment suggestions are to be read as guidelines; many other factors will be involved in the optimum treatment plan for any specific child. In the higher risk areas, it is important that any borderline situations be deemed a higher risk category rather than lower risk.]

References

- Avalon Associates. (1986). *The Oregon Report on Juvenile Sexual Offenders.* Salem, OR: Department of Human Resources.
- Burgess, A.W., Groth, A.N., Holmstrom, L.L., & Shroi, S.M. (1978). *Sexual Assault of Children and Adolescents.* Lexington, MA: Lexington Books.
- Di Leo, J.H. (1973). *Children's Drawings as Diagnostic Aids.* New York: Brunner/Mazel.
- Finkelhor, David (1984). *Child Sexual Abuse, New Theories & Research.* New York: Free Press.
- Groth, A.N., Longo, R.E., & McFaddin, J.B. (1982). Undetected recidivism among rapists and child molesters. *Crime and Delinquency, 28,* 450-458.
- Groth, A.N., Hobson, W.F., Lucey, K.P., & Pierre, J.S. (1981). Juvenile sexual offenders: Guidelines for treatment. *International Journal of Offender Therapy and Comparative Criminology, 25,* 264-272.
- Johnston, F.A., & Johnston, S.A. (1986). Differences between human figure drawings of child molesters and control groups, *Journal of Clinical Psychology, 42,* 638-647.
- Longo, R.E. (1982). Sexual learning and experience among adolescent sexual offenders. *International Journal of Offender Therapy and Comparative Criminology, 26,* 234-241.

- O'Brien, M., & Bera, W. (1986). Adolescent sexual offenders: A descriptive typology. *Preventing Sexual Abuse, 1 (3),* 1-4.
- Smith, W., & Monastersky, K. (1985). Sex offender reoffending. *Criminal Justice and Behavior,* 115-139.
- Wysocki, A., & Wysocki, B. (1977). Human figure drawings of sex offenders. *Journal of Clinical Psychology, 33,* 278-284.
- Wenet, G.A., & Clark, T.F. *Juvenile Sexual Offender Decision Criteria.* University of Washington.
- Ziegler, D.L. (1987). Inappropriate Sexual Behavior Scale [monograph]. The Assessment and Treatment of Sexual Abusers Conference, Association for the Behavioral Treatment of Sexual Abusers.

ATTACHMENT DISORDER ASSESSMENT SCALE

Introduction

With increasing frequency, children are showing up in our schools, treatment programs, foster homes and caseloads with an inability to connect or bond with others. The causes for this are complex, as is the extent of the increase, both in numbers and severity, of children with attachment problems.

Although attachment problems have been recognized for some time, there is a new emphasis on early diagnosis and treatment to maximize the potential of successful intervention. As with any disorder that becomes more prevalent, not all children that may fit some of the symptoms have an attachment disorder.

Directions

Although anyone familiar with the child could complete the scale, it is highly recommended that the child's full-time caretaker -- parent, grandparent, adoptive parent, foster parent, or kinship caretaker (aunt or uncle, etc.) -- answer the following three-part ADA Scale. Read each of the statements and circle the number that *BEST* describes the child's development history, and how often the child demonstrates a trait or interaction. It is important to answer all questions since items will help determine the presence or absence of specific traits.

A-16

Section One -- *Developmental History*

The child has encountered a significant disruption in the natural bonding process in the first twelve to eighteen months of life. This may involve some form of child abuse.

SCORE: **0 - FALSE**   **1 - UNKNOWN**   **2 - TRUE**

0 1 2 (1) The child received inadequate prenatal care.

0 1 2 (2) The mother had a history of substance abuse (drugs, alcohol, nicotine, caffeine) during the pregnancy.

0 1 2 (3) The mother was raised in an abusive environment.

0 1 2 (4) The mother was seventeen or younger at childbirth.

0 1 2 (5) The mother had a poor personal support system during pregnancy.

0 1 2 (6) The child was premature at birth (at least 3 weeks).

0 1 2 (7) The child was colicky for physical or emotional reasons or other significant medical issue.

0 1 2 (8) The child was physically separated from the mother for more than two consecutive weeks on one or more occasions during the first twelve months.

0 1 2 (9) The mother abused drugs or alcohol following pregnancy.

0 1 2 (10) The child was physically and/or sexually abused during the first two years.

0 1 2(11)   The child was moderately to severely
                neglected during the first two years.

Section Two - *Quality of Relationships*

The child produces overall pain, discouragement and heartache in his/her care providers.

SCORE:

0 - Infrequently   **1 - Occasionally**   **2 - Frequently**

(less than 10% of the time)   (about 25% of the time)   (50% or more)

0 1 2 (1)   I do not feel like I really know this child
                as a person.
0 1 2 (2)   I and/or members of my family are
                afraid of this child.
0 1 2 (3)   This child does not seem to understand
                the meaning of remorse or giving a
                sincere apology.
0 1 2 (4)   I do not feel like I have a significant
                connection with this child.
0 1 2 (5)   Despite his/her background, this child
                should respond with more genuine
                feeling than he/she does.
0 1 2 (6)   I wonder if this child really cares for me
                or anyone in my family.
0 1 2 (7)   Sometimes this child makes me feel like
                there is something wrong with me,
                when there is not.
0 1 2 (8)   I have trouble explaining to others what
                this child is really like.
0 1 2 (9)   This child cannot/will not accept my
                affection and love.

0 1 2 (10) No matter how much time I spend with this child I do not believe I have or can get any closer emotionally.

Section Three - *Personality Traits*

Children with attachment problems often have a number of personality traits that interfere with establishing and maintaining meaningful relationships with others.

SCORE:

0 - Infrequently   **1 - Occasionally**   **2 - Frequently**
(less than 10% of the Time)   (about 25% of the time)   (50% or more)

0 1 2 (1) This child manipulates to get his/her way.

0 1 2 (2) This child attempts to be in control over everything.

0 1 2 (3) This child is phony, shallow and has a blockage in his/her ability to form a deep relationship.

0 1 2 (4) This child possesses a serious lack of empathy for others.

0 1 2 (5) This child has self-destructive behaviors (behaviors attempting self-harm).

0 1 2 (6) This child has a lack of internalized moral reasoning and a lack of conscience.

0 1 2 (7) He/she does not accept responsibility for mistakes.

0 1 2 (8) He/she does not give genuine hugs or receive affection from others.

0 1 2 (9) He/she lies frequently and sometimes for no apparent reason.

0 1 2 (10) This child hurts or is cruel to animals.

0 1 2 (11) This child steals or takes what does not belong to him/her.

0 1 2 (12) He/she makes excessive demands and is anxious and angry or clingy when demands are not met.

0 1 2 (13) This child attacks peers and/or threatens adults.

0 1 2 (14) This child is bossy and often bullies other children.

0 1 2 (15) This child responds to a friendly overture with avoidance or isolating behavior.

0 1 2 (16) He/she does not do what they are told to do.

0 1 2 (17) He/she tends to be self-centered.

0 1 2 (18) This child has a habit of withdrawing both physically and emotionally, and has trouble with making eye contact with others.

0 1 2 (19) He/she has problems with developing friendships with peers.

Factors To Rule Out

Before scoring the ADA Scale, it is important to consider whether there are factors other than a psychological disorder causing the attachment or bonding problems. Each child should be screened by a professional on each of the following:

1. *Medical* - Has the child been evaluated by a physician to determine if there are any medical reasons that may be a factor in being distant from others? If medical issues exist they must be considered in the determination of an

attachment disorder. Step to be taken: obtain a physical exam.

2. *Active Child Abuse* - Has the question been asked if the child is currently being abused by someone in their environment? Step to be taken: ask the child if they are safe or have recently been abused and critically look at the child's environment.

3. *Environmental Pathology* - Has the child in the present, or in the recent past, been in a seriously dysfunctional family environment? This may include parental pathology and/or schizophrenia. Step to be taken: consider if the child has made a "healthy" adaptation to an unhealthy situation.

4. *Other Childhood Diagnosis* - Is there a more appropriate diagnosis such as childhood schizophrenia, post traumatic stress disorder or a genetic predisposition to symptomatic behavior? Step to be taken: rule out any other diagnosis which would be more appropriate.

Scoring the Results

Step one is to rule out the above factors. If one or more of these factors are present, a more detailed assessment of the potential of attachment disorder or other causative explanation is indicated. Step two is to add the total points by section. If any section has a point total under ten then ten points are subtracted from the total. [This is done to provide the mathematical integration all three sections as an interactive whole. This prevents a disturbed child who may not have attachment issues scoring high due to one section.] Step three is to total scores using the following formula:

Section One	total points	_____
(if under 10 subtract 10 points)		_____
Section Two	total points	_____

(if under 10 subtract 10 points) _____

Section Three   total points   _____
(if under 10 subtract 10 points) _____

ADA Scale total score _____

Score Analysis and Recommendations

60 - 80   Severe Attachment Disorder.
Recommendation - specific treatment for
this disorder in outpatient or residential
setting. Consult with all parties who work
with the child to develop a unified treatment
plan.

40 - 59   Moderate Attachment Disorder.
Recommendation - outpatient treatment
while child remains in a safe family setting.
Individual and family therapy recommended.

25 - 39   Attachment Issues.
Recommendation - outpatient treatment with
family

0 - 24   Minimal Attachment Issues.
Recommendation - family therapy would be
the treatment of choice if any treatment is
indicated or requested.

The Attachment Disorder Assessment Scale was developed by and
is copyrighted to Dave Ziegler, Ph.D, SCAR/Jasper Mountain.

References and Suggested Reading

Aicardi, J. (Ed.). (1994). *Epilepsy in Children*. New York: Raven Press.

Ainsworth, M.D.S., Blehar, M.C., Waters, E. & Wall, S. (1978). *Patterns of Attachment: A Psychological Study of the Strange Situation*. New Jersey: Lawrence Erlbaum Associates.

Ainsworth, M.D.S. (1979). Infant-mother attachment. *American Psychologist, 34*, 932-937.

Altimari, D., Weiss, E.M., Blint, D. F., Poitras, C., & Megan, K. (1998, August 16). Deadly restraint: Killed by a system intended for care. *Hartford Courant*.

American Academy of Pediatrics -- Committee on Pediatric Emergency Medicine. (1997). *Pediatrics, 99 (3)*, 497-498.

American Association on Mental Retardation (1992). *Mental Retardation: Definition, Classification, and Systems of Support*.

American Psychiatric Association (1994). *Diagnostic and Statistical Manual of Mental Disorders*, Fourth Edition. Washington, DC: American Psychiatric Association.

Barkley, R.A. (1997). *ADHD and the Nature Of Self-Control*. New York: Guilford Press.

Barkley, R. (1997). *Defiant Children: A Clinician's Manual for Assessment and Parent Training*. New York: Guilford Press.

Bates, J. E. & Bayles, K. (1988). Attachment and the development of behavior problems. In J. Belsky & T. Nezworski (Eds.), *Clinical Implications of Attachment.* Hillsdale, NJ: Lawrence Erlbaum Associates.

Bath, H. (1994). The physical restraint of children: Is it therapeutic? *American Journal of Orthopsychiatry, 64 (11), 40-48.*

Barlow, D.J. (1989). Therapeutic holding, effective intervention with the aggressive child. *Journal of Psychosocial Nursing, 27 (1), 10-14.*

Belsky, J. & Nezworski, T. (1988). *Clinical Implications of Attachment.* Hillsdale, NJ: Lawrence Erlbaum Associates.

Benjamin, R., Mazzarins, H. & Kupfersmid, J. (1983). The effect of time-out (TO) duration on assaultiveness in psychiatrically hospitalized children. *Aggressive Behavior, 9,* 21-27.

Bowlby, J. (1982). *Attachment.* New York: Basic Books Inc.

Caspi, A., Elder, G.H. & Bem, D.J. (1987). Moving against the world: Life course patterns of explosive children. *Developmental Psychology, 23,* 308-313.

Cole R. & Reiss, D. (1993). *How Do Families Cope with Chronic Illness?* Hillsdale, N.J.: Lawrence Erlbaum.

Coleman, W. (1993). *Attention-Deficit Disorder, Hyperactivity & Associated Disorders.* Wisconsin: Calliope Books.

Crespi, T.D. (1990). Restraint and seclusion with institutionalized adolescents. *Adolescence, 25 (100), 825-828.*

Crisis Prevention Institute, Inc. (1987). *Nonviolent Crisis Intervention.* Brookfield, WI: Author.

Crittenden, P.M. (1981). Abusing, neglecting, problematic, and adequate dyads: Differentiating by patterns of interaction. *Merrill-Palmer Quarterly, 27,* 1-18.

Curtis, R. (1991). The attachment model of residential treatment. In *Contributions to Residential Treatment,* 94-103. Washington, DC: American Association of Children's Residential Centers.

Daly, D.L., & Dowd, T.P. (1992). Characteristics of effective, harm-free environments for children in out-of-home-care. *Child Welfare, 71,* 487-496.

Dawson, G., Ed. (1989). *Autism: Nature, Diagnosis, and Treatment.* New York: Guilford Press.

Department of Health and Human Services. (1992). *Maternal Drug Abuse and Drug Exposed Children: Understanding the Problem.* Washington DC: Author.

Dorris, M. (1989). *The Broken Cord.* New York: Harper and Row.

Dougherty, J. (1982). Control measures. In J.L. Schulman & M. Irwin (Eds.), *Psychiatric Hospitalization of Children,* 135-150. Springfield, IL: Charles C. Thomas.

Drisko, J.W. (1981). Therapeutic use of physical restraint. *Child Care Quarterly, 10,* 318-328.

Epilepsy Foundation of America. (1983). *Epilepsy: You and Your Child, A Guide for Parents.* Landover, MD: Epilepsy Foundation of America.

Erickson, M., Sroufe, A., & Egeland, B. (1985). The relationship between quality of attachment and behavior problems in preschool in a high-risk sample. *Monograph for the Society for Research in Child Development, 50,* 147-166.

Fahlberg, V.I. (1991). *A Child's Journey Through Placement.* Indianapolis, IN: Perspectives Press.

Fowler, M.C. (1990). *Maybe You Know My Kid: A Parent's Guide to Identifying, Understanding, and Helping Your Child with ADHD.* New York: Birch Lane Press.

Garrison, W. T. (1984). Aggressive behavior, seclusion and physical restraint in an inpatient child population. *Journal of the American Academy of Child Psychiatry, 23,* 448-452.

George, C. & Main, M. (1979). Social interactions of young abused children: Approach, avoidance and aggression. *Child Development, 50,* 306-318.

Geralis, E. (1991). *Children with Cerebral Palsy, A Parent's Guide.* Rockville, MD: Woodbine House.

Greenberg, M. T. & Speltz, M. L. (1988). Attachment and the ontogeny of conduct problems. In J. Belsky & T. Nezworski (Eds.), *Clinical Implications of Attachment.* Hillsdale, NJ: Lawrence Erlbaum Associates.

Greenspan, S. I. & Lieberman, A. F. (1988). A clinical approach to attachment. In J. Belsky & T. Nezworski (Eds.), *Clinical Implications of Attachment.* Hillsdale, NJ: Lawrence Erlbaum Associates.

Herman, J.L. (1992). *Trauma and Recovery.* New York: Basic Books Inc.

Hershberg, L.M. & Svejda, M. (1990). When infants look to their parents: Infants' social referencing of mothers compared to fathers. *Child Development, 61,* 1175-1186.

Ingersoll, B. (1988). *Your Hyperactive Child: A Parent's Guide to Coping with ADD.* New York: Doubleday.

Irwin, M. (1987). Are seclusion rooms needed on child psychiatric units? *American Journal of Orthopsychiatry, 57,* 125-126.

James, B. (1994). *Handbook for Treatment of Attachment-Trauma Problems in Children.* New York: Lexington Books, Macmillan Inc.

Kennedy, P., Terdal, L. & Fusetti, L. (1993). *The Hyperactive Child Book.* New York: St. Martin's Press.

Kleinfeld, J. & Wescott, S. (1993). *Fantastic Antone Succeeds!* University of Alaska Press.

Kochanska, G. (1991). Socialization and temperament in the development of guilt and conscience. *Society for Research in Child Development, 62,* 1379-1392.

Kochanska, G. (1993). Toward a synthesis of parental socialization and child temperament in early development of conscience. *Society for Research in Child Development, 64,* 325-347.

Lamberti, J.S. & Cummings, S. (1992). Hands-on restraint in the treatment of multiple personality disorder. *Hospital and Community Psychiatry, 43 (3),* 283-284.

Leof, J. (1994). *Adopting Children with Developmental Disabilities.* Rockville, MD: National Adoption Information Clearinghouse.

Lewis, M., Feiring, C., McGuggog, C. & Jaskir, J. (1984). Predicting psychopathology in six-year-olds from early social relations. *Child Development, 55,* 1123-1136.

Lieberman, A. F. & Pawl, J. H. (1988). Clinical applications of attachment theory. In J. Belsky & T. Nezworski (Eds.), *Clinical Implications of Attachment.* Hillsdale, NJ: Lawrence Erlbaum Associates.

Lowenstein, L. (1998). The physical restraining of children. *Education Today, 48 (1),* 47-54.

Matos, L., Arend, R.A. & Sroufe, L.A. (1978). Continuity of adaptation in the second year: The relationship between quality of attachment and later competence. *Society for Research in Child Development, 49,* 547-556.

Measham, T.J. (1995). The acute management of aggressive behaviors in hospitalized children and adolescents. *Canadian Journal of Psychiatry, 40 (6),* 330-336.

Miller, D. (1986). The management of misbehavior by seclusion. *Residential Treatment of Children and Youth, 4,* 63-72.

Miller, D., Walker, M.C. & Friedman, D. (1989). Use of a holding technique to control the violent behavior of seriously disturbed adolescents. *Hospital and Community Psychiatry, 40 (5),* 520-524.

Nickel, R. (1997). *Community Consultants in the Care of Children with Special Health Care Needs: A Training Program for*

Primary Care Physicians and Nurses. U.S. Department of Health and Human Services.

Papolos, D. & Papolos, J. (1999). *The Bipolar Child.* New York: Broadway Books.

Penry, J.K. (1986). *Epilepsy: Diagnosis, Management, Quality of Life.* New York: Ravens Press.

Polansky, N.A., Gaudin Jr., J.M., Ammons, P.W. & Davis, K.B. (1985). The psychological ecology of the neglectful mother. *Child Abuse and Neglect, 9,* 265-275.

Powers, M.D. Ed. (1989) *Children with Autism, A Parent's Guide.* Rockville, MD: Woodbine House.

Reisner, H. Ed. (1988). *Children with Epilepsy: A Parent's Guide.* Kensington, MD: Woodbine House.

Rekate, H. Ed. (1991). *Comprehensive Management of Spina Bifida.* Boston: CRC Press.

Robin, M. (1982). The abuse of status offenders in private hospitals. In R. Hanson (Ed.), Institutional Abuse of Children and Youth. *Child and Youth Services, 4, 79-88.*

Rohmann, U.H. & Hartmann, H. (1985). A basic step in treating autistic children. *Zeitschrift Fuer Kinder-Und Jugendpsychiatrie,* 13 (3), 182-198.

Rolider, A., Williams, L., Cummings, A. & Van Houten, R. (1991). The use of a brief movement restriction procedure to eliminate severe inappropriate behavior. *Journal of Behavioral Therapy and Experimental Psychiatry, 22 (1),* 23-30.

Romer Witten, M. (1994). Assessment of attachment in traumatized children. In B. James (Ed.), *Handbook for Treatment of Attachment-Trauma Problems in Children.* New York: Lexington Books.

Rubin, K. H. & Lollis, S. P. (1988). Origins and consequences of social withdrawal. In J. Belsky & T. Nezworski (Eds.), *Clinical Implications of Attachment.* Hillsdale, NJ: Lawrence Erlbaum Associates.

Schopler, E. & Mesibov, G.B. Eds. (1994). *Behavioral Issues in Autism.* New York: Plenum Press.

Smith, P.A. (1991). Time-out and seclusion: Understanding the civil rights and treatment issues. *Residential Treatment for Children and Youth, 9,* 51-59.

Smith, P.A. (1993). Training Manual for P.A.R.T. (Professional Assault Response Training) - Revised.

Sonderegger, T.B. Ed. (1992). *Perinatal Substance Abuse: Research Findings and Clinical Implications.* Baltimore: Johns Hopkins University Press.

Sroufe, L. A. (1986). The role of infant-caregiver attachment in development. In J. Belsky & T. Nezworski (Eds.), *Clinical Implications of Attachment.* Hillsdale, NJ: Lawrence Erlbaum Associates.

Stirling, C. & McHugh, A. (1998). Developing a non-aversive intervention strategy in the management of aggression and violence for people with learning disabilities using natural therapeutic holding. *Journal of Advanced Nursing, 27 (3),* 503-509.

Sugar, M. (1994). Wrist-holding for the out of control child. *Child Psychiatry and Human Development, 24 (3),* 145-155.

Trickett, K. T. & Kuczynski, L. (1985). Children's misbehaviors and parental discipline strategies in abusive and nonabusive families. *Developmental Psychology, 22,* 115-123.

Troutman, B., Myers, K., Borchardt, C., Kowalski, R. & Bubrick, J. (1998). Case study: When restraints are the least restrictive alternative for managing aggression. *Journal of the American Academy of Child and Adolescent Psychiatry, 37 (5),* 554-555.

van der Kolk, B.A. (1989). The compulsion to repeat the trauma: Re-enactment, re-victimization, and masochism. *Psychiatric Clinics of North America, 12,* 389-406.

van der Kolk, B. A. (1996). The complexity of adaptation to trauma: Self-regulation, stimulus discrimination, and characterological development. In van der Kolk, B.A., McFarlane, A.C., & Weisaeth, L. (Eds.), *Traumatic Stress: The Effects of Overwhelming Experience on Mind, Body, and Society,* pp. 182-213. New York: Guilford Press.

von Stosch, T. (1986). Chances and limits of holding therapy with autistic children in day treatment: A case study. *Fruehfoerderung Interdisziplinaer, 5 (3),* 126-131.

Wadeson, H. & Carpenter, W.T. (1976). Impact of the seclusion room experience. *Journal of Nervous and Mental Disease, 163,* 318-328.

Wender, P.H. (1987). *The Hyperactive Child, Adolescent, and Adult.* New York: Oxford University Press.

Wong, S. E. (1990). How therapeutic is therapeutic holding? *Journal of Psychiatric Nursing & Mental Health, 28 (11)*, 24-28.

Ziegler, D.L. (1990). *Attachment Disorder Assessment Scale.* Jasper, OR: SCAR/Jasper Mountain.